GRADUAL RETIREMENT IN THE OECD COUNTRIES

Gradual retirement in the OECD countries

Macro and micro issues and policies

Edited by

LEI DELSEN
University of Nijmegen

and

GENEVIÈVE REDAY-MULVEY
Geneva Association

Dartmouth

Aldershot • Brookfield USA • Singapore • Sydney

© Lei Delsen, Geneviève Reday-Mulvey 1996

Published by
Dartmouth Publishing Company Limited
Gower House
Croft Road
Aldershot
Hants GU11 3HR
England

Dartmouth Publishing Company
Old Post Road
Brookfield
Vermont 05036
USA

British Library Cataloguing in Publication Data
Gradual Retirement in the OECD Countries:
Macro and Micro Issues and Policies
  I. Delsen, Lei II. Reday-Mulvey, Geneviève
331.25209177

Library of Congress Cataloging-in-Publication Data
Gradual retirement in the OECD countries : macro and micro issues and
  policies / edited by Lei Delsen and Geneviève Reday-Mulvey.
     p.   cm.
  Includes index.
  ISBN 1-85521-708-2
  1. Retirement. 2. Retirement age. 3. Old age pensions.
4. Retirees–Employment. I. Delsen, Lei, 1952- . II. Reday-Mulvey,
Geneviève.
HD7105.G7 1996
331.25'2–dc20   95-46948
                                                    CIP

ISBN 1 85521 708 2

Printed in Great Britain by Ipswich Book Co. Ltd., Ipswich, Suffolk.

Contents

PART III
GRADUAL RETIREMENT IN JAPAN AND
THE UNITED STATES

PART IV
POTENTIAL FOR GRADUAL RETIREMENT AND
RECOMMENDATIONS

List of tables

List of figures

Acknowledgements

The editors, Lei Delsen and Geneviève Reday-Mulvey, would like to thank the authors of the country chapters: Noriyuki Takayama and Isao Shimowada (Japan), Yung-Ping Chen and Harold Sheppard (USA), Winfried Schmähl, Rainer George and Christiane Oswald (Germany), Philip Taylor and Alan Walker (UK), and Eskil Wadensjö (Sweden), for having so readily agreed to this study. It is their thoughtful and carefully-crafted research, their enthusiastic understanding of the purpose of this study that have made it possible.

The editors further would like to state their gratitude to the European Commission (DG V) and to the Geneva Association for their generous financial support with this project and for the encouragement those institutions have proferred from the very outset.

As country authors themselves – of the chapters on the Netherlands and France – the editors would like to take this opportunity to thank all the firms, government agencies, professional associations and representatives of many academic bodies, who have willingly provided valuable information, a wealth of statistical data, and stimulating suggestions.

Finally this comparative survey could not have been achieved without the linguistic expertise, sensitive understanding of the subject-matter and pains-taking drafting of the reviser, Michael Mulvey.

All the aforementioned institutions and individuals are responsible for any worth this study may possess; the editors remain wholly answerable for all of its defects.

Editors' preface

Around the mid-1970s, demographic factors in OECD countries began to cause pension obligations to rise sharply. This fact against the prevailing background of slow economic growth, rising unemployment and large government deficits, brought finally into focus the realisation that an 'easing-up', of the expansion of social security programmes might be necessary. And yet, for demographic reasons – the sharp decline in fertility rates from the 1970s onwards, the constant increase in life expectancy and the steady aging of the population – and social reasons – the desirability of extending coverage of pensions and of increasing benefit levels – expenditure on pensions continued to rise, at a rate exceeding even that of unemployment expenditure. Today, total social security related expenditure accounts for almost 30 per cent of the GDP of our economies and pensions alone for around 10 per cent. The demographic outlook and its implications for future pensions oblige us today to reconsider what the economic and social contribution of older workers and people to our service economy in the decades to come should be.

In 1987 the International Association for the Study of Insurance Economics, commonly known as the Geneva Association, launched its Research Programme on Work and Retirement. This initiative was to make a signal contribution to rethinking the role of 'third agers' in society, and to promoting the idea that an aging population – most of whose members are, in our day and age, in good physical and mental health – can be an asset for our firms and communities provided we are ready to transform 'problems' into 'opportunities'. Out of this original Research Project the Geneva Association has now developed a fully-fledged fourth pillar Studies Programme for promoting flexible extension of working life as one of the answers to the future pensions crisis; the idea being that a part-time income (or a 4th pillar) could be added for some years after retirement to the three existing pension pillars. This study is, therefore, very much in the tradition of the seminars and reports on the development of 4th pillar policies and practice that have been made in a number of OECD countries. Several of its contributors have indeed been associated with the research, seminars and publications of the Geneva Association.

For its part the European Commission in Brussels is deeply concerned by the issue of the Union's aging population and had already adopted, in 1982, a recommendation on the principles of a Community Policy on a retirement age. That recommendation invited Member States to acknowledge flexible retirement for employees as one of the aims of their social policies. In 1986 the Commission proposed that emphasis be placed on the need for phased or gradual retirement and, in its report of December 1992, was able to state that good progress had been made in this field. With the growing acceptance of subsidiarity, however, the aim of convergent policies towards older workers and people has been largely abandoned. Even so, the European Commission in its various initiatives and more recently in its 1995 Proposal for a Council Decision on Community Support for Action in favour of Older People, continues to stress that the transition from work to retirement and the management of an aging work force are two areas in which it is crucial to promote best practice. It is in the spirit of such initiatives that the Commission saw fit to give financial support and encouragement to the authors of the current study.

Over the last two decades work and retirement patterns have undergone major changes. Evidence now suggests that the incentives of public and company labour market policies have so far been unbalanced, have been designed mainly to address the problems of youth unemployment and corporate downsizing, and in so doing have merely disguised unemployment and severely restricted the work opportunities of the active elderly.

Spurred by the prediction of a welfare crisis and by the weight of this evidence, legislators in most of the countries selected for this study have begun to contemplate ways of extending working life and reducing the generosity of pensions.

It is the editors' conviction that such legal initiatives should reflect a coherent and combined social-security/employment policy, whose focus would be to promote gradual retirement, into which can be articulated the hitherto sporadic and uncoordinated efforts of governments to address a whole range of problems – the future financing of old age benefits, unemployment, 'pension' shock, the average aging of the work force, predicted skilled shortages, etc. It is, therefore, the purpose of these pages to awaken curiosity about the reach and content of policy articulation in the domain of gradual retirement and make recommendations as to possible approaches to such an exercise.

But gradual retirement may also, indeed must, be seen in the context of the labour market challenge facing all OECD countries, that of increasing labour force participation rates, or more realistically, of devising new ways of redistributing employment at existing levels. In this context, the existence of an established and growing internal market in Europe is of importance, since it adds to the competition created by the globalisation of economies. Increasing competition means that a nation's welfare system might become a selling point in attracting investments from abroad, and hence also jobs. The question, then, arises as to which policy mix or institutional arrangements will allow for more individual choice and will make best use of the labour resource of persons of 55 years and older. What role can gradual retirement play in accomplishing this? What essential conditions have to be met? And what are the obstacles at the macro and micro levels? These are some of the questions the chapters of this book attempt to answer.

Both the macro and micro aspects of gradual retirement are examined country by country, providing an important study not otherwise available in report or book form. *Macro issues* include demographic trends and labour market participation of older workers, pension provision (the four pillars), the retirement age, government social-welfare and employment policy, pension reform in relation to new and flexible employment modes, and the call for a new-style consensus in industrial relations among the social partners. Where do the selected countries stand in relation to these issues? Are there common trends for which common policies could be devised? *Micro issues* cover personnel and wage policies, training opportunities, employee aspirations and employers' needs, and the new work environment with its flexible, information technology-driven occupational patterns and schedules. A major focus of attention will be the practical problems of gradual retirement and examples of best practice to promote it in firms across the selected countries.

Given the growing internationalisation of the economies of industrialised countries, our study covers the three major trading areas of OECD Member States. But given also the state of research in the countries potentially available for consideration and because of inevitable constraints of time and space, the editors have selected 7 countries in all for scrutiny: five countries of the European Union, Japan and the United States.

Of the European countries chosen for study, Sweden, a new EU Member State and Nordic country, is the most interesting case of gradual retirement. We shall see in the chapter devoted to the Swedish experience that it passed legislation in this field as early as 1976 and has successfully implemented its policy for gradual retirement through, among other things, a working partnership between the State and enterprise. We have included France, Germany, the United Kingdom and the Netherlands as well since in all of these countries there is documented evidence of development of gradual retirement in varying degrees.

As to the Southern European region, it had been our intention to include this area in our study, but in all the potential candidates in this region – Italy and Spain are examples – although legislation on gradual retirement has recently been adopted, research is as yet not sufficiently advanced for us to be able to draw significant conclusions. It is, however, the editors' intention to cover this area, and Italy more particularly, in a follow-up to the current study. A European seminar and possibly even a network on gradual retirement are being planned for this purpose.

For each of the countries selected, the macro and micro issues and policies related to gradual retirement are addressed within a common frame according, that is, to a single set of guidelines devised by the editors for use in preparing the country chapters. Each country survey has, therefore, a similar structure in order to allow for inter-country comparison, but beyond the guidelines each author has been allowed a free hand. The resulting differences in approach are marked and, as much as anything else, the editors believe, reflect differences in the actual country situations on the ground. In the case of the two countries at either end of the comparison range, Japan and the United States, that difference, as readers will discover, is as surprising as it is revealing. Indeed, even the title of the second part of the American chapter, on Micro Issues, is different since, due chiefly to the collapse of the main career employment system in corporations and to their widespread downsizing, there can exist no significant gradual retirement practice within firms; but the development of part-time patterns, especially for workers at the end of career, represents a specific form of gradual retirement in practice and in potential.

Part I   Touches briefly on the recent evolution of work and retirement, introduces gradual retirement and, across the countries considered, examines the current situation regarding the various macro and micro issues chosen as the focus for the study. Problems and challenges are identified in general terms.

Part II   Contains the 5 EU country studies as outlined above:
Sweden, by E. Wadensjö
France, by G. Reday-Mulvey
Germany, by W. Schmähl, R. George and C. Oswald
The United Kingdom, by P. Taylor and A. Walker
The Netherlands, by L. Delsen.

Part III   Contains the country studies for Japan and the USA, each of which is divided into two separate parts provided each by a separate author:
Japan: Macro Issues and Policies, by N. Takayama
Japan: Micro Issues and Policies, by I. Shimowada
The United States: Macro Issues and Policies, by Y-P. Chen
The United States: Micro Issues and Policies, by H. Sheppard.

Part IV In this section the editors attempt to provide a gradual retirement typology of countries based on the material contained in Parts II and III. They draw tentative conclusions as to the potential for gradual retirement and suggest areas for future action in this field which could be used as a starting point for cogitation, discussion and debate and, hence, as pointers perhaps to future legislation, public policy-formulation and recommendations, ways of integrating public strategies with corporate policies, and to codes of good and best practice for firms. The conclusions and recommendations made in this section, though considered, are, however, no more than the personal views of the editors. The reader, with the introduction as a guide, enlightened, it is hoped, by the information contained in the country chapters will judge as to their validity.

PART I

THE BACKGROUND
TO GRADUAL RETIREMENT

1 Macro issues and policies

Lei Delsen and Geneviève Reday-Mulvey

This chapter deals with macro issues and policies relating to gradual retirement. It will attempt a definition of the term gradual retirement and a brief examination of some of the concepts underlying it. Our main purpose, however, will be to focus on the following major factors: demographic and pension prospects, labour market participation and the policy and practice of early retirement over almost the last two decades, new patterns of work and retirement, and finally recent public policies which reflect the emergence of new trends.

1.1 Demography

We shall not dwell here at any great length upon demographic factors since these are already very well-known. We would merely state in this context that they exercise crucially significant pressure on pension and health systems and on the labour market, and have most often been described in pessimistic terms. If things remain the way they are now, it is argued, the pressure demography exerts on our social security systems will become intolerable. The need to transfer an increasing amount of resources to the elderly, through pensions and health care, will have major consequences for the inter-generational distribution of income. As with many aspects of gradual retirement, the demographic situation differs significantly from country to country. Countries such as Germany, Japan and the Netherlands, which, in just 30 years, will have over one third of the population over the age of 60 will be subject to greater pressure than those with only 20 per cent or 25 per cent of over 60s.

In fact, however, in many respects enhanced life expectancy is highly positive, for the potentially catastrophic arithmetic of demographic projection must be viewed in the context of the enhanced physical and mental health of the aging population many of whose members will be able, and will desire, to remain active much later in life. Japan, with a population that has aged earlier than that of any other OECD country, is a good illustration of this point. The median age of its workers rose significantly in the eighties without any apparent loss of productivity.

By the end of the century, a number of European countries and Japan are expected to show a decrease in the absolute number of working age people. Thereafter, projections indicate that a progressively larger number of countries will begin to experience shrinkage of the working age population, particularly during the second and third decades. This will affect state pensions and welfare programmes which are financed largely from taxes and social security contributions paid by the working population. But, at the same time, it will create more potential for extension of working life. With increased life expectancy a pension designed to cover ten or fifteen years of retirement might generate intolerable upward pressure on contribution rates were it to be maintained over 25 years, especially in countries like France where currently the average level of pensions is almost as high as the average wage. Indeed, contributions and rates of taxation cannot continue to rise without significant repercussions for wages, for the competitiveness of businesses, and hence for employment. In addition, all problems arising from population aging are aggravated by reduced economic growth. Lower growth rates make it more difficult to secure jobs and to finance social security programmes. The number of people employed, productivity per worker and trends in their real earnings will all be key elements in coping with expenditure increase.

1.2 Pension provision

The Geneva Association, in choosing a metaphor to describe pension provision, has likened the income security structure to an edifice resting on three pillars to which it has been proposed a fourth one be added. The first is the compulsory state or basic pension usually known as social security. The second is the supplementary employer or occupational pension. The third is income from personal pensions, life insurance, individual savings and assets. And the proposed fourth pillar, in a sense the 'raison d'être' of the present study, is the option open to older people to work part-time with a partial pension in order to supplement the income from the other three sources. Our concern at this point is with the first three pillars and their relation to the fourth.

In Europe, Japan and the United States, basic pensions are financed on a pay-as-you-go basis, either through social security contributions or from taxes, while occupational pensions are financed by funding (with the exception of France). Public pension spending in Europe is currently higher than in the USA and Japan. It is, however, as N. Takayama will show in his chapter, set to rise considerably in Japan as well. As a percentage of GDP it ranges from 5 per cent in Japan to over 10 per cent in most of the EU countries selected for this study. The combination of an aging population and a declining work force is particularly alarming for public pensions. Under the assumption of constant rates of replacement (benefits as a percentage of labour earnings) and of labour force participation, public expenditure on pensions as a percentage of GDP would be expected to double across the OECD area between 1985 and 2040 (Holzmann, 1988). Since, for obvious economic reasons, this will be impossible to achieve, there will be a relative decrease of the size of the 1st pillar public pensions in most countries, and this is reflected in recent public pension reforms which have raised the pension age (or number of contribution years), and provided for a reduction over time in the relative level of pensions to wages.

Not all OECD countries have well-developed multi-pillar systems, since until recently, only the public pillar has been mandatory. Although the relative sizes of the mandatory and voluntary pillars – as measured by their relative shares of old people's income – differ widely, public pay-as-you-go plans still represent high proportions of the elderly's income. However, as the World Bank's 1994 Report observes, occupational and personal pensions have grown fast and there is also a significant trend towards replacing pay-as-you-go systems by funding, so as to relieve the pressure on the active population which, as we have seen, is decreasing relative to the dependent one. This trend towards funding is expected to continue, since in countries with flat-rate basic pensions (such as the Netherlands and the UK), there is obviously more need for supplementary second pillar provision – and hence for funding – than in Germany or France where basic pensions are earnings-related. It will be observed that, in some countries such as the UK and the USA, a proportion of the work force (at least a third) is still not covered by any form of second pillar pension provision. This means that, in these countries, state pension provision will continue well into the next century to be crucial for at least this third of the population, and important for the average citizen. The first pillar pension will have to be maintained at a reasonable level, and where, as in the UK, policies have been introduced to reduce it, it will sooner or later have to be restored to an acceptable level, unless second pillar provision is made compulsory with enough government support to make it viable as far as the average wage-earner is concerned.

As to the third pillar, it is well-known that the rate of personal savings of most OECD economies is far too low for that pillar ever to be able, for the average citizen at least, to constitute a significant source of income during old age. That is why, from the standpoint of pension financing, in the medium and long-term, a flexible extension of working life is seen as highly advisable and by the less optimistic as altogether unavoidable.

However, more crucial to the immediate issue of promoting gradual retirement are the portability of pension claims and the terms of pensions at end of career. Individual and defined-contribution pension claims are fully portable from one employer to another. Claims on the state pension are fully portable as well, because the schemes are nationwide. Defined-benefit plans operated at the firm or industry level have neither of these two characteristics, and are thus not fully portable. Limited portability hinders labour mobility, which is an impediment for forms of gradual retirement outside main employment. Moreover, if pension claims are not fully portable, because of long vesting periods, labour becomes less mobile. Arguments in favour of more funded systems see the latter not only as ways of diminishing inter-generational transfer, but also as a means of increasing internal and external labour market flexibility and of improving economic performance (see Holzmann, 1992; Bovenberg, 1994; Delsen, forthcoming; World Bank, 1994).

Finally, we come to the terms of pensions at end of career – and these will be analysed for each country. Suffice to say at this point that these terms, together with the degree of portability, are factors which can facilitate or hinder the development of gradual retirement. The final-salary, as opposed to average-salary, base upon which pension terms are frequently constructed in a number of countries (for example, the Netherlands, the USA and the UK) is a major obstacle to gradual retirement. An average-salary base of twenty years or more is gradual retirement neutral.

1.3 Labour market participation and early retirement

Over the last twenty years, in all industrialised countries, the employment situation has been characterised by an increasingly early exit from the labour market at end of career. While a continuous increase in life expectancy in good health and a steady extension of schooling for the young have been observed, employment has been entered into later and quitted earlier and, as a consequence, occupational life has shrunk considerably. In some countries such as France where the young enter employment especially late and the older worker leaves his or her job especially early, the average citizen now spends more time outside employment than within it!

A large number of OECD countries took special measures for older workers – non-wage income provision in the form of unemployment benefits, disability benefits and early retirement schemes – which have enabled older workers to withdraw from the labour market prior to being eligible for a public pension. These early retirement policies have resulted in decreasing rates of labour market participation which, as the chapters will show, have been exceptionally marked in France and the Netherlands, very marked in Germany, relatively less so in the UK and the USA and least of all in Japan and Sweden. Of the active male population in the 55 to 59 age-group in the first two of these countries, in 1993 less than 60 per cent were in employment, while this rate was around 20 per cent for those in the 60-64 age-group. At the other end of the spectrum, these rates for Sweden and Japan were respectively and approximately 80 and 50 per cent. As a consequence, there has been a growing gap between the statutory age of retirement – which is 65 in the countries studied except Japan and France where it is 60 – and the effective age at which workers leave the labour market, voluntarily or not. The country authors in Part II and III of this study will be examining this issue in some detail.

It is an established fact that the significant trend towards early retirement has been the result of a deep consensus – which we shall dub the 'old' consensus – part of a social contract between the State, enterprise, trade unions and the community. For the State, the main purpose of early retirement has been to reduce youth unemployment – which was high in the 1970s and 1980s – since in many schemes, at least until recently, there was a replacement condition. Moreover, it should be noted that, in most of the countries studied, the duration of unemployment benefit for older workers has lengthened, the latter not being required, prior to retirement, to register at labour offices. This has tended to result in an under estimation of unemployment. For enterprise, early retirement has had a two-fold advantage – productivity can be enhanced through modernising the process of production and the firm restructured without the cost and the embarrassment of rising redundancies. For the trade unions, it has been a coveted prize in the long struggle to lower the retirement age and so leave workers, who so often started their working life young and frequently in strenuous jobs, some years of respite in good health. And last, the average citizen has greatly benefitted from this trend particularly in countries where the financial terms of early retirement have been generous.

1.4 New patterns of employment and retirement

There is little doubt that some of the main trends observed in employment over the last two decades constitute very favourable factors for gradual retirement. The development of services as a key factor of the modern economy has radically altered the existing work environment and in some respects created an entirely new one. If we consider not only tertiary-sector service activities *per se* but also service funtions in manufacturing and agriculture (such as research, planning, marketing, maintenance, storage, quality control, safety measures, distribution), between 70 and 80 per cent of jobs in our economies are now in services, and this trend is set to increase further in the years to come.

The very nature of service activities has brought into being a widening range of flexible job options. The rigidity that was so characteristic of the older manufacturing production chain contrasts starkly with the suppleness of the work patterns, flexible in both time and space, of our information age. There has, as a result, been an overall growth in the amount of work performed in part-time jobs, which, in some countries such as the Netherlands, the UK and Sweden, now constitute almost a third of jobs. Most of these part-time jobs are no longer of the old 'industrial' type (i.e. related to lower and frequently unprotected employment profiles) but increasingly involve the deployment of qualified experience which, for various reasons, people cannot or will not exercise in a full-time job.

Flexible work, a category which includes also self- and temporary employment, will become the norm in the professions and even in management over the next fifteen or twenty years. For instance, millions of people will be working from home at some time during the week, achieving a considerable improvement in productivity and a considerable reduction in office and transport costs. Moreover in most countries, especially in the USA, Japan and the UK, the frequency of part-time and self employment increases with age. Often self employment assists individuals to remain economically active.

In most of the countries studied, employees in the services sector tend to retire later than those in the secondary sector. Statistics, both in the USA and in Europe, provide evidence that employees in manufacturing retire earlier than in the service sector (e.g. French Ministry of Labour, 1994). One reason for this trend is certainly that restructuring has so far been more radical in manufacturing industries and has led to stronger early retirement policies. Another important reason is that the content of work in most service activities is increasingly intellectual or mental. This crucial fact is supported by scientific studies which show that mental abilities decrease much more slowly with age than physical ones and that, as a result, productivity declines with age faster in manual work than in most white-collar activities (Charness, 1985). That is why qualified employees tend to retire later than non-qualified ones, both productivity, and frequently motivation, remaining high much later in life.

1.5 Gradual retirement

In the past, most workers, whether peasants or craftsmen, used to retire gradually, i.e. in stages. With diminishing physical strength, they would work less and less. Gradual retirement of this kind was, as it were, a natural and progressive, sometimes imperceptible, downsizing of the workload and even today many self employed people – doctors, architects, lawyers, craftsmen and farmers – would, given the choice, not dream of retiring in any other way. However, with the industrial revolution, work conditions had to be regulated and progressively the idea of retiring people when they grow old and less useful became established. Retirement came to be fixed at a certain age, earlier, obviously, for miners and others doing physically demanding jobs than for clerks. Almost everywhere, however, retirement was soon to be viewed as 'overnight' and irrevocable – 'la retraite couperet' or guillotine retirement, as the French were later to call it. Most people did not live for many years after retirement; a few years of rest, hopefully in good health, before death was all that could be expected. More recently, however, while the age of retirement has been lowered, so has life expectancy been increasing rapidly which means that, especially since the last World War, retirement has ceased to be a residue and has progressively become a period of life in its own right, a new stage and a fresh departure that can be planned and prepared for. And so, little by little, the idea of flexible retirement, of a transition period between a full-time career and full retirement, better suited to the needs of both the individual and the firm, has come into being.

Gradual retirement, often called phased, partial or part-time retirement, has been advocated, introduced and used for various reasons. By reducing work hours according to graduated and agreed schedules, it constitutes a way of avoiding the pension shock, following an abrupt transition from full-time work to full pensioning; it is also a way of achieving greater flexibility and individualisation of working life by distributing work and free time more evenly over the latter part of the occupational cycle, and a potential means of redistributing the available work supply. It further provides a 'soft' form of personnel reduction, a means of reducing growing exclusion of older employees from the labour force and, for management, cost-effective opportunities to retain people with valuable corporate knowledge and precious technical skills. Finally, actuarially, it reduces retirement and unemployment costs not only by reducing the relative volume of benefits but also by lengthening the contribution period and by increasing the contribution base (Delsen, 1990; Reday-Mulvey, 1993).

Many formulae for workload downsizing exist and the transition periods during which this occurs can run for anything from one to ten years. As we shall see in the country chapters, approximately five years is the transition period most commonly encountered in the countries studied.

But gradual retirement, it should be understood, can mean a reduction or an extension of working life. In Sweden, where the retirement age has long been a relatively late one at 67, we shall see that gradual retirement was originally designed to facilitate a reduction in working life. In France, to mention another example, current public policies designed to reverse the early retirement trend use gradual retirement as a kind of part-time early retirement in substitution of full early retirement. The net effect of such policies, however, is to extend working life. The same may be said of Japan, as indeed of most of the countries studied. It is, in fact, the editors' contention that gradual retirement constitutes a flexible extension of work life, and should be promoted as such.

Often, at present, a bridge between the official and the effective retirement age, it is, we believe, destined to become the standard mode for extension of working life beyond any notional retirement age. It is precisely for this reason that the authors strongly advocate that there be no overall and absolute age limit to work and employment.

1.6 New public policies towards reversing the early retirement trend

Already in the early eighties, there were signs that the 'old' consensus on early retirement was not as solid as it had been; the State was becoming anxious about its cost. And although the change occurred at different times in different OECD countries – earlier in countries like France where it had started early and had been strongest or in Japan where there is an established tradition of working late – there was generally a rising awareness that the early retirement trend could not continue for ever.

In many countries apprehensions about intolerable future pressure on pension systems became particularly acute – as early as 1983, the USA passed a law to raise the official retirement age. Most countries (Germany, Japan, France, Italy, Sweden, the UK) have followed suit by increasing either the pension age or the number of contribution years to social security, and by making conditions for retirees less favourable.

With regard to the specific issue of this study, public legislation has been passed in most countries allowing for more flexible retirement, the possibility of combining a pension with earnings from employment and various possibilities for phased retirement, or what we call gradual retirement. During recent years, six EU Member States have adopted measures for gradual retirement: Denmark (1988, but reinforced in 1995), France (1988), Germany (1989, effective from 1992), Italy, Luxembourg and Spain. The new Member States, Sweden, Finland and Austria, adopted measures respectively in 1976, 1987 and 1993. Japan, for its part, adopted legislation in 1986, reinforced by measures in 1994. The overall trend of these public reforms is clear: they enable mature workers to leave employment gradually and remain active later. As we shall see, gradual retirement goes some way towards bridging the gap between the effective age and the statutory age for retirement, particularly in cases where the age for admission to phased retirement is lower. The advantage of gradual retirement over other forms of policy (early retirement, unemployment or invalidity insurance) much used over the last two decades is, in our view, that gradual retirement can be built into retirement schemes and, thereby, is more easily incorporated into overall employment policy, and can thus be considered a 'permanent' system.

For its part, enterprise is slowly becoming wise to the fact that jettisoning older employees sometimes incurs a net and irreparable loss of skills and corporate expertise. Early retirement is coming to be seen as a short-term or quick-fix solution to the problems of redundancies and of an aging active population, but also as a costly solution in terms of its increasing the rate of contribution for welfare. However, it will be shown how much most corporate policies, thus far, are still greatly affected by the early retirement culture and difficult labour market conditions.

Many trade unions are becoming aware that the needs of the employee in the service economy are different from those of the worker in manufacturing, and that, with entrenched aging of the work force, continuing training and adjusted work conditions are issues to be addressed. As to the older workers themselves, surveys show that they often desire some kind of transition between a full-time career and full retirement even if the vast majority still expect eventually to enter the latter at an earlier age and on very generous terms.

At the time of writing, therefore, a 'new' consensus appears to be emerging to replace the 'old', but the process of its formulation, by no means ubiquitous, varies from one country to the next, as our comparison of OECD countries will show. Although overall there has been a relative bottoming-out of the fall of employment rates for older workers, we shall see that, where not securely articulated into company policies, public policies have not yet necessarily produced the expected results. Raising the retirement age alone is, for example, decidedly no more than a partial answer to the problem.

In this context, the main macro questions which the country chapters will attempt to answer are the following: What incentives have been provided for implementing new public policies and what have been the results? How can the current gap between the broader economic and social design of public policy and the needs of the corporation as reflected in company policies be narrowed, and how can the partnership between the State and enterprise be improved? What will be the shape of the 'new' consensus and how can it be developed in the years to come?

References

Bovenberg, A.L. (ed.) (1994), *The Economics of Pensions: The Case of the Netherlands*, Papers and Proceedings 9401, Research Centre for Economic Policy, Rotterdam.

Charness, N. (1985), *Studies in Human Performance*, John Wildey and Sons.

Commission of the European Communities (1993), *Older People in Europe: Social and Economic Policies, The 1993 Report of the European Community Observatory*, DG V, Brussels.

Delsen, L. (1990), 'Part-time Early Retirement in Europe', *The Geneva Papers on Risk and Insurance*, 15, pp. 139-157.

Delsen, L. (1995), *Atypical Employment: An International Perspective. Causes, Consequences and Policy*, Wolters-Noordhoff, Groningen.

Delsen, L. (forthcoming), 'Gradual Retirement: Lessons from the Nordic Countries and the Netherlands', *European Journal of Industrial Relations.*

Holzmann, R. (1988), *Pension Policy in the OECD Countries: Background and Trends,* IMF Working paper WP/88/85, International Monetary Fund, Washington.

Holzmann, R. (1992), *Economic Aspects of Pension Reform in OECD Countries,* Paper presented at the 48th Congress of the International Institute of Public Finance 'Impact of Demographic Changes for the Public Finances', August 24-28, Seoul.

Ministère du Travail, de l'Emploi et de la Formation Professionnelle (ed.) (1994), *Emploi et vieillissement,* La Documentation Française, Paris.

Reday-Mulvey, G. (1993), 'Facing Social Uncertainty: Towards a New Social Policy' in Giarini, O. and W. Stahel, *Limits to Certainty,* Kluwer Academic Publishers, Dortrecht.

World Bank (1994), *Averting the Old Age Crisis. Policies to Protect the Old and Promote Growth,* Oxford University Press, Oxford, New York etc.

2 Micro issues and policies

Lei Delsen and Geneviève Reday-Mulvey

Not only will the aging of the work force in OECD countries result in a smaller body of workers with which to finance social welfare and public pensions, but the work force itself as it ages will need to remain efficient and productive if it is not to jeopardise the competitiveness of our economies. Moreover, with the fall in new entrants to the labour market, it may well prove essential to keep older employees longer at work so as to avoid qualitative and quantitative bottlenecks in the provision of personnel.

In this chapter, micro issues and policies relating to gradual retirement are reviewed. An extensive literature exists on most of the areas involved, yet it is not in any way the purpose of this chapter to summarise them. We shall, therefore, indicate only those issues we believe most relevant to gradual retirement, more particularly those which country authors will be examining in their respective chapters. Of relevance, we believe, are: work performance, age discrimination, personnel management, training, the wage-cost profile, part-time and flexible work, employee preferences and the life-cycle of the worker.

2.1 Work performance

The whole notion of capacity for work, i.e. for productive activity, is changing dramatically. To cite but one rather obvious example, today somebody who in traditional industrial society suffered from severe disadvantage through physical handicap can now become a perfectly competent computer programmer, whereas the athlete, in spite of the traditional advantage of exceptional physical fitness, will remain computer illiterate unless he or she take steps to remedy that deficiency. Education, health status, experience and psychological attitude, then, are combining in new ways to engender new notions of capacity for work.

Scientific research seems to be moving in new directions also, causing long-held prejudices to change. The evidence of biological studies now points to the possibility of regeneration of neurons and brain cells. It is now well established that mental abilities decrease much slower and later than physical ones and can, especially with training, remain viable much after 60 or even 65 years. It is becoming obvious also that work, especially when part-time and in moderation, has a positive effect on the health of people after 60 years.

There exists a great number of studies on this issue and it is here only possible to touch upon one or two examples. According to surveys in the United States (Commonwealth, 1991), and contrary to conventional corporate opinion, the general perception of older workers is positive: lower turnover, more conscientious, possessed of better judgement and more flexible. There is strong evidence that older workers are more flexible in their attitudes to work assignments and conditions than younger ones. Indeed, it is thought that because they possess long experience, they can perform multiple tasks and, as the Japanese experience will show, frequently welcome mobility. Having often benefitted from good material conditions during most of their career and with career prospects behind them, they are more ready to accept conditions which would not be acceptable to younger colleagues who have future promotion in mind. A British survey (Warr, 1994) on the topic shows that the performance of older workers surpasses that of younger ones on six accounts: they are reliable, work hard, are effective in their job, think before they act, possess interpersonal skills and work well in teams. On the other hand they fare less well than younger workers in four areas: the ability to grasp new ideas, adaptability to change, acceptance of new technology and the ability to learn quickly. In France, according to the survey made for the French chapter in this study, it appears that in many firms the greater flexibility of older workers is perceived as something which, in years to come, should favour an extension of working life.

There are many work activities in which age is a definite advantage or, at least, neutral (Warr, 1994). We shall see that American firms which have made wide use of older workers and retirees are, as a rule, entirely satisfied with them (H. Sheppard in his chapter). The same appears to be true of Japanese firms, especially the smaller ones, where the long experience of older workers and their ability to perform multiple tasks are highly appreciated. In the UK, such firms as make use of older workers state that they do so for sound commercial reasons: older employees, it is found, establish contacts with aging customers more easily. In many firms, for instance in Japan, we shall see that qualified employees are working as part-time consultants in the firm they used to work for or in an affiliate.

2.2 Age discrimination

There is abundant literature in this area also. One of the most complete studies (Eurolink Age, 1993) revealed that there is substantial discrimination, either direct or indirect, at various stages during the end of career and that it takes, among others, the following forms: early exclusion from the work force, for older unemployed re-entry to the market is virtually impossible, lack of training opportunities and discrimination at retirement age. Discrimination against older workers takes the form of differential treatment based upon prejudices or stereotypes. These include the view that older workers are more expensive, less productive and less adaptable than younger ones. Such prejudices may be held by employers, the public, policy-makers and even by older workers themselves. Sometimes these views reflect real facts, which is why it is crucial to modify wage costs and increase adaptation, for example, through training. Gradual retirement, because it involves part-time work in some shape or form, has been viable particularly in firms where the latter is established or common practice. Part-time work seems to have a number of advantages: it often increases productivity, reduces absenteeism, and enables the firm to retain 'within its walls' the older worker's corporate knowledge and experience while allowing for a reduction of costs and promotion of younger employees.

Age discrimination legislation is the focus of much debate currently and doubtless specific and/or general measures will be forthcoming in the not too distant future. For the time being, however, only the USA (with Spain) has adopted significant measures to protect older workers' rights in employment and reduce blatant forms of discrimination. But, such legislation has not brought about any general improvement in employment opportunities for older workers. This shows to what extent age discrimination is part of the early retirement culture dominant in the USA and in most OECD countries. In countries like Japan and Sweden, by contrast, where different cultures obtain, the authors of the respective chapters will show that there is much less discrimination.

2.3 Personnel management

While until a few years ago personnel management had concentrated mostly on employees between the age of entry to the firm and 40 or 45 years, with the aging of the work force there are signs of a new awareness of age-specific problems within firms and this is beginning to influence the design of human resource management strategies. The sort of end of career problems that tend to crop up around 55 years should in the normal course of events have been foreseen and catered for several years previously. For it is when the employee reaches around 45 that questions about the future role he or she is going to play within the enterprise or outside should begin to be asked. Therefore, the new 'prospective' staff age-management techniques are not designed to produce job security *per se* but rather the added human resource value of constantly updated skills buttressed by experience. The Skills and Aptitudes Review and the Training Plan are two of the main instruments employed in 'prospective' management (Entreprise et Progrès, 1993). The Skills and Aptitudes Review provides a full description of the employee's professional capacities and his/her future potential, the overall aim being to draw up a personal end-of-career plan which, while fully meeting the needs of an enterprise, enables the employee to shape his/her professional future and where necessary acquire any additional training he/she may require to suit his/her or the firm's needs. According to several of the country authors, firms are starting to adopt this approach, and not only the big firms which can more easily afford the costs involved, but also some of the smaller, more dynamic ones.

In some cases it has been found that certain functions are better suited to end-of-career employees and these are being developed in some of the firms surveyed for this study: trainers, tutors, in-house and outside consultants, negotiators. Some firms are starting to adjust structure and practices so as to be able to take full advantage of their older employees. Meanwhile experiments have been conducted on manual workers, for example in France at Renault and Aérospatiale, to introduce modern ergonomic techniques into the workplace and to deploy workers in a differentiated and positive fashion until retirement age.

Personnel age-management also includes managing new kinds of flexibility, reduced time schedules, and working from home part of the week, etc. None of these flexible options is without special problems and yet, once the initial steps have been taken, they often prove to be a source of savings for the employer and of considerable satisfaction for both parties.

2.4 Wage costs

Traditionally, older workers have been more expensive because of the seniority rule which has existed in most firms worldwide. Young workers have, in fact, been subsidising the higher wages of older workers. In principle, there is nothing wrong with this rule; it is an incentive for higher productivity and has led to the life-employment we have known for decades in large corporations and in the public sector. However, it causes problems when the average age of the work force increases and when workers approach the end of career. To the extent that older workers are paid more than their effective productivity, enterprise will have an incentive to get rid of them or, when redundancy occurs, to shed them first. That is the reason why the seniority rule has thus far been, and will remain until abandoned, an obstacle to gradual retirement or to any extension of working life. Moreover, in a few countries, pension rules cause pension contributions to increase with age.

However, as most of our authors will show, there have been profound changes over recent years in adapting pay profiles to performance, first in American and British firms and subsequently, although to a lesser extent, among German, Dutch, French and even Japanese firms. The new performance-based remuneration, especially for professional categories, will promote a different wage profile and should thus make the older employee more competitive.

It is, at all events, now known that productivity per hour in many work functions increases when a worker moves from full- to part-time (see Delsen, 1995). Moreover, experience of part-time work and partial retirement in Swedish firms has shown that part-time work tends to reduce absenteeism which is generally rather high for full-time older workers.

The experience of Japanese and American firms in some sectors has been to retain older workers or re-employ retirees, often on a part-time basis, but performing different tasks, less demanding than the ones they did previously, and, therefore, to pay them considerably less. This practice should not necessarily be encouraged. It is, however, a fact that older workers, especially those drawing a pension or a partial pension, have smaller financial needs. Nevertheless, with continuing training, skilled workers remain productive late in life, especially when working part-time, and could well continue to be active in their field and to be paid according to their performance.

As far as pensions are concerned, rules which make them more expensive for older employees should be modified and should at very least be rendered gradual-retirement or extension-of-working-life neutral.

2.5 Training

The globalisation of the economies will imply that a country's competitiveness largely depends on the quality of its supply side. Investment in human capital becomes a condition *sine qua non* for future competitiveness. Employment adjustments that are too rapid and rely on the external labour market to a large extent, as in the USA, may not prove as satisfactory in the long run as the lower transaction-cost 'employment retention' model prevalent in Japan (Koshiro, 1992). What appears to be increasingly important is the functional flexibility which the new technologies have made necessary. The modern enterprise requires the deployment of higher level skills and performance of a much broader mix of tasks/functions than did the traditional firm.

By extending training opportunities, making employees more effective in their current firms but also more employable in other firms, and by easing thereby the consequences of job loss, the stage can be set for more flexible and hence more productive employment systems. However, what appears to be crucial for gradual retirement is for enterprises to extend training or retraining opportunities until end of career and not to reduce them from the age of 40 or 45 onwards, as has hitherto generally been the case. In the chapters that follow the reader will discern the beginnings of a reverse trend. In many firms early retirement has escalated the demotivation of workers already in their early 50s who see no sense in continuing training since their career prospects are very short. Any form of extension of working life, therefore, has a positive psychological effect on workers who have a reason to invest efforts as well on management which sees training as a longer investment. Greater psychological content will have to be given to training if is to help older workers to remain mobile, motivated and adaptable. Continuing training now has to be adapted to suit the older worker, whose learning and pedagogical needs are known to be different from those of younger cohorts. Training of older workers, then, must be designed to take full advantage of their experience and knowledge in introducing to them new ways of thinking, doing, or being.

Moreover, early retirement policies, it should be noted, have had negative consequences for firms because of the loss of experienced workers who have a capacity for training younger employees and who in general have more to contribute to enterprise culture. Many firms in the USA, France and the UK have recognised these facts and, as we shall see, are now beginning to reverse the trend. Older qualified workers have indeed an important role to play in the training of younger employees whether it is in formal teaching courses or simply by working in teams. It is also becoming quite common to see qualified engineers, economists and insurance experts pursue a second career as teachers in their field of knowledge and work experience.

2.6 Part-time and flexible work

The development of part-time employment which has been rapid over the last two decades has, as it were, prepared the ground for gradual retirement and greatly enhanced its potential for the years to come. In countries where rather traditional attitudes to part-time work have for long existed, such as Germany, France and Japan, employers' attitudes have started to change and the need for flexible work patterns has at least been recognised. Employers' objections to part-time work, job sharing or gradual retirement are invariably the same: a job cannot be 'split', organisational problems, failures to communicate, decreased work commitment, poorer output. However, where part-time work has been developed or job sharing used, supervisors generally welcome it. Where it has not been experienced, people tend to be sceptical (Delsen, 1995). Practice shows that many more functions could be performed by part-timers than is currently the case, that even jobs hitherto considered to be totally 'unsplittable' e.g. management functions can in fact be viably divided.

Experience in Europe with gradual retirement thus far shows that where managers view part-time work positively, reduction of work time has caused few problems, once the initial organisational and adaptation stage is passed. Against the extra administrative, planning and sometimes equipment costs, must be set reduction in absenteeism, higher flexibility, improved morale and raised productivity. The benefits gained from retaining the skills of older workers outweigh their costs, and this will be especially the case when the supply of new entrants to the work force diminishes. Where a job can be shared between a younger and an older worker, not only will the employer be able to retain the human resource capital of the older worker but the system may also provide – as practice in French firms will show – a cost-effective way of imparting a specific skill endowment to young workers.

Both working conditions and pension provision should be sufficiently flexible to enable the transition from work to retirement to take place smoothly. But, in principle, there are structurally no business or economic obstacles to the introduction of gradual retirement (Hart 1984; Delsen 1995). The latter could also be a useful praxis for developing part-time and flexible work patterns in enterprise and could, finally, prove an ideal way of lengthening working life.

2.7 Employee preferences and the life-cycle

The rigid, linear, three-phase life cycle – youth and training, adult life and work, withdrawal from work and retirement – that has predominated throughout the period of the mature industrial revolution is today gradually being replaced by a cycle which is less certain, less predictable and of necessity more creative. Among other things it is characterised by more flexible work patterns, more training throughout professional life, periods of unemployment and sabbatical leave, and more active retirement. Gradual retirement is therefore very much part of this new approach to the life cycle.

Workers who have retired over the last twenty years had usually begun what proved a long and arduous working life at an early age. They have been part of the long pattern of economic growth and, while largely benefitting from exceptional material well-being, they have often had little time to devote to activities outside the work place. Retirement comes, then, as a well-deserved rest, a kind of golden period with time to enjoy the leisure a good pension makes possible. However, many surveys have already revealed that overnight or 'couperet' retirement has proved a difficult experience for many retirees who have not had time to adjust before entering it. Many have switched from a position of social prestige within their company into what has been called 'social oblivion' (Guillemard, 1990). If only for this reason, a fair proportion of retirees wish to remain mentally alert and socially integrated.

People retiring in 2000 and beyond will, for the most part, have enjoyed much longer periods of education and training. Their working life will have often been interrupted by unemployment or part-time employment, for a few, by sabbatical leave. On the whole, most of them will have experienced much more flexible work patterns than their parents' generation. Indeed, new categories of employee nowadays – other than mothers of young children or young people in training – are concerned to organise their work in new ways and frequently quite simply to work less. These new categories include workers in the mid-life period who wish to combine regular work with meeting other requirements (e.g. self employment, a return to training, community service of one sort or another, caring for elderly parents, etc.), and workers at the end of their career who wish gradually to move from a full-time working life into healthy retirement. Since their youth, this generation has had much more leisure time and a majority has had continuing training in service or outside the firm. Often they have had two or three different careers (Gaullier, 1992).

When these workers, the baby-boomers, are questioned about their wishes with regard to retirement, many – particularly if they are qualified and sense that they are making a valid contribution – would wish to keep a foot in the occupational door for some years after the legal retirement age. As was so aptly observed, the relative utility of leisure and retirement to that of work will tend to diminish in the years to come (Kessler, 1990). However, a majority of baby-boomers will wish to alter their work rhythm and will, therefore, be attracted by part-time work as part of a gradual withdrawal from full-time employment. Recent European surveys (Eurobarometer, 1993) confirm that most people are in favour of flexible retirement, and American surveys have shown that, for men, the desire to work part-time increases with age (Sheppard in his chapter).

References

Delsen, L. (1995), *Atypical Employment: An International Perspective. Causes, Consequences and Policy*, Wolters-Noordhoff, Groningen.

Entreprise et Progrès (1993), *La gestion des fins de carrière – La préretraite n'est pas un acquis social*, Paris.

Eurobarometer (1993), *Age and Attitudes*, Commission of the European Communities, DG v, Brussels.

Eurolink Age (1993), *Age Discrimination against Older Workers in the European Community*, London.

Gaullier, X. (1992), 'The Changing Ages of Man', *The Geneva Papers on Risk and Insurance,* no. 62, January, pp. 3-25.

Guillemard, A-M. (1990), 'Les nouvelles frontières entre travail et retraite en France', *La Revue de l'IRES,* no. 2 (Hiver), pp. 41-98, Paris.

Hart, R.A. (1984), *Shorter Working Time. A Dilemma for Collective Bargaining,* OECD, Paris.

Kessler, D. (1990), *Les quatre piliers de la retraite,* Etudes et Dossiers, no. 144, The International Association for the Study of Insurance Economics, Mars, Geneva.

Koshiro, K. (ed.) (1992), *Employment Security and Labor Market Flexibility: An International Perspective,* Wayne State University Press, Detroit.

The Commonwealth Fund (1991), *New Findings Show why Employing Workers over 50 makes good financial Sense for Companies,* New York.

Warr, P. (1994), 'Research into the Work Performance of Older Employees', *The Geneva Papers on Risk and Insurance,* no. 73, October, pp. 472-480.

PART II

GRADUAL RETIREMENT
IN SELECTED
EU COUNTRIES

3 Gradual retirement in Sweden

Eskil Wadensjö

Up to the mid-1980s, both the coverage of State welfare in Sweden and the level of the benefits it provided improved steadily. New schemes were established and income replacement, by international standards, remained high. Generous benefits were, however, accompanied by a strong commitment to keeping the active population in work, as was, for example, illustrated by the country's active labour market policy. While low take-up rates with some welfare schemes demonstrated that high benefit levels do not always lead to high overall expenditure, with many of the other income transfer systems, sickness benefit being one example, both take-up rates and replacement rates rose. The cost of earnings related pensions (ATP) also climbed as the system matured and as a result of demographic trends. So that, in the second half of the 1980s, the cost of transfer programmes became the focus of public debate and attempts were made to curtail expenditure and increase work incentives, health insurance and survivors' pensions being two of the benefit schemes affected.

The 1980s were, indeed, characterised by a prolonged period of economic expansion with labour force participation climbing to a high level and unemployment dropping very low. But, in 1991, a fall in domestic demand and a drop in exports caused the economy to switch rapidly from a state of overheat to recession. The contraction in domestic demand was due mainly to badly-timed changes by the Government in regulations governing financial markets and foreign payments and in the tax system which combined to trigger a sudden rise in private savings and a crisis in the property market and construction industry. An overvalued *krona* and an international recession were responsible for the drop in exports, and fear of inflation caused the Government to delay with counter-cyclical measures such as public relief works. This already unsatisfactory situation was worsened by action, taken during the early stages of the recession, to solve long-term structural problems. Unemployment reached high levels, unprecedented in the post-war period, and labour force participation declined. The resulting fall in tax returns, together with increased expenditure on social transfer programmes, especially unemployment benefits, led to a huge deficit and a rapidly rising public debt. By way of response, the Government introduced several changes to income transfer systems, tightened the rules on eligibility, and lowered replacement rates.

3.1   Macro issues and policies

Recent trends

The development of the Swedish labour market over the post-war period can roughly be divided into two: an extended period from 1945 to 1990 with low unemployment and gradually rising labour force participation, followed by the current crisis with high unemployment and a huge fall in labour force partici-pation. The first period was marked by gradual expansion of the coverage and benefit levels of most public welfare programmes, and the crisis that followed it, by rapid contraction in the coverage and benefit levels.

Over the decades prior to the current crisis, labour force participation for those aged 16 to 64 increased steadily from 72 per cent in 1963 (the first year of the labour force survey) to 85 per cent in 1990. For those aged 65 and over, however, participation diminished. Over the same period also the composition of the labour force changed: female labour force participation increased greatly (from 54 to 83 per cent) while male labour force participation contracted slightly (from 90 to 87 per cent).

The latter contraction of male labour force participation was mainly confined to the young and the old. The decline among young people can be explained largely in terms of the lengthening duration of formal education since today most children remain in school for at least 12 years. As to the labour force participation of older workers, one might be tempted to hold the change in the official retirement age – which in 1976 was lowered from 67 to 65 years – largely responsible for its decline. It should be noted, however, that participa-tion has decreased also among those below 65 and the decline in the 65 to 67 age-group commenced prior to 1976.

From 1991 to 1993 labour force participation plummeted for both men and women, unemployment reaching altogether unprecedented levels. In 1994, however, both labour force participation and employment began slowly to pick up. Even so, in 1995, unemployment is still at a very high level.

Labour market position of older workers

Increased basic pensions in the late 1940s and a major pension reform in 1960 are factors behind the reduction in the labour force participation of those over the official retirement age in the post-war period. In 1990 only a fifth of all men aged 65-69 participated in the labour market and many of those who worked did so only part-time (see table 3.1).

Table 3.1
Long-term development of male labour force participation rates in Sweden

	50-54	55-59	60-64	65-69	70-74	75+
1960	95.1	92.3	82.5	50.6	20.3	7.3
1965	94.5	91.9	82.4	45.7	16.8	5.7
1970	91.9	88.4	75.4	31.3	5.0	—
1975	90.2	85.5	68.5	21.8	7.3	2.3
1980	89.9	84.4	65.9	14.4	7.4	2.6
1985	90.3	85.3	63.2	19.1	10.1	5.4
1990	89.5	84.1	63.9	19.5	9.8	4.3

Note: Over the period considered, there have been several changes in the definitions and methods used in the census.
Source: Statistics Sweden, Population censuses.

Since the mid-1960s, there has been a marked decrease in labour force participation among those aged 60-64 and to a lesser extent also among those aged 55-59 years. The changes in the 1980s, however, were smaller than in the previous decades.

Labour force participation has increased among women in all age-groups except for teenagers and for those 65 years and older (see table 3.2). Note that labour force participation increased considerably also among women aged 60-64 and 55-59 in the 1970s and 1980s.

The unemployment rate was low among older workers, 1.4 per cent for men and 2.5 per cent for women aged 60-64, and 1.1 per cent for men and 0.9 per cent for women aged 55-59 in 1990.

Modes of labour exit
In the 1990s labour force participation has fallen among all age-groups, most among young people, and more among older workers than among those aged 25-54. For men aged 60-64 the labour force participation rate decreased from 63.2 per cent in 1990 to 56.3 per cent in 1994. For women of the same age the participation rate decreased from 53.9 to 46.7 per cent. For those aged 55-59 the changes were smaller; from 87.8 to 82.0 per cent for men and from 79.2

to 77.6 per cent for women. Labour force participation according to age in 1994 is shown in table 3.3.

Table 3.2
Long-term development of female labour force participation rates in Sweden

	50-54	55-59	60-64	65-69	70-74	75+
1960	35.2	31.3	21.1	9.6	2.8	1.0
1965	41.9	36.2	24.7	9.7	2.8	0.8
1970	50.3	41.1	25.5	7.6	0.9	—
1975	68.8	57.7	35.1	8.5	1.8	0.5
1980	77.8	66.4	41.4	6.1	2.1	0.5
1985	83.1	72.5	45.6	6.9	2.6	1.1
1990	85.8	76.8	53.1	9.3	2.9	0.9

Note: see table 3.1.
Source: Statistics Sweden, Population censuses.

Table 3.3
The labour market situation in 1994 according to age in Sweden

Age	Men			Women		
	Labour force participation (%)	Unemployment (%)	Part-time work* (%)	Labour force participation (%)	Unemployment (%)	Part-time work* (%)
16-19	25.5	17.7	54.7	29.0	15.5	71.3
20-24	66.8	19.3	16.1	64.8	13.9	38.6
25-34	86.8	10.9	6.9	80.9	8.8	38.2
35-44	91.5	7.4	5.0	88.6	5.3	42.1
45-54	91.2	5.3	4.7	88.7	3.7	34.8
55-59	82.0	7.0	8.7	77.6	3.8	44.0
60-64	56.3	9.3	44.6	46.7	7.0	65.7
60	70.7	7.9	32.9	65.6	5.8	57.6
61	62.2	8.7	45.4	53.3	6.3	62.9
62	55.8	9.4	48.8	47.0	5.1	67.2
63	48.1	9.0	49.7	39.0	10.1	73.0
64	44.9	12.4	51.0	30.1	9.7	73.9
65-74	14.1	—	76.8	4.3	—	83.6

* Part-time workers – 34 hours a week or less – as a percentage of those employed.
Source: Statistics Sweden, Labour Force surveys.

For older workers the decrease in labour force participation is chiefly due to an increase in early exit. Until 1994 the drop in labour force participation was parallelled by an increase in the number of new disability pensions and occupational injury annuities. However, in 1994 the number of new disability pensions dropped drastically to its lowest level since changes to the disability pension system were adopted in the early 1970s. The number of new occupational injury annuities also decreased dramatically.

As labour force participation has decreased, so unemployment among older workers has increased. The unemployment rate for those aged 60 to 64 increased to 9.3 per cent for men and 7.0 per cent for women in 1994, and to 7.0 per cent for men and 3.8 per cent for women for those aged 55-59. Unemployment reached a peak in 1993 and has since then slowly decreased, especially among young people. Among older workers unemployment has continued to rise.

Age of retirement
The official retirement age was 67 up to July 1, 1976, and has been 65 thereafter. It has, moreover, been the same for men and women since the introduction of a basic old age pension in 1913. However, some groups, for example policemen, nurses and miners, have been governed by regulations or agreements which stipulate a lower retirement age. In recent decades, there has been a general tendency to cancel such rules and to raise the retirement age to 65. The most obvious explanation for retirement before the age of 65 is that many use various options for early exit from the labour market.

One crude measure of the development of the effective age of retirement is the age at which 50 per cent of a given cohort remain in the labour force. See figure 3.1. Figure 3.1 shows that the effective male retirement age has gradually decreased. The decline was strongest in the early 1970s and in the 1990s. The effective retirement age now stands at around 63 years, lower than the official retirement age but higher than the effective age of most other countries. The effective retirement age of women measured in this way increased up to the early 1990s as part of the general rise in labour force participation among women. However, in the early 1990s, the effective retirement age declined even for women. The difference in the effective retirement ages of men and women has gradually narrowed and is now only one year compared to more than ten years in the mid-1960s.

Pensions and social security[1]

Pension system
Payments from social insurance and occupational insurance schemes are the most important forms of income support for older workers who have left the labour market.

Figure 3.1 The age at which 50 per cent are in the Swedish labour force
1965-1994; men and women

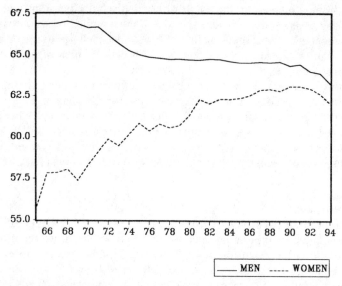

Source: Statistics Sweden, Labour Force Surveys.

Sweden has a national pension system which provides basic support for those
aged 65 years and over (35,200 SEK in 1994). From the age of 60 it is possible
to choose a reduced old age pension (a reduction which will continue after 65).
The pension may also be delayed up to the age of 70, in which case it is
increased. Few, however, use the option of drawing an old age pension at any
other age than 65. Those who retire early tend to use other options which we
shall be examining below.

Over and above the national basic pension, most people obtain the ATP
pension which is national, supplementary, earnings-related and compulsory. For
a person who has been in the labour force at least 30 years and who retires at
65, the replacement rate of the basic pension and ATP combined is about 65 per
cent. Those without or with a low ATP receive a supplement to the basic
pension and thereby achieve a higher replacement rate. The 10 per cent of the
population with highest income receive – because of a ceiling in the ATP-
system – a replacement rate lower than 65 per cent from social insurance
pension, but the shortfall is, in substantial measure, made up from occupational
pensions.

For the vast majority of people, pensions from the national social insurance
or 1st pillar schemes are supplemented by payments from occupational or 2nd
pillar insurance schemes. The scheme for blue-collar workers in the private

sector was introduced in the 1970s, those for the other groups in earlier decades. With the exception of the above-mentioned scheme for blue-collar workers, occupational pension schemes compensate for earnings over the ceiling in the ATP pension. When occupational pensions are added to pensions from the social insurance schemes, the replacement rate at the official retirement age is 75 per cent for most people.

Disability pensions and labour market programmes
Most of those who leave the labour market before the age of 65 do so on being awarded a disability pension (more often than not the decision to grant a disability pension is preceded by a period during which sickness cash or unemployment benefit are drawn). Up to September 1991, it was possible to be awarded a disability pension for three reasons: 1) on medical grounds (for those aged 16 to 65 years), 2) on medical and labour market grounds (for those aged 60 to 65), and 3) on labour market grounds (for those aged 60 to 65 who have exhausted their right to unemployment benefit). If a person has been employed before receiving a disability pension (or employed before the prior sickness or unemployment period), the latter is generally combined with benefits from occupational insurance schemes. Disability pensions on exclusively labour market grounds were discontinued in September 1991. They were often called '58.3 pensions'. The explanation for this peculiar name is a specific combination of various insurance schemes. When a firm had redundancies and wanted to initiate lay-offs, according to the Law on Employment Protection (from 1974) those with the lowest seniority should go first. However, firms and trade unions can make exceptions to the rule if they agree and did so in most cases so that older workers from 58 years and 3 months and older were laid off. If a worker of that age was laid off, he obtained unemployment benefits up to the age of 60 and thereafter a disability pension for labour market reasons was granted. This system of '58.3 pensions' had become very popular.

Another early exit option of which use rapidly increased in the late 1980s is exit with an annuity from the occupational injury insurance scheme. Once again, national social insurance is supplemented by occupational insurance. In this case the replacement rate was always one hundred per cent until changes were introduced in 1993.

Labour market policy is also an important part of social policy for older workers in Sweden. None of the labour market programmes is exclusively for older workers but all, except those specifically aimed at the youth labour force, are open to them. Not surprisingly, older workers are under-represented in labour market training. People from most age-groups are placed in public relief work, but rather few are 60 years or over. However, in the last two years, a new public relief programme, ALU, has been extensively used for older workers also. Workers from all age-groups are eligible for placement in disability programmes, of which the two most important are sheltered workshops owned by the Government and subsidised work in the private sector. Both programmes mean long-term placement for many, in some cases up to the age of 65. The relative importance of disability programmes has tended to grow and with it the older workers' share of them in labour market programmes. Labour market programmes may, moreover, combine with a benefit from social insurance, so that, for example, a beneficiary may work half-time in a sheltered workshop and draw a half disability pension.

Part-time pensions in Sweden[2]
An important difference between Sweden and most other countries is that in Sweden it is possible to combine part-time work with a part-time pension, thus facilitating gradual withdrawal from the labour force. There are three possible ways of doing this:

1 between the ages of 60 and 65, a partial early old age pension may be drawn, i.e. one may combine part-time retirement with work part-time. Between 1960 and 1993 the only alternative to a full-time early old age pension was a half pension. From July 1993 onwards, however, it has been possible to draw ¼, ½ and ¾ of the pension. An early partial drawing of the pension means that the latter is reduced, a reduction that continues after the official retirement age at 65. Conversely a delayed drawing of part of the pension, i.e. starting or continuing part-time work after that age until 70 years, increases the pension;

2 combining a disability pension with work is also possible. Between 1970 and 1993, three forms of disability pension were possible: the full pension and, for those retaining some work capacity, a 2/3 and a ½ pension. As of July 1993, two new forms were added: the ¾ and ¼ pensions, and no new 2/3 pensions were granted;

3 a partial pension scheme was launched in July 1976 with the following eligibility requirements: i) the candidate had to be between 60 and 65 years, ii) work time had to be reduced by at least 5 hours a week, iii) remaining work time had to amount to at least 17 hours a week, iv) the candidate must have worked at least 10 years since the age of 45, and v) had to reside in Sweden. Provided the employer's consent had been obtained, a partial pension would be awarded on application by a candidate. The income replacement rate under the scheme was 65 per cent up to 1981, when, until 1987, it was lowered to 50 per cent, after which it was restored to 65 per cent.

In 1994 the *Riksdag*, Sweden's Parliament, made certain changes as part of a plan for a new old age pension system. The starting age for entitlement to a partial pension was raised from 60 to 61 years, the replacement rate was lowered from 65 to 55 per cent, and the maximum reduction compensated for was set at ten hours.

The impact of these changes on the number of people with pensions can be seen, first, from a comparison of the number of part-time pensions in 1980, 1986 and 1993, and second, from the development in the awarding of new partial pensions over this period.

It will be observed that, as a result of the lowering of the partial pension replacement rate just referred to, the number of people with a part-time pension decreased between 1980 and 1986 (see table 3.4). It will also be seen that restoration of the replacement rate to 65 per cent in January 1987 led to a fresh increase in the number of partial pensions from 32,180 in 1986 to 48,608 in 1993.

Table 3.4
People aged 60-64 in various part-time pension schemes in Sweden
in 1980, 1986, and 1993

	1980		1986		1993	
	Men	Women	Men	Women	Men	Women
Disability pension						
3/4				183	99	
2/3	1,400	2,512	1,110	2,246	873	953
1/2	4,219	2,854	7,214	6,030	8,591	8,584
1/4					74	144
Early old age pension						
3/4					7	2
1/2	416	79	2,927	310	1,985	437
1/4					150	35
Partial pension	46,504	21,333	18,560	13,620	29,907	18,701
Total	52,123	23,929	29,811	22,206	41,770	28,955

Sources: Riksförsäkringsverket 1981 and 1985/86; Riksförsäkringsverket, Statistisk information 1994:2 and 1994:14; Information from the Riksförsäkringsverket.

The inflow of new partial pensions has varied with the replacement rate and the business cycle (see figure 3.2). It has been higher in periods of higher replacement and of high unemployment, and especially so in 1980 and 1992. In 1980 it was announced that, as of 1981, the replacement rate for new partial pensions would be reduced from 65 to 50 per cent and many people chose to apply for a partial pension before that reduction took place. In 1992 the Government first tried to discontinue the granting of new partial pensions and later

Figure 3.2   New partial pensions in Sweden, 1976-1994

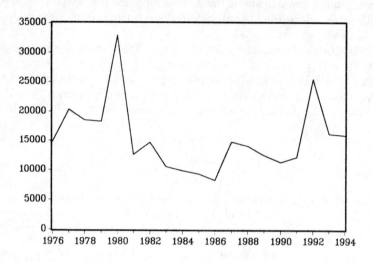

Source: Riksförsäkringsverket (National Social Insurance Board), 1995.
Delpensioneringen t o m 1994. Statistikinformation 1995:1.

to lower the replacement rate. On both occasions many people made applications before the intended dates of change, and on both occasions the Government failed to get support for the proposals in the *Riksdag*. The number of partial pensions increased somewhat in 1994, probably as a response to changes in the rules for compensation and in the number of hours compensated.

As already stated, from 1995 onwards, only ten hours reduction will be compensated for. The majority, 72 per cent of men and 53 per cent of women in June 1994, had reduced their work time by more than 10 hours. A reduction from 40 to 20 hours, from full-time to half-time, has proved to be quite common. It is likely that employers have found this form of reduction easy to handle by letting two persons share a full-time job. Under the new rules, however, in most cases this will no longer be possible.

To sum up, then, part-time pension schemes, especially the partial pension system, have led to shorter working hours on average for workers aged 60-64. This is especially so for men in this age-group as part-time work for other reasons has been relatively unusual among adult men in general. Figure 3.3 shows the development in work hours for older men. Work hours for those aged 60, 62 and 64 are compared to those aged 59 (who are not entitled to part-time pensions except under the disability pension system). The figure shows that in practice there was no difference in working hours in the years just preceding the introduction in 1976 of the partial pension system, and that the differences after 1980 have gradually increased, the difference being greater the higher the age.

Figure 3.3 The difference in average work hours between men aged 59 and those aged 60, 62, and 64 in Sweden, over the period 1963-1993

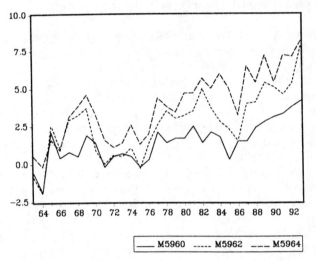

Source: Statistics Sweden, Labour Force Surveys.

New public policies

Even if, by international standards, labour force participation is high in Sweden, it has been decreasing among older men. The authorities have been very concerned about this decline as also about the increased utilisation of social insurance schemes by older workers. Several of the recent or proposed changes to social insurance schemes have been introduced with the intention of influencing labour market participation, and some, at least, appear to have had this effect. Hereafter, I list and briefly comment on some of the more significant of these changes:

1 since September 1991 disability pensions are no longer granted on labour market grounds only. The abolition of disability pensions on labour market grounds was offset by disability pensioning on combined medical and labour market grounds. The total number of new disability pensions increased

rapidly to reach an all-time high in 1992 and 1993 but decreased strikingly in 1994;

2 as part of the new pension system which was agreed upon in spring 1994 between the Government and the Social Democratic party, from July 1994 the partial pension system was changed: the replacement rate and the number of hours compensated were lowered, and the minimum age raised. Under this agreement the law will later be altered so that no new partial pensions will be awarded from the year 2000. The intention is that part-time pensioning should continue but in the form of early old age pensioning;

3 the main direction of labour market policy changed in the 1980s from public relief work (with many older participants) to labour market training (with few older participants). The resulting decrease of older workers in labour market programmes was hardly an intended consequence. In the last three years different forms of public relief works have been expanded and with them the participation of older workers in labour market programmes;

4 a change in the official retirement age from 65 to 66 was a part of a crisis agreement involving the government and the major opposition party in the fall of 1992. The plan was later abandoned and the retirement age will continue to be 65 years. In practice, however, steps have been taken to raise the retirement age in the new pension system which was adopted in 1994 by the *Riksdag* and will be launched in 1996. Features of this new pension system are:

i   according to the job security law, the seniority rule is valid at lay-off up to the age of 65. People aged 65 and over are not protected by the law. Under the new pension reform, that age will be increased to 66 years from 1997 and to 67 from 1998;

ii   the pension system has been changed so that the pension is lower than previously for those who stop working at 65. On the other hand, the replacement rate will be maintained for those who continue to work until they are 67;

iii   the earliest age at which an old age pension (partial or full) can be drawn is to be raised from 60 to 61 when the new pension system comes into force in 1996;

iv   under the current system, average earnings over the best 15 years between the ages 16 to 65 provide the base for pension calculation, and 30 years or more with at least one (price-indexed) basic amount in earnings including social transfer income (the amount was 35,200 SEK in 1994) suffice for entitlement to a full pension. Under the new system, pension calculation will be based on lifetime earnings. Earnings in all years bear upon the pension, even after the age of 65.

The above changes, (i) to (iv), will doubtless act as incentives for people to retire later;

5 in 1991, legal changes were introduced to promote the rehabilitation of long-term sick employees (SFS 1991:1040);
6 in 1993, several changes were made to the occupational injury scheme. The most important were a stricter definition of an occupational injury and a lowering of the compensation level from 100 per cent to that of sickness cash benefits. The number of new annuities granted has also decreased as a result of changes to the law;
7 in July 1995, a new wage subsidy programme for older unemployed workers started. Employers receive up to 50 per cent of wage costs if they hire long-term unemployed older workers.

The changes to pension schemes described in this section will influence retirement behaviour in the years to come. Other changes will doubtless be introduced over the next few years since several government committees are currently working in the area of social insurance and labour market legislation.

3.2 Micro issues and policies

Recent trends

Company pension regulations

In Sweden the replacement rates in social and occupational insurance schemes are high – around 75 per cent on average for most people receiving an old age or disability pension. The pensions from the first and second pillars are augmented to some extent by either group pensions or by personal pensions. Although at present they account for only a tiny portion (approximately 1 per cent) of total pensions paid out, they are increasing and over the coming decades their coverage is expected to expand.

This means that company pensions are of very little importance in Sweden. There are two minor exceptions: 1) personal pensions for key personnel and top management designed to retain personnel and secure tax relief, and 2) personal pensions paid by the employer to staff who have been laid off with a view to smoothing the severance process and facilitating exceptions to the seniority rule. Under this arrangement, employees are paid a pension until the official retirement age of 65. This type of pension exists in several forms, called 'guarantee pensions', generally offered to selected individuals or to all those over a certain age.

Age discrimination

Sweden has no law against age discrimination which has thus far not been an issue of public debate. Age bars in personnel advertisements, for example, are not forbidden but not very common either. Public employers and large firms almost never indicate age bars in advertisements. When they do occur, they are chiefly to be found in advertisements for personnel by retail firms and restaurants. Statistics from the National Labour Market Board show that older people who become unemployed in many cases obtain jobs even if their unemployment spells are longer than those of younger people. This does not mean that age discrimination does not exist, most companies probably have a preferred age span for a vacancy, but age discrimination is not openly stated and is probably not as strong as in many other countries.

In the last few years, however, company policies towards older workers in Sweden and more generally the situation of older workers in the labour market has become a political issue. One manifestation of this is the founding of a new organisation, '50+', which aims to strengthen the labour market situation of older workers. '50+' was started with the support of the unions as well as of employers and employers' organisations.

New company policies

Pay policy

By comparison with most other countries, Sweden has a very even wage structure. This is to a great extent the result of the solidaristic wage policy pursued by the LO (the Swedish Confederation of Trade Unions), the central trade union organisation for manual workers. The unions of salaried employees also have to a considerable extent followed a policy of the same type. This means that the age-wage profile is less steep in Sweden than in most other countries and therefore economic incentives to get rid of older workers are weaker. The obstacles to taking on older workers may also be lessened if age and wage are unrelated or only weakly related.

Since the early 1980s the employers' organisations have attempted to discontinue the solidaristic wage policy by trying to avoid central wage agreements which cover the entire private sector. They have succeeded to some extent and the wage spread has increased even if, by international standards, it still is limited. The employers' policy, however, has not been to increase the wage spread according to age (with the exception of a lowering of youth wages) but to strengthen the relation between productivity (education, skill) and wages. The increased wage spread may not, therefore, have negative employment consequences for older workers.

Part-time and flexible work

Part-time is frequent among older workers in Sweden. As we have seen many combine part-time work with a partial pension. Most of those in receipt of a partial pension start to draw it at the age of 60. Of those who started drawing a partial pension in December 1991, 1992, and 1993, 60.6, 65.3 and 80.4 per cent were 60 years of age. Many receive a partial pension from the same month in which they reach the age of 60 or a few months thereafter. Most of those who are granted a partial pension continue to receive it until the age of 65. Few people increase their work hours to the extent that they are no longer eligible for a partial pension, few forfeit their right to belong to the partial pension system by reducing their work time below the 17-hour limit, and few leave in order to draw another type of pension. This means that prior to the recent changes to the rules, those with partial pensions were about equally divided among those aged 60, 61, 62, 63 and 64.

It can be said, then, that many employees reduce their work hours at the age of 60 and continue to work part-time up to the age of 65. It is the employee who must apply for the partial pension but with the consent of the employer as regards reduction of work hours. Figure 3.4 shows the work hours of those receiving a partial pension for those who worked 40 hours before the reduction (as the majority of those with partial pensions did).

This figure shows very marked concentration on 20 hours (half-time), 32 hours (4 working-days a week), 24 (3 working-days a week), and to a lesser

Figure 3.4   Work hours in 1994 after receiving a partial pension for those who had been working 40 hours a week in Sweden

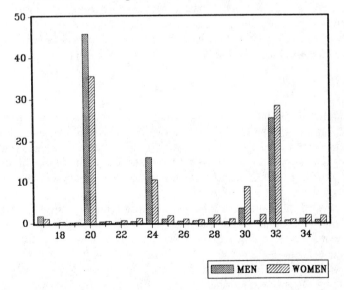

Source: Computations for this study by Riksförsäkringsverket.

extent on 30 hours (¾ of full-time). Very few reduced from a 40 hour week their work hours to other lengths of work-week.

There are no statistics on the distribution of partial pensioners by industry and occupation. Data on the distribution of partial pensioners who are members of unemployment insurance societies can be used as a proxy. The unemployment insurance societies are organised by the unions and the majority of partial pensioners (c. 85 per cent) are members of unions and thereby of unemployment insurance societies. The unions are mainly organised by industry, with separate unions for white-collar and blue-collar workers. The number of partial pensioners who are members of an unemployment insurance society account for 1.3 per cent of the total membership of unemployment insurance societies overall. Among the larger unemployment insurance societies (more than 30,000 members) the percentage varies between 0.4 and 2.4 per cent. The percentage is highest among the unions in manufacturing, somewhat higher among white collar-workers than blue-collar workers, but in all unions in this sector higher than the total average of 1.3 per cent. In all other unions the percentage is lower than the average. The lowest percentages being found among bank employees and those employed in hotel and restaurants. The low percentage among bank employees is probably the result of the crisis in the banking sector in the early 1990s which initiated the frequent use of various types of full-time early pension. In the public sector partial pensioning is more frequent among members of white-collar than among blue-collar unemployment insurance societies.

The general conclusion is that partial pensions are used in all industries, for both white-collar and blue-collar workers, but they have tended to be more frequent in manufacturing than in other sectors and more frequent among white-collar than among blue-collar workers in all sectors.

Training

One indicator of company policy towards older workers is the extent to which their training programmes are open to older workers. Since 1986, Statistics Sweden has conducted surveys of firms' training of employees. From 1988 onwards this has been achieved by adding extra questions to the labour force surveys. Training is defined in these surveys as that which has been fully or partially financed by the employer.

The extent of the training is impressive. From January to July 1994, 2.8 per cent of all work hours were devoted to training and 38 per cent of all employees took part in at least some training during this period. Surprisingly, the percentage who were given training varies only slightly with age – 36 per cent of those aged 55-64 took part in training compared to the average of 38 per cent, and the average number of days of training is 5.5 for those aged 55-64 compared to 6.7 for all irrespective of age (see table 3.5).

The impression that the extent of training varies only slightly with age is strengthened by the fact that those with higher education and those who work full-time are substantially overrepresented among those trained. Older workers are certainly underrepresented among the above groups but, even so, only slightly underrepresented among those trained overall.

Table 3.5
Personnel training in Sweden, January-June 1994

Age	None	5 days or less	6 days - 1 month	More than one month
16-24	77	18	4	1
25-34	63	28	7	2
35-44	57	31	9	2
45-54	56	33	10	2
55-64	64	28	7	1
All	62	28	8	2

Source: Statistics Sweden, Statistiska Meddelanden, Education and training of the labour force 1993 and 1994, U39 SM9501.

Company policy in times of restructuring

Restructuring within a firm often has major implications for the employment of older workers irrespective of whether the firm closes down or not. Two examples will be presented here.

In 1991 *Folksam*, one of Sweden's largest insurance companies, undertook major reorganisation of its structure which entailed a large reduction in personnel. To achieve this reduction, employees with health problems were asked to apply for disability pensions (available from social insurance) and all employees aged 55 years and older were given an opportunity to apply for a pension which would yield 72 per cent of their salary up to the age of 65 provided they volunteered to leave the company. Later the offer was increased to 80 per cent of the salary. The overall result was that some 357 out of 633 aged 55 or over left the company with a 'guarantee pension' that they would continue to draw until the age of 65 (see Isaksson and Johansson, 1994).

A study by Donald Storrie (1993) of workers who were laid off when the Uddevalla shipyard was closed in 1985-87 shows how different programmes were used for different age-groups. Younger workers who could not imme-diately find new jobs were often placed in labour market training or public relief works. Older workers, especially those between 50-58 years, were very often placed in disability programmes (43 per cent of all those laid off who were between the ages of 50 and 54). The oldest ones, 58 years and over, in practice all left the labour market through various forms of disability pension. It is important to note that placement in most disability programmes means long-term placement.

These two examples show how labour market programmes, social insurance, and supplementary payment from firms may be used to encourage early exit from the labour market. The changes in the social insurance systems we have referred to may lead to increased reliance on supplementary payments from firms and probably also thereby to a decrease in the number of early exits.

3.3 Potential for gradual retirement and recommendations

At the beginning of the 1960s retirement behaviour was fairly uniform in Sweden. Most male blue-collar workers continued to work up to the then official retirement age of 67, while male white-collar workers retired at the age of 65 with an occupational pension covering the period up to 67. Since then a system of gradual retirement has successively developed. It is gradual in two senses: 1) many, especially blue-collar workers, leave the labour force before the ordinary retirement age which is now 65, and 2) many leave after a period of combined part-time work and part-time pension.

The combination of part-time work and part-time pension has now become very common among those aged 60 to 65, much more so than in other countries. Part of the explanation for this may be the existence of relatively generous replacement rates and part also the fact that before the introduction of the partial pension system firms were already familiar with the organisation of part-time work. Female labour force participation started to expand as early as the 1960s in Sweden with many women working part-time.

As described in some detail in this chapter, major changes to the system have been introduced since January 1995. These changes are leading to a drastic reduction in the number of new partial pensions. In January and February 1995 only 232 new partial pensions were awarded compared to 2,134 in the same period in 1994. This is mainly due to the rise in the minimum partial retirement age from 60 to 61. No new cohort will become eligible for partial pensions in 1995 (and most of those who applied for a pension before 1995 did so in the same year they reached the minimum age). The number of new partial pensions will probably increase in 1996, but because of the more stringent terms will most likely not reach the same levels as before 1995.

The reduction in the number of new partial pensions may lead to an increase in the number of part-time early old age pensions, to increased frequency of full-time work (at least until the age of 65), but also to increased pressure on existing full-time early exit pathways, and also to the construction of new pathways financed by firms or under agreements on new occupational insurance schemes.

In conclusion, Sweden already has a functioning system for gradual retirement – part-time work and a part-time pension for many of those aged 60-65. Several changes have recently been introduced in this and related systems, but the consequences of these changes are still unknown.

Notes

1 See Wadensjö (1991) for a more detailed presentation.
2 See Ginsburgh (1985), Wadensjö (1994) and Wise (1990) for more information on the part-time pension systems.

References

Ginsburgh, Helen (1985), 'Flexible and Partial Retirement for Norwegian and Swedish Workers', *Monthly Labor Review*, 108, no. 10, pp. 33-43.
Isaksson, K. and G. Johansson (1994), Gå i pension eller fortsätta jobba ..., Department of Psychology, Stockholm University and Folksam, May.
Riksförsäkringsverket (National Social Insurance Board), *Allmän försäkring* 1981 and 1985/86.
Riksförsäkringsverket (National Social Insurance Board) (1994a), Delpensioneringen t o m 1993. *Statistikinformation*, 2.
Riksförsäkringsverket (National Social Insurance Board) (1994b), Förtidspensioner utbetalade i december 1993. *Statistikinformation*, 14.
Riksförsäkringsverket (National Social Insurance Board) (1995), Delpensioneringen t o m 1994. *Statistikinformation*, 1.
SFS 1979:84, *Lag om delpensionförsäkring*.
SFS 1987:364, 1990:671, 1992:1743, *Lag om ändring av lagen om delpensionförsäkring*.
SFS 1991:1040, *Lag om ändring i lagen (1962:381) om allmän försäkring*.
Socialförsäkringsutskottets betänkande 1991/92: SfU8, *Socialförsäkring – inriktning och anslag* (April 9, 1992).
Socialförsäkringsutskottets betänkande 1992/93: SfU9, *Besparingar i socialförsäkringssystemet* (December 9, 1992).
SOU 1994:20, *Reformerat pensionssystem*.
Statistics Sweden, *Labour Force Surveys*.
Statistics Sweden, *Statistiska Meddelanden*, Education and Training of the Labour Force 1993 and 1994, U39 SM9501.
Storrie, D. (1993), *The Anatomy of a Large Swedish Plant Closure* (diss.), Department of Economics, Gothenburg University, Gothenburg.
Wadensjö, E. (1991), 'Partial Exit: Sweden', in Kohli, M., M. Rein, A.M. Guillemard, H. van Gunsteren (eds.), *Time for Retirement: Comparative studies of early exit from the labor force*, Cambridge University Press, Cambridge.

Wadensjö, E. (1994), 'Partial Exit Options in Sweden: Recent and Future Changes', *Generations*, 17, no. 4, pp. 15-19.
Wise, Lois (1990), 'Partial and Flexible Retirement: The Swedish System', *The Gerontologist*, 30, no. 3, pp. 355-361.

4 Gradual retirement in France

Geneviève Reday-Mulvey

The recent economic and social situation in France has been marked by the following features:
- until 1990, rapid expansion of production (a growth rate of 4.3 per cent in 1987, 3.9 per cent in 1989, 2.4 per cent in 1990, 0.6 per cent in 1991, 1.1 per cent in 1992, -1 per cent in 1993 and 2.5 per cent in 1994);
- compared to the expansion of GDP, only slight growth in employment. Over the 1970-1992 period the total growth percentages in output and employment were respectively 75 and 7 per cent. It should be noted in passing that this trend, almost uniform in Europe, was very different in the USA where the percentages in question were 76 and 45. The French economy, then, along with those of other European countries, is characterised by a marked dissociation between growth and employment;
- rapid transformation from a manufacturing to a service economy with, over the last 20 years, widespread modernisation of the tools of production. Employment is now distributed as follows: 64.5 per cent in services, 29.6 per cent in the secondary sector and 5.9 per cent in agriculture;
- high levels of well-organised social welfare. By way of example, and by comparison with neighbouring countries, the benefits paid in France to the unemployed, early retirees and retirees are generous. The State pension has increased fivefold over the last three decades while wages have tripled. People have spoken of this time as the 'golden age of pensions' even though glaring inequalities across the system have persisted. In 1982 French early retirees were on average receiving almost the equivalent of a mean working

wage while percentages elsewhere were substantially lower: 71 per cent in Germany, 65 per cent in Sweden and 31 per cent in the UK (Gaullier, 1993, Age et Emploi). The cost of welfare overall in 1993 was estimated to be 2,500 billion francs, 35.4 per cent, that is, of the GDP. Despite its cost, the French remain enthusiastic admirers of their system of social welfare. What is true, then, of most industrialised countries, where public spending on retirement has become a sizeable item in social welfare budgets, is remarkably the case in France. In 1992 the cost of social benefits for the elderly reached 12 per cent of GDP and 49 per cent of social welfare expenditure overall. Moreover, it was estimated in the early nineties that public expenditure on the elderly – pensions, the funding of early retirement, medical costs, etc. – accounted for almost 60 per cent of the nation's total social welfare budget at a time when unemployment had reached record levels;

– finally, over the last twenty years employment policies that have concentrated on unemployment and particularly youth unemployment which has been more marked in France than in other economies.

4.1   Macro issues and policies

Recent trends

In 1993, the active population was 25 millions and that in work was 22.2 millions. Activity rates were 63 per cent for men and 46.8 per cent for women. Several features of the employment situation in France are worth mentioning:

– unemployment is high and, in 1994, affected 11 per cent of the active population;

– the growth of women's employment has been rapid – 36 per cent of women were working in 1962 and 46.8 per cent in 1993. An expansion of on-going careers (regular and/or permanent employment) for women can be observed above all among managerial staff, women in commerce, farm personnel and craftswomen;

– there is a low percentage of atypical forms of employment. For example, part-time employment has been low compared to other EU countries (UK and Netherlands). Over very recent years, however, it has increased fast owing to new legislation and in early 1995 was estimated to affect around 15 per cent of jobs. The number of 'insecure' jobs has also increased over the last ten years: 750,000 in 1985, and more than 1,300,000 in 1993, approximately, that is, 7 per cent of employment. Worthy of mention also is the fact that the full-time career which has been the norm for three decades is beginning to become a privilege;

– a late average-age of entry on the labour market and an early age of withdrawal can be observed. As mentioned in Chapter 1, over the last 15 years

early retirement in France, together with the Netherlands, has been the strongest in Europe. This situation has followed decades of good protection and integration of older employees;
- as elsewhere, there is an overall 'greying' of the active population as the 'baby-boom' generation joins the 45-55 age-group so that by 2010 more than half the active population will be 40 years and over.

Labour market position of older workers

The last twenty years have been marked in France by very early retirement policies. Along with the Netherlands, France, of all industrialised countries, has the lowest activity and employment rates for the 55-64 age-group. Since 1984, less than half this group has been effectively employed. Among industrialised countries again, France has probably pushed furthest ahead with its policy for early retirement. Since 1972 a series of steps have been taken to permit the lay-off of workers at increasingly early ages, up until 1982, at 62 or 60 years while 65 remained the legal retirement age, and since then throughout the 1980s at 58 and 55 years even when the legal age was brought down to 60 years. As we shall see later, since 1989 there have been important measures to reverse this trend.

Age of retirement
On 1 April 1983 the official retirement age was brought down to 60 years, at which age employees became entitled to the basic (1st pillar) pension. For supplementary pensions the qualifying age has remained 65 years, but one can begin drawing a pension before this if payment of contributions over 150 quarters (see below) can be substantiated. An exception is made for the unemployed, handicapped persons and mothers of families for all of whom the requirement is 120 quarters. In all cases, the pension is reduced if retirement is entered before the pension age. Lowering the official age has in fact merely hastened slightly the already rapid downward trend in the number of older wage-earners.

The gap between the official age of retirement and the actual age of exit from the labour market is a sizeable one in France and is estimated in industry and building to amount on average to over two years. Workers retire later in the tertiary sector (Ministère du travail, 1994) where in some professional branches the age of retirement is 65 years.

Modes of labour exit
Table 4.1 shows for 1992 the number of workers employed full- and part-time by age-group.

In 1992, the total number of workers aged 55 and over was 2,148,400. These figures yield rates of employment around 64 per cent for the 55-59 age-

Table 4.1
Work after age 50 in France in 1992, by age-group (in thousands)

Employed	Full-time	%	Part-time	%
50-54 years	1,731.5	9	215.4	8
55-59 years	1,264.8	7	223.2	8
60 years and over	496.9	3	163.5	6
All 50 years and over	3,493.3	18	602.2	22
All 15 years and over	19,280.5	100	2,798.6	100

Source: INSEE Surveys, 1992.

group and 19 per cent for those in the 60-64 age-group. Until quite recently, the vast majority of part-time workers aged 55 and over were women. But with the current adoption of measures on gradual pre-retirement and part-time a better balance between the sexes is emerging (Ministère du Travail, 1994).

In the tertiary sector, full retirement remains the main (for more than two/thirds) mode of exit for aging workers, in contrast, that is, to the secondary sector where for many years early retirement and more recently gradual early retirement were predominant. According to a very thorough Ministry of Labour survey of 1991 (the most recent of its kind), of all employees aged 55 and over, full retirement was the mode of exit from the workplace for 64 per cent of them, pre-retirement for 20 per cent, while close on 9 per cent were laid off and 7.5 per cent left with negotiated redundancy pay. It is an established fact that the self employed, for their part, not only enter retirement later than wage-earners but also reduce their work hours gradually.

The number of early retirement beneficiaries, which was 100,000 in 1978, rose to a peak of 685,000 in 1984 and by 1991 had fallen back to 400,000. By beneficiaries we mean the accumulated 'stock' of beneficiaries in the year in question, and not the number of those entering early retirement. In 1991, the total number of employees aged between 55 and 59 in the private sector, the only one involved in this scheme, was no more than 750,000. As of 1992, the number of new entrants in the schemes began to fall. By the end of 1993, 67,000 additional beneficiaries had entered the scheme (58,000 in full early retirement and 9,000 in gradual early retirement) bringing the total number to 191,800. In 1994, entry to gradual early retirement speeded up with 16,000 new beneficiaries (Ministère du Travail, 1995). In all, the number of workers benefitting from early retirement since the late seventies is in excess of 1.3 million.

The pattern of distribution by activity sector of modes of exit into early retirement is most revealing (see table 4.2). The figures of the Ministry of Labour survey of 1991, although not as recent as they might be, do give a clear picture of the prevailing situation which, it should be added, has since

Table 4.2
Distribution of early exit modes into early retirement by economic sector in
France in 1991

%	Industry	Building	Commer-cial tertiary	Non-commer-cial tertiary	Total
Full early retirement (unsupplemented)*	60	53	32	37	51
Full early retirement (supplemented)	24	47	7	7	20
Gradual early retirement	12	–	50	42	22
Part-time (subsidised)	3	–	12	14	6
All	100	100	100	100	100

Deviations from 100 per cent are due to roundings.
* not supplemented by an enterprise facility.
Source: Ministry of Labour, DARES, 1992.

altered due to the new public and firms policies described later (see New public and company policies).

Data by firm size from the same survey show that it is above all the firms with 200 employees or more that use the FNE scheme (see below). Use of this facility by firms with from 10 to 49 employees is much less frequent. Retirement accounted for eight departures out of 10 in small firms and for half that number in the bigger ones. In the tertiary sector, with its less concentrated distribution of the work force, in contrast to manufacturing and building, three out of four departures are to retirement and the incidence of gradual withdrawal is much higher.

It is the large enterprises – above all the industrial undertakings – which made greater use by far of early retirement programmes. Surveys have shown that between 40 and 50 per cent of early retirees come from firms with work forces of over 500, two thirds of them in industry and less than one third in services (Ministère du Travail, 1994).

Since 1984, the financing of early retirement or early withdrawal from the workplace has been based on two systems: the FNE (National Employment Fund) on the one hand and the UNEDIC (National Interprofessional Union for Industrial and Commercial Employment)-managed system of unemployment insurance on the other. The first of these two systems is based on what are known as the ASFNE (Special FNE benefits) agreements concluded between the Government and enterprise which define a 'social plan' whose purpose is to monitor and slow-up the lay-off of older workers. The second system, the UNEDIC, is managed by the social partners and functions as a pre-retirement fund.

For some years now, both systems have been competing, some firms having greater recourse to one or other of the systems, although their respective shares of the total number of early retirements catered for has been reasonably well balanced. In 1992, early retirement benefits accounted for 45 per cent of total UNEDIC expenditure. However, in that same year and in 1993, two new agreements made access to both these early retirement systems more costly and more difficult (see New public policies). It should finally be noted that early retirement in France, as in the Netherlands but contrary to what occurs in other countries, has never been financed from pension funds, and only to a very limited extent, although increasingly since 1992, by enterprise. Financing has been rather by the State or by the social partners under special unemployment benefit agreements.

Overall, early retirement has proved very expensive. Since 1984, UNEDIC and FNE combined, it has cost France some 50 billion francs annually, more, that is, in certain years than unemployment benefits. For the FNE alone in 1994, it was estimated to have cost more than 15 billion francs.

Not only have the authorities woken up to the cost of early retirement and tried to modify these policies as we shall see, but some enterprises also are waking up to the disadvantages of policies for compulsory early retirement. They have learnt that there is a price to be paid in terms of loss of expertise and enterprise culture for the early jettisoning of certain categories of management and skilled employees. They have found that replacing 55-60 year-olds by younger staff only postpones the problem a few years (Entreprise et Progrès, 1993).

In spite of the fairly wide range of facilities available, all these early withdrawal routes in France have certain characteristics in common. They all provide for a replacement income to be paid, over a given period prior to the official pension age, to all persons having withdrawn from the labour market for good, generally for reasons beyond their control. The replacement rate of the income in question is invariably high: 70 per cent at least of the last earned wage in the 1970s, and around 65 per cent more recently. This income is based on final pay and is, therefore, as a rule better than that of average-wage pensions. These early retirement schemes 'à la française', it should be noted, are hybrid and place their beneficiaries in a special category, the latter being neither wage-earners, nor unemployed, nor retirees. The placing of an employee in early retirement is a kind of laying-off but of a special kind, since it depends on the existence of an agreement between the enterprise and the government or the social partners, the terms of which apply to that employee when the latter renounces part of his redundancy entitlement. Laying-off of a special kind also since the early retiree in question is not allowed to seek further employment. As in the Netherlands and Germany, there is no stigma attached to early retirement.

Life cycle and attitudes to work and retirement
Generally speaking, the French are very much wedded to the idea of official retirement at the age of 60. This entitlement is in many ways a symbol of

social progress, something the French have fought for through long years and that was granted them with the advent of a socialist government in 1981. Surveys reveal a wide range of perceptions of early retirement, the manual labourer's view of the latter diverging substantially from that, for example, of the technician or manager. The vast majority of employees in manufacturing and un- or low-skilled workers in general view 'compulsory' early retirement as a liberation, a significant step up the ladder of social progress. Such perceptions are by no means always shared by white-collar and skilled workers. As in some other countries, the Netherlands being one exemple, studies, which unfortunately are not very recent, have shown how more than half the beneficiaries in the latter categories would have wished to continue their professional lives or, at very least, to have been able to enjoy a period of gradual change (Guillemard, 1990).

Over time, however, attitudes began to evolve and early retirement for a period began to be viewed as a kind of new right or entitlement. Many employees were waking up to the fact that early retirement had its advantages, that not only did it confer a social status close to that enjoyed by the retiree, but it was also comfortably different from the plight of the unemployed in that it brought with it a guaranteed income until the early retiree in question was of an age to draw a pension.

Today, however, things have moved even further on. Once again workers must learn to live with the fact that early retirement is neither as commonplace nor as early as it used to be. Pension reform and the nationwide debate on the vexed question of financing pensions has now brought workers face to face with the fact that overall they will have to go on working later than has been the case over the last two decades.

This debate is indeed part of a broader pattern of change in France affecting the entire life-cycle: longer studies, more frequently now a bout of unemployment before a steady job is found, job changes interspersed with periods of unemployment, continuing training within and outside the firm throughout one's career, the 'second career', greater leisure time, and earlier and more varied patterns of exit from working life (Gaullier, 1993). According to our survey and recent literature (Futuribles, 1995), people in France are beginning to adjust to these life-cycle phenomena to the extent that a well-paid, secure full-time job is tending to be deemed a privilege rather than a right.

Pensions and social security

Finance of social security
As stated earlier, in 1993 social welfare expenditure was estimated at more than 2,500 billion francs, 35.4 per cent, that is, of GDP. Welfare is funded mainly from contributions: employers 51.8 per cent, employees 28.4 per cent, and from public taxes 17.5 per cent. These contributions and taxes combined

are used to fund welfare provision which entails covering the population at large in four major risk areas: first, old age insurance (i.e. pension provision, the top-up pension and the old age minimum) which accounts for 49 per cent of overall welfare expenditure; second, health insurance at 27 per cent, then family insurance at 13 per cent and finally unemployment insurance (mainly unemployment benefit) at 11 per cent of that total.

Pensions specifically are financed from employer/employee contributions only. As at 1 January 1994, the rates for old age insurance contributions were: employers 8.2 per cent and wage-earners 6.5 per cent. In 1992 nationally, the bulk of old age insurance benefit costs were as follows: 854 billion for the basic state pension and 594 billion for supplementary pensions.

Pension system

The pension system in France is based, as in most other industrialised countries, on three pillars but, even so, has a number of unique features. The *first pillar*, as elsewhere, is the basic state pension but in France this is proportionate to income. Payment is in the form of an annuity whereby accumulated entitlements are expressed as a percentage of earnings over a given period (10 best years for the time being) and depends on the number of contribution years (for a long time 37.5 years and more recently moving up to 40 years). Paid benefits amount to approximately 50 per cent of the 10-best-years (see also New public policies) wage but are subject to a ceiling.

The *second pillar* comprises the compulsory (since 1972) occupational pension schemes financed by both employers and employees, but in France, in contrast to many other countries, on a pay-as-you-go basis. Two large funds handle these supplementary or occupational schemes: the AGIRC (the General Association of Pension Funds for Professional Personnel) and the ARCO (the Association of Supplementary Pension Funds). Supplementary schemes are based on points accumulated over an entire career free of any upper limit.

Together these two full-career pillars (I + II) generate a pension whose replacement rate is approximately 75 per cent of the wage.

The *third pillar* is optional and covers the various forms of pension provision which are privately arranged with insurance firms, banks and, to a lesser extent, through mutual funds. Such pensions schemes take the form of collective professional agreements which have yet to be defined by a proper legal framework. This third pillar – which some studies consider part of the second pillar, since they assimilate the pay-as-you-go compulsory supplementary schemes to a second strain of the first pillar – has been under discussion for a number of years now and is set to expand. There are plans to make this pillar the subject of draft legislation focusing on pensions funds and retirement savings. Mention in this context should also be made of the various kinds of contract between individuals and banks and insurance firms which have also been developing fast. The growth rate of life-assurance premiums and of pension investment (by 15 per cent in 1992 and by more than 20 per cent in 1993) is evidence of the average French householder's concern to save.

Pension benefits

Taken together, the first two pillars yield a comfortable pension and a satisfactory rate of replacement, of about 75 per cent as has just been stated. In 1993 the average income of retirees was around 7,000 francs per month. According to a recent CERC (Incomes and Costs Study Centre) survey, this average is above that of the active population and is approximately 5 per cent higher than that of working households. For those who have had a full career (at least 37.5 contribution years) this average is in excess of 7,600 francs per month (INSEE, 1994). The survey also reveals that more than 80 per cent of pensioners' resources come from the basic and supplementary schemes (65 per cent for farmers), with own-assets income accounting for no more than 10 per cent. With the exception of the old age minimum, all pension benefits are liable to income tax. As at 1 January 1995, the old age minimum which rose considerably during the 1980s stood at 3,200 francs per month for a single person and 5,700 francs for a couple.

New public policies

Pension reform

On 22 July 1993 a new law on pension reform was adopted. The law provides, on the one hand, for the creation of an Old Age Solidarity Fund and, on the other, for modification of the criteria for pension entitlement. The above Fund is responsible for the non-contributive benefits dispensed under welfare provision for the elderly (old age minimum, etc.) and for disbursement of benefits under the solidarity schemes. It is state-financed. The criteria for pension entitlement have been changed as follows: between 1994 and 2003 the number of compulsory quarterly contributions will gradually (at a rate of one per year) increase from 150 to 160 (i.e. from 37.5 to 40 years). The base period for calculation of the annual average wage will also be raised from the 10 to the 25 best years (between 1994 and 2008). Even if retirement at 60 years is now an established right, many are those who will have to work well beyond that age in order to clock-up the requisite 40 contribution years.

The supplementary pensions system also is beset by financing problems. ARCO's technical deficit (contributions/benefits ratio) was 1.9 billion francs in 1993 and is expected to reach the 4 billion mark in 1994, in spite of a rise in the contribution rate from 5.4 to 5.5 per cent in that same year. The other Fund, the AGIRC, recorded a 6 billion franc deficit in 1993. In addressing this problem both Funds have had to broaden their financing base and increase their reserves. These measures, though very necessary, will doubtless not suffice and funding by capitalisation – a practice already established in a number of sectors notably insurance and banking – is widely advocated as the solution.

The early retirement dissuasion policy

Since 1987 and especially since 1989, steps have been taken to reverse the pronounced trend towards early retirement. The measures concerned have been designed to achieve four main objectives.

First, to make early retirement less attractive. Financial penalties have been imposed (a law of 1987, for example, although there are still exceptions, increased the cost of lay-off employees over the age of 55; in 1992, a measure increased the employers' contribution to unemployment benefit for workers aged 50 and over) and the age at which it is now possible to lay-off workers who will be entitled to state early retirement benefits has been raised from 55 to 57 years.

Second, to encourage gradual retirement. The law of 5 January 1988, for example, promotes tapered retirement by allowing an employee of 60 years who has paid the full quota of contributions to receive a partial pension while continuing to work part-time with no age limit set for full retirement. Thus far, in the current labour market circumstances and due mainly to complicated regulations and inadequate information to those potentially concerned, no great use has been made of this facility with only 10,000 employees involved in schemes of this sort in 1994. Another measure has been the new provisions for gradual withdrawal from the workplace (i.e. gradual retirement) established under the Law of 31 December 1992 (along with its implementing Decrees and Order of March 1993). This law considerably simplifies and renders more attractive earlier arrangements for gradual retirement. From now on, early retirees of 55 years and over will be able to work 40 to 50 per cent of their previous workload instead of merely taking or leaving the half-time option available under earlier agreements.

The rigid work force replacement rule has now been abandoned and enterprises are encouraged to make their own contribution to the gradual retirement schemes financially or by guaranteeing compensatory recruitment, priority being given to certain special categories of job-seeker. The special categories in question are: young persons under 26 years of age who have been unemployed for at least a year, the unemployed aged 50 years and over, disabled workers, lone-parent employees and beneficiaries of the RMI (minimum income allowance). The Five-year Law of 20 December 1993 (see below) now makes possible calculation of the workload of gradual retirees on a pluriannual basis subject to certain conditions. The latter can now, therefore, enjoy work schedules equivalent to between 20 and 80 per cent of their former workloads provided that, over the period during which the gradual retirement benefit is available (for example the five years between the ages of 55 and 60), the workload reduction be on average 50 per cent. The State (FNE) offers 25 to 30 per cent compensation of the previous wage, which gives a 75 to 80 per cent replacement rate.

Third, to promote part-time work. The Decree of 11 September 1989 encourages part-time employment as a substitute for lay-offs on economic grounds. This facility is designed to run for two years, the employee receiving a supplementary allowance equivalent to 40 per cent of loss of income during the first year and to 20 per cent during the second. The law of 31 December 1992, followed by the regulations of February 1993, changes unequivocally the status of part-time workers and recognises part-time work as a regular, permanent form of employment, giving part-timers equal legal rights to those working full-time regarding all aspects of work: promotion, training and social benefits.

The Five-year Law of 20 December 1993 on labour, employment and vocational training introduced a number of interesting measures, establishing, *inter alia*, the principles and conditions of work reduction, employment sharing and part-time work on an annual basis. The overall effect of these measures has been to render the organisation of part-time work more flexible.

In 1992, a measure provided for a 30 per cent reduction in the employer's contribution where the creation of part-time jobs made compensatory recruitment possible.

Pursuant to the Law of 25 July 1994, the creation of time-saving accounts enables employees to accumulate a work-hour capital over an entire career. Annual leave can in this way be saved up and financial entitlements transformed into leave savings. The above Law stipulates that periods of accumulated leave shall be not less than 6 months, shorter periods being negotiable by the parties under gentlemen's agreement.

Fourth, to promote continuing training through to end of career, and so facilitate the employment of older workers. The Law of 2 August 1989, for instance, provides for the funding of continuing training of employees over the age of 45; it is completed by a measure of 18 January 1991 which exempts from social costs any enterprise taking on a worker over 50.

The Government's overall purpose in serving the above four major objectives has been, together with pension reform, to reverse the prior and costly trend towards early retirement by progressively promoting an extension of working life. It aims, then, to replace full early retirement by gradual early retirement or by gradual retirement and to diversify the end of career. The kind of early retirement that has been common over the last fifteen years must now be reserved for exceptional firms or regions. Gradual early retirement is now developing and currently affects several thousands of workers, often employed by big firms. A fair number of recent contracts between the social partners contain agreements to keep employees in the firm until the legal retirement age but at the same time to offer them several alternatives for reducing their work hours.

4.2 Micro issues and policies

Recent trends

Work performance

As in most countries, a wealth of research exists in France on age, health, aptitudes and *productivity*. Just to cite one, the largest current study is the ESTEV survey into Health, Work and Aging. Longitudinal in design and extremely comprehensive, the study is based on a representative sample of 25,000 employees and was begun by a team of occupational doctors in 1988. It is not expected to be finished before the year 2000 at the earliest. The first phase of the study was undertaken in 1990 and the second is scheduled for 1995. Results to date already confirm a number of hypotheses (Deriennic *et al.*, 1994):

– physical and mental suffering increase with age but the increase is by no means uniform;
– identifying and understanding the impact of work on health involves examining the psycho-social dimension of what is done in conjunction with the physical and environmental conditions prevailing in the workplace;
– no dynamic scrutiny of the 'age-health' process can afford to disregard the trajectory of a professional career, if only because the causes of certain 'age effects' may have commenced very early on in a career.

Other scientific research carried out in France, as indeed elsewhere, has stressed the varigated character of the aging phenomenon and the fact of its limited aggregate impact on work by reason of its highly progressive and unpredictable nature. It is an established fact that 'the effect of aging on industrial productivity is marginal and variations from one age-group to the next are less significant than those within a given group' (OECD, 1990).

Moreover, a Ministry of Labour survey of 1992 into more than 2,000 representative enterprises showed that the aging of the work population is not considered a problem in the tertiary sector in very stark contrast to what occurs in manufacturing and building (Guillemard, 1994). It is true that the age structure within the tertiary sector is characterised by an inflated median age-group but, as yet, not normally by any high proportion of elderly workers. Probably more significant is the fact that the higher mental abilities specifically required in the tertiary sector diminish less rapidly with age than manual capacity and can be kept 'in shape' longer with continuing training.

The same Ministry of Labour survey provides a clear account of the perceptions of heads of firms regarding the strengths and weakness of their older employees. To one very searching question in this connection:

Question: What would the effect of a relative increase in the proportion of employees over 50 years in your work force be?
answers were as follows:

A *negative effect*

1	Difficulties in adapting new technologies	61
2	Resistance to change	61
3	Additional wage costs	58
4	A fall in productivity	43
5	Career prospects of younger employees jeopardised	43
6	Would compromise the firm's image	10

A *neutral effect*

1	Would alter organisation of work	30

A *positive effect*

1	Greater handing-on of knowledge	67
2	Greater expertise/memory retained within the firm	62
3	Enhanced complementarity among work-teams	47

It is interesting to note that less than half the respondents mention a drop in productivity.

Company pension regulations

The situation with regard to company pension regulations is fairly straightforward. Neither basic old age insurance (1st pillar) nor the supplementary occupational schemes (2nd pillar) penalise reduction of work hours at end of career or, thereby, gradual pre-retirement. As was mentioned before, the amount of the first pillar pension is based on the 10 best years (but is being raised) within a career, and that of the supplementary pension on 'points' accumulated throughout a career. The employee who transfers from full- to part-time work during, say, the last five years of his professional life would see a slight drop in the number of points clocked-up, but this in any case would occur were a change to be made at any other time in the career. Moreover, under the terms of many of the agreements on gradual pre-retirement currently in force, the employer more often than not continues to pay pension contributions as if the employee were working full-time.

Age discrimination

Non-discrimination is one of the mainstays of the French Constitution, and yet nowhere does the latter, either generally or in relation to work, refer to age.

This state of affairs is confirmed by jurisprudence (Gaullier, 1993). There have been one or two attempts to modify the Constitution, to incorporate the notion of 'age' under discrimination so that the text should read:

> 'None shall be discriminated against in work or employment by reason of origin, creed or *age*.' The grounds for these intitiatives are 'the advances in biology, medicine and surgery and improvements in living and working conditions which have so rejuvenated the adult population ... that there is no comparison between a 60 year-old today and 50 years age.' (Gaullier, 1993)

Negative age-discrimination in firms and in the Administration in France is, more often than not, the result of stereotyping which, according to some studies, is less prevalent today than it was some years ago. There appear to be two main reasons for this progress:

– over the last twenty years France has transformed from an industrial to a service economy. The image of industrial production has remained alive in peoples' minds while the reality of jobs and work conditions today has radically altered. Age will doubtless become a decreasingly significant factor in today's service society with its increasingly mental mode of operation;

– French society in particular had enormous difficulties in getting its young-sters, even when well qualified, into the workplace. As a result, a social understanding had been reached among enterprise, the Government and the unions to favour recruitment of young labour market entrants to the detri-ment of employees at the end of career. Age discrimination was thus the consequence of a deliberate, and, therefore, reversible, choice. This situation is now changing and looks set to change even more over the coming years. In comparing France with her neighbours it must be stressed that she has adopted at least two sets of measures to combat age discrimination (Eurolink Age, 1993):

– legislation which bans age limits in recruitment advertisements in the private sector;

– special assistance for the unemployed aged 50 and over (see also New public policies).

Unfortunately, enforcement of the first set of measures has not been very energetic.

New company policies

In this section, we recap briefly on some of the main ideas contained in the previous part on recent trends, and then go on to examine practical illustrations of these policies in best practice in gradual retirement.

Personnel policy

There is no question that awareness of the aging phenomenon and an understanding of its importance in personnel management have as yet been achieved only by the larger and more dynamic firms in France. According to the Ministry of Labour survey referred to above (Guillemard, 1994), only a tiny proportion of firms (8 per cent) have the wherewithal systematically to predict employment trends in their enterprise three to five years into the future. The vast majority of firms, even when faced with staff shortages, seem for the time being reluctant to keep or take on older workers. In such circumstances, gradual retirement is frequently the only tool cited by those searching for an alternative solution.

Even so, more and more firms are now giving attention to management of their aging personnel and are beginning to redesign their practice. Again the above-mentioned survey – and this was found to be the case in the firms visited by the author herself – records that the strategies chosen by firms for managing aging personnel are principally: the extension of continuing training until end of career, the expansion of gradual retirement, and a more widespread use of part-time and flexible work hours. Another practice rapidly spreading in French firms today (Renault is a good illustration) is the drawing up of a 'career plan' based on a 'skills and aptitudes review' for employees aged from 40 to 45 years which takes stock of skills and experience to date and outlines a project for the individual staff-member defining end of career prospects and his/her training and job-mobility potential. At Thompson's, for example, a review of this kind is made for every employee, especially for those in the last third of their career, who, over the previous five years, have not been promoted or have not benefitted from any training (Gaullier, 1993).

Pay policy

It is now perfectly clear that seniority-based pay policy, by raising the wage costs of workers at end of career, constitutes a very real obstacle to all forms of extension of working life (see Ministry of Labour survey mentioned before). This is why there is, according to our survey, a growing trend in wage calculation today towards reducing the weight of the seniority factor and increasing that of performance. In some sectors like insurance, there has recently been a thorough review of policy on wage components resulting in the removal altogether, except for certain categories of unskilled worker with very limited career prospects, of the seniority criterion. Some banks have now reduced the weighting of the seniority component by half, and similar sorts of practice are beginning to take on in various branches of industry.

Redesigning work and lightening the workload

In the enterprises surveyed, end of career is frequently a time when adjusting the functions of a job or changing to a new one is felt to be necessary. This is typically the case in the tertiary sector where, for commercial reasons for example, part-time work would be inappropriate, or because of overmanning in administrations, or again in industry on technical grounds. Some firms broaden the functions expected of their staff at end of career by employing them as tutor-trainers. But even if adjustment of existing job functions or changing to a new job mean that the work expected of the pre-retiree is less burdensome and involves less responsibility, such change is not normally accompanied by loss of salary. Firms like Aerospatiale, Renault, Usinor-Sacilor, Thompson and Otis are renowned for their highly differentiated and ergonomic approach to job organisation for employees of 50 years and over. The very interesting experiments of these firms in 'holistic' job design have been monitored by CREAPT (The Research and Study Centre on Age and the Working Population) with a view to developing new ideas 'on the design of technical systems and the adjustment of work conditions to suit the needs of the aging employee'.

Part-time and flexible work

Until quite recently France was among those countries where part-time work was least developed, hovering as it did between 7 and 10 per cent of employment. However, the grave employment situation has subsequently changed all this giving rise to a certain number of proposals regarding work-sharing and the need for encouraging part-time employment patterns. The Law of 1992 gave to part-time work a regular employment status and proper social protection and the Five-year Law on Employment provided the framework for flexibility that employees and employers alike had so earnestly demanded. As a result, part-time work is now expanding rapidly, and in January 1995 accounted for around 15 per cent of employment overall. Some firms have concluded collective agreements committing themselves to developing part-time work, *inter alia* and notably, through the provision of financial incentives. Part-time work being already commonplace with women, firms are now anxious to develop the practice with men as well. It exists in various forms such as part-time work according to the academic calendar or week-end work.

In addition, other flexible work patterns are emerging. 'Time sharing' is one particular form this takes and more especially concerns skilled workers aged around 55 years. The idea here is for a worker to have several employers all offering very low part-time work schedules. He, or she, is thus able to service with special skills or functions a number of small firms which individually would never be able to offer a full-time post. There are, as yet, no statistics on this kind of flexible work, but interviews with professional groups using such work patterns reveal that those involved in 'time sharing' constitute in certain fields a sizeable body of managerial staff and skilled workers. A recent survey of 1994 into 100 insurance companies revealed that almost half of them found this kind of time sharing work very useful; more than one third are ready to expand it, especially for loss assessment purposes (Observatoire sur le Temps Partagé, 1994).

The recent Law on time-saving accounts, for its part, is evidence of a much broader desire to organise work not only on monthly and annual bases but also in such a way as to comprehend the entire life-cycle.

Training

In most French firms one observes a fall in training costs for employees over 45 years (CEREQ, 1992), but the statistics do not really make it possible to identify different age-groups. An improvement in the relative training situation of those aged 45 and over is, however, the apparent pattern in recent years. For example, in 1992, the over 45s constituted 24 per cent of all wage-earners and 21 per cent of all trainees (Reday-Mulvey, 1993), and in 1993 this situation improved further. Continuing training seems to be strongly related to cohort effects. And the Law of 2 August 1989 increased Government aid for long-term training initiatives for employees aged 45 and over.

The firms surveyed by the author are for the most part dynamic and lead the way in the formulation and implementation of policies for continuing training until end of career. In France, training costs account for a not inconsiderable portion of the overall wage mass; anything from 3 to 7 per cent. The Law of 1971 (modified since adoption) stipulates a compulsory expenditure of at least 1.5 per cent. In none of the enterprises visited did the author find any evidence of age discrimination in training. One frequently noticed, even so, a tacit or *de facto* agreement between bosses and employees to limit such training, the case of specific needs excepted, during the years running up to retirement, and especially during the gradual pre-retirement phase. A number of firms, the GAN among them, pursue the both interesting and effective policy of retraining staff around the age of 40 years in cases where their initial training had been fairly rudimentary. The idea with this policy is to make possible a second start either within the firm or, since the retrainee if successful is awarded a diploma recognised outside the firm, elsewhere.

Best practice in gradual retirement

Gradual early retirement (GER) which up to 1993 affected very few workers, has since that time spread rapidly. By December 1994, 31,000 workers benefitted from this facility, 20 per cent, that is, of all part-timers (working between 15 and 29 hours per week) aged 55 and over. This percentage is set to increase further in 1995. The above figure does not cover the gradual early retirement practice of firms not benefitting from government aid. Such firms, though numerous, are not identified in current statistics. Indeed, a large number of firms are now beginning to taper the workload of end-of-career employees on what in general are proving to be excellent financial terms.

Gradual early retirement agreements have become commonplace in the tertiary sector (47 per cent), but it will also be observed that their use is becoming widespread in industry as well – 40 per cent in 1993, a percentage which climbed even higher in 1994. The main tertiary-sector branches affected by GER are banking, and medical, computer and catering firms. Enterprises resorting to GER tend to be faced with two different types of situation:

– they may be forced to make lay-offs on economic grounds – or, for example, due to improvements in productivity – in which case GER serves as a useful social-planning tool in reducing over-staffing and government aid is available to help with the cost of operating such GER schemes;

– GER is also used by firms needing to rejuvenate their age-pyramid and update their skills in which case firms will take on job-seekers to fill the positions freed by senior employees transferring to part-time employment. A proportion of such job-seekers will be drawn from 'priority' categories of the unemployed experiencing special difficulties in entering the labour market. Most of the agreements concluded in 1993 contained clauses committing firms to compensatory recruitment, 45 per cent of the latter on average being earmarked for the so-called special or 'priority' categories of the unemployed. Another feature worth mentioning is that 16 per cent of GER agreements concluded specifically refer to the use of part-time early retirees in traineeship schemes.

Case studies

Our survey conducted in 1995 provided information about several interesting and representative experiments in the services sector and in industry. From the firms visited, we have selected two in the insurance sector, one in banking, and four in industry. Among major insurance companies at least three have agreements on gradual pre-retirement: UAP, AXA and GAN. GAN's contract, while very interesting, involves for the time being only a small number of gradual pre-retirees.

UAP: UAP recently negotiated a contract to provide for gradual retirement during the five years before full retirement (which occurs between 60 and 65 years). Employees of all categories can work half-time for a year (but with a spread workload) for a salary of around 75 per cent (of which 25 per cent is paid by the National Employment Fund), retain all rights in the firm and draw social benefits as if full-time. In addition, UAP is launching a four-day week for qualified mature employees and professional workers with a view to creating new jobs for qualified younger people seeking employment. The philosophy, here, is to share employment in a new way since it is believed that further growth will not create enough jobs to reduce significantly the rate of unemployment. Many female and some male employees already work 80 per cent of the time, and the new contract also includes a new work-year based on the 'academic' calendar.

AXA: Rather than laying them off or having the community pay (with early retirement funds) for its overstaffing, AXA 'releases' its workers aged 55 and over (with the requisite number of contribution years and having worked at AXA for 15 years at least) from regular work and calls on them when they are needed. The aim is to enable employees over 55 from all categories to benefit from a transition between full career and full retirement. The firm offers this scheme to employees during the last five years before they are entitled to full pension. The employees concerned are 'released' from work until the legal retirement age on a voluntary basis. They receive 65 per cent of their salary, but remain members of the staff and retain all their welfare benefits. They do not have the right to take another job. The company has the option to call them back when the need arises: a sudden increase in the work load, replacement of staff on leave, expertise in a specific area, training of a new recruit or supervision. The employee then works in the same or similar job as before and receives 100 per cent of his salary in proportion to the time he spends back in the company. Over 150 employees are currently benefitting from this measure which has been practiced for two years. However, for the time being, very few workers are being called back and only in specific situations.

The Credit Agricole: In 1993, this large bank (69,000 employees in France in 1994) concluded with the government an interesting GER agreement which breaks new ground in the banking sector. The Bank in implementing the agreement has a threefold purpose: to rejuvenate the age-pyramid, stagger exits into retirement and promote part-time work. The long-term aim is to be able to devise a number of tools for age-management which meet the specific requirements of the Credit Agricole's regional branches. In 1994/95 more than 600 employees will have entered the GER scheme the firm is running enabling it to take on more than 300 new recruits, many of them young apprentices or job-seekers. One of the more interesting features of this scheme they call the 'contract for progress' is that it creates a positive link between GER on the one hand and training and apprenticeship schemes on the other through the taking-on of new recruits and the active role the partial early-retirees are encouraged to play in training them. A fresh round of negotiations is scheduled for end 1995 on the duration and organisation of work hours. The French Banking Association foresees some expansion of GER into other banks which have recently been successful in reducing overall levels of early full-retirement. At present there seem to be two major challenges facing all those involved: to facilitate the take-on of new recruits and encourage the use of part-time work patterns.

Rhône-Poulenc: Part-time pre-retirement in Rhône-Poulenc has been growing rapidly since 1987 with positive effects. During the period 1987-92, over 1000 employees – of which 70 per cent were qualified and unqualified blue-collar workers and 10-15 per cent professional workers – benefitted from it. Since 1993, the number of total early retirements has been very small (only 90 in 1994) and the practice of gradual early retirement has been developing fast; early 1995 around 1,000 people had chosen it and between 2,000 and 2,500 people will be concerned in the three years 1994/95/96. Most employees are over 55 and benefit from this measure during the three years before full retirement. Employees work half-time, flexibility depending upon the nature of work, the department and the desires of the worker. Some employees work one week in two, others two or three days per week. With the possibility of annualising work time, there is a new trend to work 80 per cent of the time the first year, 50 per cent the second year and only 20 per cent the third year, which might become a source of concern were it to be generalised. Gradual early retirement is on the whole welcomed more by manual than by professional workers, and certainly more by people working in smaller towns than by those in Paris. Positive effects have been rejuvenation of the age-pyramid and of human resources and greater flexibility in work patterns. The management feels that such a formula is progressively leading to reorganisation of the end-of-career phase, indeed, of the entire career. In spite of traditional drawbacks, there is a strong desire to reorganise work by integrating part-time work in a new way. Overall the experience has been very positive for both employees (who enjoy a real transition between a full-time career and full retirement) and for management. Professional workers, now, need to develop the kind of flexible outlook that their less qualified collegues already seem to possess.

Hewlett-Packard: Since 1991, this firm with a very young work force (35 years on average) of 3,750 employees has been, with government support, running a GER ('phased withdrawal from the workplace') programme which provides the firm's employees between 55 and 60 years with a generous deal over the five years preceding full retirement. In 1994, for example, of the 73 employees eligible for the programme, some in positions of great responsibility, 47 volunteered to join. Those involved are accorded considerable freedom in making up their own part-time work schedules on a weekly, monthly, annual or pluriannual basis. Redeployment to new functions has been possible, where, as with salesmen and women a part-time work pattern would be inappropriate. At present, negotiations are underway in an attempt to reorganise work hours so as to encourage part-time work (which to date involves only 7 per cent of employees) and permit greater diversity in available work-schedule options (e.g. based on the academic calendar).

Aérospatiale: This firm is replacing its early retirement policy (from the age of 56) by a pre-retirement policy for employees aged from 56-57 for a period between two and five years. This policy extends until employees are 60 or, in the case of professional workers, over 60 even. Aérospatiale is one of the big French firms committed to lengthening working life in a way which is positive for the employee and for the firm. Their gradual early retirement scheme currently concerns over 300 employees but is expected to expand. Under this policy, employees work a 59 per cent workload for the three years of the GER programme (the distribution of this workload varying from case to case, often 80 per cent the first year, 59 per cent the second year, and 20 per cent the third, for example) but are paid 80 per cent of their earlier wage (50 per cent of this cost being borne by the firm and 30 per cent by the National Employment Fund which, prior to the programme, used to defray almost 100 per cent of the cost of early retirement). Aérospatiale offers 'gradual early retirees' half redundancy pay as incitement to join the programme. In the case of one of Aérospatiale's subsidiaries, the programme has created opportunities for compensatory recruitment. Parallel to this programme, Aérospatiale is promoting other forms of part-time work in an attempt to achieve a more satisfactory allocation or division of available employment. This particular policy has proved more successful in the Provinces than in Paris where work functions do not easily lend themselves to division and/or compression. The people at Aérospatiale mentioned the problems they had encountered with certain social security institutions because of red-tape and lack of flexibility; the URSAF (Social Security Contributions Collection Service) in its calculation of employer/employee contributions and the tax authority in computing tax bases for employees moving from full- to part-time were examples of this. Aérospatiale remains convinced that these bureaucratic barriers must be removed and gradual retirement encouraged as a *de facto* extension of working life. It needs, they believe, to become part of the 'in-firm system' and a positive corner-stone of enterprise HR management policy and not just another facet of state/enterprise cost-sharing arrangements.

Framatome: This firm specialises in the construction and maintenance of nuclear reactors, and mechanical engineering and employs 5,800 persons in France. With the help of the Government, but independent of any financial rehabilitation programme, Framatome recently set in motion a GER pilot project designed to rejuvenate the firm's age-pyramid and update skills, but also to provide some indication of how appropriate GER would be for the end-of-career management of certain categories of highly qualified personnel. In 1995, some forty older workers (aged 57.5 years) – out of a potentially eligible force of some 240 employees – have joined the scheme which will run for 2½ years.

Other examples of innovative end-of-career management schemes are to be seen in Pechiney-Rhenalu, La Générale Sucrière, Otis, Renault (the latter includes part-time work and the tutoring of the younger workers in the end-of-career envelope).

4.3 The potential for gradual retirement and recommendations

The situation that has prevailed in France for over twenty years has been marked by increasingly early retirement generously funded largely by the State. It was brought into being by policies which reflected the country's economic needs at a given point in time, and was founded on a solid consensus shared by the State, enterprise, the unions and the majority of workers. Except for youth unemployment – which because of rising productivity was not sufficiently reduced – those policies largely achieved the purposes for which they were designed. But their cost proved very high in financial terms to the State and in other ways to many enterprises which found it difficult to fill the gaps in expertise and corporate culture left by departing early retirees. A sizeable number of employees also, more often than not the highly qualified ones, who retired early have left with the distinct impression that they had become the solution to a social-economic problem.

For several years now, since 1989 and more especially since 1992, this policy has been extensively modified, though not abandoned altogether. As we have shown, pressure on State expenditure has rendered the terms of early retirement less generous, making the latter a more costly option for both firms and employees and, as result, gradual early retirement is tending to replace full early retirement. Elsewhere in this chapter we have reviewed the numerous public measures to promote both the extent and flexibility of working life. A viable partnership between the authorities and enterprise is now being established, with the latter becoming aware of the importance of new age-management models, of continuing training until end of career, of a more realistic wage curve and of the advantages of being able to offer a varied range of schedules for part-time work and for the transition from a full-time professional life to full retirement. The examples of enterprise good practice we have examined show that practical and satisfactory solutions can be found to the problems of redesigning retirement, although thus far, such practice has been confined to far too small a number of firms and to far too small a portion of the older labour force.

Gradual early retirement 'à la française' may be approached from two different angles. Sometimes a way of shortening or at least lightening an individual's working life, especially in the services sector (e.g. insurance, banking, etc.) where overstaffing is common, gradual retirement is, perhaps, more importantly a way of lengthening professional life, especially in industry where it can advantageously replace full early retirement, a practice which was both widespread and costly during the 1970s and 1980s. It is, moreover, highly germane, if not indispensible, to solving two of the major concerns exercising French minds at present:
- the need and wish to extend working life for very sound reasons which have to do with the financing of pensions and the proper management of HR and skills; and
- the need to develop part-time work as part of an overall redesign of employment and of its more proper division nationally.

France's potential for gradual retirement, therefore, is considerable, most of its preconditions having already been largely met. However, many of those preconditions will need to be strengthened further, and particularly, the cultural mind-sets of the institutions which represent workers and employers will need to change before retirement begins to be widely perceived and accepted as a progressive, phased and delayed phenomenon. And currently, the focus of attention in the 'unemployment debate' must be moved away from the rather sterile, problem-generating 'zero sum game' of shortening work-life at both ends of the life-cycle. Growth, of course, will need to continue, but in a consistent sustainable fashion, and redistribution of employment rethought to make gradual retirement and a flexible extension of working life large-scale realities.

References

Aznar, G. (1990), *Le travail (à plein temps), c'est fini*, Belfond, Paris.
CEREQ (Centre d'Etudes et de Recherches sur les Qualifications (1992, 1993, 1994), Brefs et Documents de Travail, Marseille.
DARES (Direction de l'Animation de la recherche, des études et des statistiques (1993), *Contributions pour le Colloque Européen 'Emploi et Vieillissement' des 22-23 novembre 1993*, Ministère du Travail, de l'Emploi et de la Formation Professionnelle, Paris.
Deriennic, F., A. Touranchet and C. Monfort (1994), 'Age, Travail, Emploi', *Gérontologie et Société*, no. 70, October, Paris.
Dictionnaire permanent social (1994), *Préretraite progressive: organisation pluriannuelle de la durée du travail*, Bulletin 522, 12 septembre, Editions Législatives, Paris.
Entreprise et Progrès (1993), *La gestion des fins de carrière, La préretraite n'est pas un acquis social*, Paris.
Eurolink Age (1993), *Age discrimination against older workers in the European Community*, London.

Féderation Française des Sociétés d'Assurances (1991), *Assurer l'avenir des retraites,* Paris.

Fondation Nationale de Gérontologie (1994), *Age, Travail et Emploi,* Cahiers no. 70, Paris.

Futuribles (1992), Numéro spécial Temps du Travail, no. 165-166, mai-juin, Paris.

Futuribles (1995), Numéro 195 et 197, Paris, February and April.

Gaullier, X. (1990), *Modernisation et gestion des âges, Les salariés âgés et l'emploi,* La Documentation Française, Paris.

Gaullier, X. (1993), *Age et emploi, De la discrimination à la gestion des âges,* Laboratoire de Sociologie du changement des institutions (CNRS), Paris.

Gaullier, X. (1993), *Salariés âgés: Conditions de travail et transition vers la retraite. Rapport sur la France pour le Bureau International du Travail,* Laboratoire de Sociologie du changement des institutions (CNRS), Paris.

Gaullier, X. (1993), 'The Changing Ages of Man', *The Geneva Papers on Risk and Insurance,* no. 62.

Guillemard, A-M. (1990), 'Les nouvelles frontières entre travail et etraite en France', *La Revue de l'IRES,* no. 2. Hiver, Paris.

Guillemard, A-M. (1991), 'France: Massive exit through unemployment compensation' in Kohli, M., M. Rein, A-M. Guillemard and H. van Gunsteren (eds.), *Time for retirement,* Cambridge University Press, Cambridge.

Guillemard, A-M. (1993), 'Travailleurs vieillissants et marché du travail', *Travail et Emploi,* no. 57, Ministère du travail, Paris.

Guillemard, A-M. (1993), *Vieillissement et politiques sociales et économiques en France,* Rapport réalisé pour la CE – DG V, dans le cadre de l'Observatoire Européen, Centre d'Etude des Mouvements Sociaux, Paris.

INSEE (1994), *Tableaux de l'Economie Française,* La Documentation Française, Paris.

Ministère des Affaires Sociales, Ministère du Travail (1994), 'Ages dans l'emploi, Ages dans le travail', *Revue Française des Affaires Sociales,* no. 1, janvier-mars, Paris.

Ministère du Travail, de l'Emploi et de la Formation Professsionnelle (1994), *Emploi et Vieillissement,* La Documentation Française, Paris.

Ministère du Travail, de l'Emploi et de la Formation Professsionnelle (1995), *Travail et Emploi,* no. 63/2.

Ministère du Travail, de l'Emploi et de la Formation Professsionnelle (1995), *Délégation à l'Emploi, Document interne sur les préretraites progressives,* Paris.

Observatoire du Temps Partagé (1994), *Enquête sur le temps partagé dans l'assurance,* Association Nationale des Directeurs et Cadres de la Fonction Publique (ANDCP), Paris.

OCDE (1991), *La transition de la vie active à la retraite, La France,* Groupe de travail sur la politique sociale (SME/ELSA/WP1 (91)09).

Le Particulier (1993), *Un temps choisi, des emplois partagés,* Spécial 73, Paris.

Reday-Mulvey, G. (1993), 'Facing social uncertainty: towards a new social policy' in Giarini, O. and W. Stahel (eds.), *Limits to certainty,* Kluwer Academic Publishers, Dordrecht.

Reday-Mulvey, G. (1994), 'Continuing training until end-of-career: A key policy for the Fourth Pillar', *The Geneva Papers on Risk and Insurance,* no. 73, October, pp. 481-489

Reday-Mulvey, G. (1994), 'A flexible extension of working Life: A new social policy for the service economy', *Paper prepared for the International Research Meeting of the ISSA (International Association for Social Security, Geneva),* 9-11 November, Vienna.

5 Gradual retirement in Germany

Winfried Schmähl, Rainer George, Christiane Oswald[1]

When and how to retire have become an important focus of economic and social policy in Germany. As in many other European countries, the reasons for this are population aging, labour market problems, particularly, a high rate of unemployment, and the financing of social security, especially pensions. In Germany, however, in contrast to other countries, there is an important additional factor which makes the search for appropriate solutions to the challenges of structural change much more difficult. That additional factor is the process of German unification.

In Germany, as in other countries, the issue of gradual retirement is of the utmost relevance to gerontologist and economist alike. But it also touches in a very practical way on the economic objectives of firm and household and of the state in the design and implementation of economic and social policy. Such objectives may frequently be in conflict or relate to the circumstances of different time horizons – the prevailing situation with its high unemployment, for example, as against the expected future shortage of qualified manpower due to demographic change.

The design and organisation of gradual retirement can be undertaken at various levels: by individual firms, under collective agreements, or by the state with legislation. And gradual retirement schemes themselves can vary enormously, in terms, for example, of their time-frame or of their effect on the income of employees. The latter will depend on alternatives for combining reduced work-time with earnings from employment and with the benefit payments that emanate from a variety of different sources. Our purpose hereafter will be to describe the most important of such alternatives as exist in Germany and so provide a picture of the country's practice of, or potential for, gradual retirement.

Our chapter will start with some data on the labour market situation of older workers in Germany and on the legal frame-work more especially of statutory old age insurance. We shall review the various options for labour market exit and take a look at the new instruments introduced under the Pension Reform Act of 1992. We shall then turn to firm strategies providing examples of past and current models of gradual retirement and finally, in light of the new possibilites opened up by the 1992 Act, we shall attempt briefly to assess the prospects for gradual retirement in Germany in the future.

5.1 Macro issues and policies

Recent trends

Labour market position of older workers

Older workers in Germany constitute a minority in the labour market. In 1993 people aged 55 and over accounted for only 11 per cent of the total labour force (table 5.1).

Table 5.1
The age structure of the labour force in Germany, 1993

Age	Total %	Men %	Women %
< 20	3.9	3.8	4.0
20-24	10.2	9.6	11.1
25-29	13.7	13.2	14.5
30-34	13.8	13.8	13.6
35-39	12.5	12.1	12.7
40-44	12.3	11.9	12.7
45-49	10.1	10.0	10.2
50-54	12.6	12.9	12.1
55-59	8.0	8.8	7.0
60-64	2.2	2.9	1.3
> 64	0.8	0.8	0.8
	100	100	100

Source: Mikrozensus (deviations from 100 per cent are due to roundings).

Since the early 1970s, labour force participation rates (LFPR) of men aged 55 and over dropped drastically (see Jacobs and Schmähl, 1989). This can clearly be seen from figure 5.1: in West Germany the LFPR of men aged 63 was 67 per cent in 1970. After the introduction of a flexible retirement age in statutory pension insurance (in 1973) the LFPR went down within 2 years by 20 per cent and within 10 years by 40 per cent. During recent years the LFPR of men aged 63 has been fairly stable around 20 per cent.

Figure 5.1 Labour force participation of different male cohorts in Germany

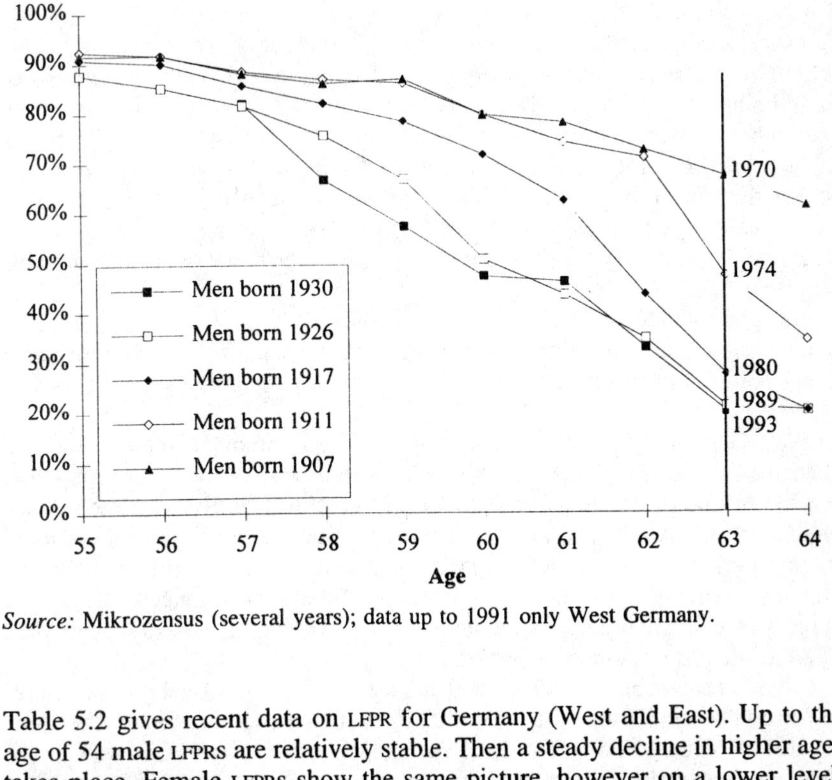

Source: Mikrozensus (several years); data up to 1991 only West Germany.

Table 5.2 gives recent data on LFPR for Germany (West and East). Up to the age of 54 male LFPRs are relatively stable. Then a steady decline in higher ages takes place. Female LFPRs show the same picture, however on a lower level. A sharp drop of LFPRs occurs at 60, when female employees become eligible for an old age pension. In 1993 only 40 per cent of men and 11 per cent of women were still working as employees at the age of 60.

About half of the women working between the age of 55 and 60 were on a part-time contract. For the 60 to 65 age-group this figure is slightly higher even. For men part-time work is of little importance except that, of men still in the labour force after 65, 40 per cent work part-time.

Table 5.2

Labour force participation rates of older men and women aged 55
and over in Germany, 1993

Age	55	56	57	58	59	60	61	62	63	64	> 64
Men	83	76	72	67	61	47	39	31	20	16	4
Women	55	46	42	36	32	15	12	10	8	6	2

Source: Mikrozensus.

Modes of labour exit

LFPRS are influenced by a variety of factors. The modes of retirement available
to those aged 55 and over will very much depend on social-security provision,
there being a range of possible pathways for transition from working life into
retirement. In what follows, we first examine the options for exit from the
labour market before eligibility for an old age pension and, thereafter, we
review the various options available within statutory pension insurance for both
blue- and white-collar workers. Figure 5.2 provides a comprehensive overview
of existing options. The principal modes of labour market exit prior to drawing
a pension are:
- pre-retirement arrangements (Vorruhestand);
- unemployment benefit up to the pension-insurance special early-retirement
  age, often topped up by additional payments by the employer.

In West Germany, *from 1984 until 1988*, the Pre-Retirement Act was in force.
It enabled workers aged 58 and over who withdrew from the labour market to
receive bridge payments from their former employer until such time as they
were able to draw a social-insurance pension. The law served to relieve labour
market pressures since older workers could quit the labour force without the
stigma of unemployment. The Act required that such arrangements be the
subject of collective agreements under which the employees concerned were
eligible for pre-retirement benefits.

Provided such benefits constituted at least 65 per cent of final gross earnings
and provided the vacated job was refilled, then the Federal Labour Office paid
a subsidy of up to 35 per cent of the pre-retirement benefit as well as the
employer's contribution to statutory health and pension insurance. About 70
per cent of employees entitled to take up pre-retirement benefits under collective agreements actually did so. Many branches, however, the public sector
being one example, did not offer this alternative to their employees.

From the beginning of *1989 until end 1991 only*, this Act was replaced by
the Part-time Work in Old Age Act which was a first attempt to establish a
phased retirement system at the federal level. Employers who concluded a part-
time work agreement with an employee aged at least 58 could receive a

Figure 5.2 Options for transition into retirement provided for under social insurance legislation in Germany

Age limit		58	59	60	61	62	63	64	65	
Pension because of vocational disability 3 yrs compuls. contrib./last 5 yrs	main- ly em- ployed		disabilitiy pension and reduced employment						Old age pension	
Invalidity pension 3 yrs compuls. contrib./last 5 yrs	main- ly em- ployed		Invalidity pension and marginal employment at most						Old age pension	
"59" Regulation 52 wks unemploym./last 1 1/2 yrs. 8 yrs compuls. contrib. /last 10 yrs	57J+4mo mainly employed		unemploy- ment benefit	Old age pension for unemployed persons						
Pre-Retirement 1990-92 in the 5 new states (the former GDR)	55 Special pre-retirement benefit			Old age pension for unemployed persons						
Pre-Retirement for women 1984-88 by law since then by collective agreement	mainly employed		Pre-retire- ment benefit	Old age pension for women * insured for a longer period						
Pre-Retirement for men 1984-88 by law since then by collective agreement	mainly employed			Pre-retirement benefit	Old age pension for persons insured for a long period *					
Full pension at 60 for women 10 yrs compul. contrib. from age 40	mainly employed			Old age pension for women insured for a longer period						
Full pension at 60 Disabil./Invalid./severe disablement 35 yrs contribution	many years in employment			Old age pension in the event of reduced fitness to work						
Full pension at 63 35 yrs contribution	many years in employment					Old age pension for persons insured for a long period				
Full pension at 65	prior employment								Normal old age pension	
Partial pension entitlement to a retirement pension fewer hours/less pay	Employment			individual combination of employment and partial pension					Full pen- sion	

* if the respective requirements are met. If not, entitlement for pre-retirement only 3 years before the normal retirement age of 65 years
yrs = years
wks = weeks

subsidy from the Federal Labour Office provided certain conditions were met (see Schmähl and Gatter, 1994, p. 441):
– the employee had to reduce his weekly hours by half, and work at least 18 hours a week on average;
– the employer was obliged to supplement pay by at least 20 per cent;
– the employer also had to make up the difference in pension insurance contributions between part-time pay and 90 per cent of the previous pay level;
– the vacant job had to be filled with someone who was unemployed.

This law was not financially attractive either for employers or employees and failed.

For many employers the Pre-Retirement Act was less attractive than the following alternative. For older workers who become unemployed, statutory pension insurance provides an opportunity for early transition into retirement, whereby, after receipt of unemployment benefit, an old age pension can be drawn at 60 years. A large number of employer/employee agreements made use of this pathway, many of them providing for additional financial compensation by the enterprise. The maximum period during which unemployment benefit can be received is now 32 months, and the older unemployed are now eligible for the latter without being obliged to look for a new job. Under certain circumstances employers have to reimburse part of the unemployment benefit. In other cases, if financial compensation is paid by the employer, the benefit is reduced.[2]

After the socialist economy of former East Germany collapsed in 1989 the number of the regularly employed in East Germany dropped by 2.3 million between 1990 and 1993 (28 per cent). Nevertheless, the 'official' number of unemployed in East Germany was only 1.2 million. The reduction in the number of the unemployed was in large measure due to the very wide coverage of pre-retirement measures (Schmähl, 1992b, with further references). Even before the introduction of the DM (July 1990) and unification (October 1990), the East German Government in February 1990 had brought into force an initial act which offered pre-retirement benefits to men from the age of 60 and to women from the age of 55. The benefit was 70 per cent of the last net earnings until the drawing of an old age pension under the social insurance system of the German Democratic Republic, namely at 60 for women and 65 for men.

After unification of the two German states, this was replaced by a special pre-retirement benefit, which was paid to women from the age of 55, to men initially from the age of 57 and later also from 55. Benefits were 65 per cent of individual average net earnings over the last three months, and were paid by the Federal Labour Office. In July 1993 the number of pre-pensioners in East Germany peaked at 857 thousand. This was almost one third of official and 'hidden' unemployment combined. These benefits will continue to be paid until 1997, but in the meantime many beneficiaries will reach 60, which will enable them to claim an old age pension.

In contrast to West German pre-retirement agreements, workers who were pensioned off in this way in East Germany seldom chose this route of their own accord, but were mostly forced to retire early because the only other alternative was to become unemployed. Beside financial reasons, such as lower incomes resulting also in lower retirement benefits, people in East Germany expected to retire much later. In former socialist society, life at the workplace was a much more important facet of everyday existence than in market economies. Therefore, some cohorts in East Germany have been profoundly affected by structural change after the collapse of the socialist economy and society.

Pensions and social security

Pension system and pension benefits
The German statutory pension scheme is a mandatory pay-as-you-go public pension insurance for all white- and blue-collar workers. Only permanent civil servants and certain groups of self employed are not covered by this system. Craftsmen are insured on a compulsory basis, other self employed on a voluntary basis. Eighty per cent of revenue is from income-related social-security contributions from earnings up to a contribution ceiling. Contributions are paid half by the employer and half by the employee. The other source of finance is federal grants. These are intended to compensate for pension-insurance expenditure aimed at interpersonal redistribution. Retirement benefits depend on the average relative earnings (i.e. individual gross earnings to average gross earnings in every year of insurance) and the number of contribution years. Benefits are linked to the actual earnings level of all currently employed people and adjusted regularly to the net average earnings of all employees. Therefore, pension policy is not primarily aimed at avoiding poverty, i.e. in principle no minimum pension exists, but to maintaining to a given extent the former standard of living (earnings replacement). Statutory pensions are by far the most important source of income in old age for most elderly German citizens.

The German statutory pension scheme makes a clear distinction between disability and old age pensions. While for old age pensions a certain age is required, this is not a precondition for disability pensions. Only five years of insurance and three years of contribution payments within the last five years are required. There are two types of disability pension. Pensions for vocational disability are awarded to people who are no longer able to carry out the job for which they are qualified. The disability pensioner is expected to work part-time in another job in addition to the pension in order to secure a full income.

Invalidity pensions are awarded if the individual is no longer able to work at all. If a worker eligible for a disability pension is unable to find a part-time job within a certain time the disability pension is usually transformed into an invalidity pension.

Age of retirement

In Germany a range of retirement ages for claiming an old age pension exists, offering certain flexibility in the transition from work to retirement. Table 5.3 gives a broad view of the different types of pension: vocational disability, invalidity and old age pensions. In 1993, 30 per cent of all new male pensioners claimed a vocational disability or invalidity pension and 70 per cent an old age pension (women 80 per cent). As far as old age pensions are concerned, more than 1/3 of men and as many as 50 per cent of women claimed an early old age pension at 60. One quarter of male old age pensioners used a flexible old age pension at 63, and about 40 per cent (men) and 50 per cent (women) took up an old age pension at the official retirement age of 65. But of all new pensioners in 1993 take-up at the official age was only 1/4 for men and less than 40 per cent for women. Therefore, the average retirement age even in statutory pension insurance is below 60 years. The average age of exit from the labour force, however, is even lower.

It should be noted that up to now, pensions claimed prior to the official retirement age are not reduced, as might be expected, by deductions because of the longer period of pension receipt. This is in principle a strong incentive to retire as early as possible.

Table 5.3
Use of different retirement options in Germany, 1993

	Men			Women		
	absolute	in%	in%	absolute	in%	in%
Old age pensions	391,477		100	396,343		100
for severely handicapped persons (60)	39,058	7	10	6,707	1	2
for long term unemployed (60)	102,203	18	26	9,635	2	2
for insured women (60)	–	–	–	182,721	37	46
for long-term insured (63)	95,098	17	24	12,050	2	3
regular pension (65)	153,403	27	39	185,224	37	47
Disability and invalidity pensions	170,800	30		100,741	20	
Sum (pensions of insured)	562,277	**100**		497,084	**100**	

Source: VDR (1994) and own calculations (deviations from 100 per cent are due to roundings).

New public policies

Pension reform of 1992

Introduction of partial pensions

The 1992 Pension Reform Act makes it possible for all old age pensions in Germany not only to be taken up as full pensions but from now on also as partial pensions. By combining one third, one half or two thirds of full retirement benefits with earnings from a part-time job, a more flexible exit from the labour force for older workers has been created, thus providing a model of late phased exit from the labour market into retirement. This was done because one objective of the reform act was to extend working life, to postpone retirement. Models which favour gradual exit before the earliest age of retirement in statutory pension insurance have been advocated by both trade unions and employers.

For partial pensioners before the age of 65 there exist ceilings for earnings beside the partial pension which depend on the individual's former earnings and the type of partial pension chosen.[3] The individual earnings ceiling is higher the lower the percentage of the full pension claimed as a partial pension, and the ceiling is linked to increases in average net earnings of all employees. Table 5.4 shows ceilings for supplementary earnings for a so-called 'standard pensioner', a person who has 45 years of insurance and who earned average earnings during this period. If we assume that this pensioner also had an average monthly gross earning from full-time employment in his last working year of 4,333 DM, his gross income from pension and employment can be seen in table 5.4.

Table 5.4
Example for calculating gross income under the partial pension scheme for a standard pensioner, West Germany, 1995

Type of partial pension or full pension (1)	Supplementary earnings limit (DM) (2)	% of last gross earnings (3)	Pension (DM) (4)	Pension and labour earnings (2)+(4) (5)	% of last gross earnings (6)
One third	3,220	74	690	3,910	90
Half	2,415	54	1,035	3,450	80
Two thirds	1,610	37	1,380	2,990	69
Full pension	580	13	2,070	2,650	61

Source: BfA-Mitteilungen, 1/95, calculated according to Viebrok, 1993, p. 98.

Concerning gross income for pensions and earnings, we can see that partial retirement seems financially attractive if earnings from part-time employment are as high as the ceiling. For individuals and households net instead of gross income is in many respects decisive. Because income taxation for pensions and earnings is different, calculating the net income effect is rather complicated and depends on the mix of pensions and earnings.

In table 5.5 some calculations are made, assuming an income-tax rate for a married sole breadwinner, and the contribution rate for compulsory social security at the beginning of 1995, which is 19.2 per cent (employee's part) of gross earnings. Income tax on pensions from the statutory pension system have to be paid only for a part of the pension, which is designed to be comparable to the 'return on capital', so pensions in fact are almost tax free. Earnings below 580 DM (1995) are not burdened by social insurance contributions. Pensioners have to pay contributions to statutory health and long-term care insurance (6.65 per cent).

Table 5.5
Sample estimates of net income under the partial pension scheme for a standard pensioner, West Germany, 1995

Type of partial pension or full pension	Supplemen-tary earnings limit (DM)	Pension (DM)	Income taxes (DM)	Contribu-tions to social security (DM)*	Net income (DM) (2)+(3)-(4)-(5)	In % of last net earnings (2,992.32 DM)
(1)	(2)	(3)	(4)	(5)	(6)	(7)
One third	3,220.00	690.00	334.33	664.13	2,911.54	97
Half	2,415.00	1,035.00	214.66	532.51	2,702.83	90
Two thirds	1,610.00	1,380.00	99.16	400.89	2,489.95	83
Full pension	580.00	2,070.00	0	137.66	2,512.34	84

* In Germany there exist different contribution rates to health insurance funds.
Source: BfA-Mitteilungen, 1/95, estimated according to Viebrok, 1993, p. 98.

Regarding net income from pensions and earnings, we can see that a full pension with only marginal employment yields an income at least comparable to that which could be achieved with a partial pension. This might be one of the reasons why little use has been made of this new regulation so far.

In 1992 and 1993 only 846 men and 1,067 women chose partial retirement as a phased exit from working life (table 5.6).

As can be seen from table 5.6, most male partial pensioners use this option at the age of 63. Some men claimed a partial pension as disabled. Females make fairly full use of the pension for women at the age of 60. About 40 per cent of pensioners claim half of the full pension (table 5.7).

Why, then, was disappointingly little use made of this new form of flexible retirement, which had been discussed and advocated before its introduction? The main reason seems to be the unfavourable labour market situation in Germany. There was a broad political and social consensus to the effect that early exit of older workers was better than unemployment of young people. When reducing the work force, total reduction is preferred. Moreover, expectations concerning early exit have developed over time, influenced also by institutional arrangements for early retirement.

Table 5.6
Transitions into partial retirement in Germany

Partial old age pensions	1992		1993	
	Men	Women	Men	Women
For severely handicapped (60)	70	14	114	14
For long-term unemployed (60)	11	-	20	1
For insured women (60)	-	342	-	541
For long-term insured (63)	248	78	378	71
Regular pension (65)	4	-	1	6
Sum	333	434	513	633

Source: VDR-Statistics.

Table 5.7
Use of the different types of partial pension in Germany, 1993

	Men		Women	
	Absolute	In %	Absolute	In %
One third	140	27	193	30
Half	211	41	268	42
Two thirds	162	32	172	27
Sum	513	100	633	100

Source: VDR-Statistics and own calculations (deviations from 100 per cent are due to roundings).

Secondly, partial pensions can only be claimed by women as of 60 and for most men as of 63 (although for some at 60). After the age of 65 a partial pension ceases to be attractive because as of that age there are no further earnings ceilings for people choosing full retirement.

The regulations on individual earnings ceilings are very complicated and compliance has to be revised regularly. This implies high administrative costs for social insurance and for the employer. The employee runs the risk of being downgraded to a lower type of partial pension or, when he earns too much, of loosing his pension altogether. But since employees in general want to earn up to the earnings ceiling, previously negotiated wage increases can result in 'excess' earnings.

On the company side, in contrast to the situation in Sweden, there is a general lack of part-time jobs especially for men. This will be discussed later in this chapter.

Age of retirement

From the year 2001 onwards the retirement ages for a pension without deductions ('reference retirement age') will gradually be increased until 2012 when 65 will become the reference retirement age for a 'deduction free' old age pension for both men and women. Earlier retirement will then still be possible and the earliest retirement age will be 62. Only disabled people will still be able to stop working at 60. For every month a person retires earlier than the reference retirement age reductions in pension benefits of 0.3 per cent will occur. A reduction of 3.6 per cent per year does not provide any strong incentive to work longer because it is still not actuarially fair (see Börsch-Supan, 1992, p. 551). For each month a pension starts after the 65th birthday, a supplement of 0.5 per cent is added to the pension.

It is by no means certain that the introduction of deductions will have a positive impact on the use of gradual retirement.[4] On the one hand, it seems desirable for people who retire before the age of 65 (the official retirement age) to compensate reductions in pension benefits by earnings from part-time employment. On the other, the calculation of supplementary earnings limits will become even more complicated than it is nowadays because deductions also have to be taken into account. If invalidity and disability pensions are also deduction-free in the future, it will be important to avoid this type of pension becoming a loophole for many of those who want to retire early.

5.2 Micro issues and policies

Recent trends

As mentioned already, the German legislator tried on several occasions to introduce gradual transition into retirement. But these attempts failed. Whether there is an opportunity in practice to establish gradual retirement in Germany will depend on decisions at the micro level of the economy, influenced by preferences of individuals and by the objectives of enterprise. The following remarks are intended to provide some information about the decision-making of employers and employees and the practical problems of implementing gradual retirement and part-time work of older workers.

Attitudes towards work and retirement

For most *employees* earnings from employment are their main source of income and it is gainful employment also that stabilises individual identity. But for many employees also, depending on working conditions, health status etc., employment is a burden. Therefore, decisions of older employees concerning transition to retirement are mainly influenced by its effect on their income, social relations, health, type of work and situation at the workplace. Workers, for example, facing high health hazards are likely to try to reduce the work load even by accepting high losses of income. Under such circumstances, a model of gradual retirement, which delays the transition to retirement would hardly be acceptable, but phased retirement at a lower age can help to decrease the pressures of work and maintain a relatively high level of income. When gainful employment implies a high level of individual satisfaction, delaying exit from work through gradual retirement meets the income aim while preserving the employee's work-dependant social status. These examples show that gradual retirement corresponds to different employee preferences and that many employees are in principle likely to be interested in retiring step by step.

Subjective data of the German Socio-economic Panel[5] show that more than one third of all men aged 50 years and over would accept a part-time job, were the loss of income to be substituted by a partial pension. Nearly 40 per cent of all women in full employment could also imagine using the partial pension option (see DIW, 1988, p. 54). A question concerning the preferred beginning and ending of phased retirement revealed a significant preference for an early transition into retirement. Male respondents on average would like to start gradual retirement at 57½ and to end it at about 60½. The actual age they expected to retire was on average about 61½ years. Women preferred beginning and ending phased retirement some months earlier than men, their expected retirement age being 60 (table 5.8). This clearly demonstrates that expectations are strongly influenced by existing institutional arrangements. The strong preference for leaving the work force step-by-step as early as possible is one explanation for the low interest in the partial pension option under the 1992 Pension Reform Act, which permits gradual retirement only when the employee is entitled to an old age pension. Moreover that partial pension is not as financially attractive as the hypothetical partial pension scheme on which the questions in the Socio-economic Panel were based. A further result from the panel survey is that blue-collar workers especially would like to retire as early as possible.

Empirical research on work in old age indicates a strong preference for a shorter working period within the life cycle (see Landenberger, 1983, p. 23). A study of the attitudes of employees aged 49-60 to reducing work time indicated that 65.5 per cent would prefer early retirement compared to fewer weekly work hours or longer vacations (see Engfer *et al.*, 1983, p. 101 or Viebrok, 1993, p. 81). Younger employees voted mostly for longer holidays and middle-aged people would like to work fewer hours per week. The Institut für Arbeitsmarkt- und Berufsforschung (IAB) asked employees aged 55 or more about their attitudes to transition to retirement: 60 per cent favoured early exit. Bad health and lack of job satisfaction were frequently cited as reasons for early retirement (see Blaschke *et al.*, 1986, p. 277). A survey by the Emnid research institute confirms that health status is an important reason for the retirement decision: 36 per cent of retired people said that they had left their job because of bad health (see Emnid, 1993, p. 41).

Table 5.8

Supposed beginning and ending of partial pensions on average and expected effective average age for full retirement according to the Socio-economic Panel

| Group | Gender | | Occupation | | | |
| | Men | Women | Blue collar workers | White collar workers | Public servants | Self employed |
Average Age						
Expected effective age for full retirement	61.4	60.0	60.6	61.3	61.9	60.8
Start of partial pension	57.5	56.4	57.2	57.3	57.6	57.0
End of partial pension	60.7	59.8	60.2	60.8	60.4	59.6

Source: DIW, 1988, p. 57.

But in evaluating such findings it is necessary to take into account that the motives mentioned may not have been the real reasons for the decision, that the people interviewed were not confronted with real and existing models of transition to retirement, and that they were mostly unaware of the financial impact of gradual retirement. Extending working life, especially when an old age pension is available, depends usually on economic incentives. Emnid (1993) asked people still working at pension age about their motives for doing so: 80 per cent mentioned that one reason was 'lack of money'.

Companies regard employee retirement as an important facet of personnel management. Every retirement, even gradual retirement, means a release of personnel and a vacating of a work place (see Stitzel, 1985, p. 120; Viebrok, 1993, p. 82). For the employers retirement can fulfil three major aims of personnel management (see Rosenow and Naschold, 1994, p. 211):

1 reducing personnel;
2 exchanging personnel, i.e. replacing older employees by younger ones;
3 changing personnel structure, i.e. replacing older employees by employees with higher education and qualification. Here (as in 2) higher productivity and/or lower labour costs are expected.

Gradual retirement can, however, serve other personnel management purposes (see Deters *et al.*, 1989, p. 36), for example:

4 retaining personnel; and
5 recruiting personnel.

The objective of retaining personnel or rather maintaining human capital was the main reason for introducing models of gradual retirement in three out of the five companies investigated by Deters *et al.* (1989, p. 219).

Complete retirement or total reduction is, however, not always the ideal answer to personnel-structure adjustment problems. In many cases gradual retirement would be the better solution. The fact that many of the models of gradual retirement currently applied were initiated by enterprises (Deters, *et al.*, 1989, p. 35) shows that employers as well are aware of the organising potential of different forms of transition to retirement. Whether gradual retirement can be made to meet personnel management needs depends on how authoritative companies are in the design and application of phased retirement (Deters, *et al.*, 1989, p. 36).

Using gradual retirement for personnel objectives further depends on the availability of strategies for complete externalisation of older employees. In recent years companies have preferred to use early retirement, especially under the Pre-Retirement Act and the so-called '59-Regulation', to reduce the number of the employed and to restructure staff. A survey by Rosenow and Naschold shows that early retirement is used not only to reduce staff, since it is used in prospering as well as in declining branches, and in the service sector as well as in industry (Rosenow and Naschold, 1994, p. 203). A study of retirement in the insurance industry in Germany indicates that early retirement is also preferred in branches with low pressure to reduce the work force and that early retirement can help to adjust the age structure and qualification of staff (Schmähl and Gatter, 1994).

Work performance

It is thanks to Thomae and Lehr (1973) that the so-called 'deficit-model of growing old', which posits a general decline of physical and psychological performance as life progresses, no longer secures any serious support in the scientific literature (see also Dohse *et al.*, 1982, p. 14). It is only common sense to evaluate an individual's work performance in the context of the operation to be performed and of working place conditions (Deters *et al.*, 1989, p. 235).

Nevertheless, personnel management theory presupposes that individual physical performance declines and experience increases with age (see Drumm, 1992, p. 122). Even though the interdependence of age and physical performance seems obvious, empirical research cannot conclusively prove decreasing work performance in older workers. Thomae and Lehr (1973) surveyed studies on the productivity of older workers. These studies carried out in different enterprises yielded different results: some indicated no differences between older and younger workers, several higher productivity for younger ones and others – surprisingly – a higher performance for older workers. The findings of Thomae and Lehr cannot claim validity for modern workplaces where new skills are required, since the studies are based on operations in traditional occupations. Older employees are said to suffer from disadvantages in learning new skills and operating new technologies (see Deters *et al.*, 1989, p. 235; Hentze, 1994, p. 152).

Another problem concerning work performance are higher wages of older workers because of increasing age-earnings-profiles. Göbel's study (1983), based on data on the German statutory pension scheme for blue-collar workers, indicates a positive correlation between wages and age. Similar results are given by Bellmann and Buttler (1989) using data of the Federal Labour Office (Bundesanstalt für Arbeit). Seniority-based wage systems (see Knoll, 1994) can be a barrier to postponing retirement (see Bellmann, 1989).

A further obstacle to the employment of older people is the investment in human capital of older employees. There exist several objections to training older workers: firstly, older employees have less accumulated human capital since they have fewer formal qualifications than younger ones (see Hoffmann, 1993, p. 323). Therefore, they have a smaller basis for occupational training activities. Secondly, older employees are said to be lacking in the ability to learn where new technologies are concerned (see Hentze, 1994), namely, they have a negative self-image regarding their own ability to learn and perform. Thirdly, the shorter period for amortising investment in human capital hinders vocational training of older employees from the point of view of both employer and employee. Fourthly, the higher wages of older workers mean higher opportunity costs for vocational training. Finally, older workers with strong preferences for early retirement are possibly not willing to 'go to school'.

Company pension regulations

In Germany the freedom to enter into contracts is guaranteed, and therefore gradual retirement could theoretically be introduced under agreements between employers and employees. In reality, however, there are only a few models of phased retirement established under the initiative of those involved. Gradual retirement has been given some emphasis only in certain collective bargaining agreements, such as in the cigarette industry, in chemicals, and in parts of the plastics and metal industries. Some firms have also individually introduced gradual retirement schemes.

Since 1978 older workers in the cigarette industry have been either entitled to reduce their work time to 20 hours weekly without any loss of income or to leave the work force completely in return for 75 per cent of the their last earnings (see Schwahn, 1988, p. 88; Jacobs, 1988, p. 4). Under this agreement it was possible for women and the severely disabled to reduce employment at the age of 58 and men at 61. It was up to the employee to claim these options. Employers were able to reject an application for gradual retirement, but had to offer full retirement to the employees instead. The use of both options rose from about 70 per cent in 1979 to more than 90 per cent in the second half of the eighties. But the choice between the alternatives had changed completely: in 1979, 70.8 per cent decided to work part-time; in 1982, only 43.8 per cent opted for partial retirement. The lowest use made of the part-time option was in 1986, when only 18.1 per cent opted for partial retirement.

In 1985 a collective agreement on part-time work in old age was signed for the chemical industry (see Prognos, 1986, p. 162; Kohli *et al.*, 1989, p. 207). Employees at 58 were entitled to choose between two alternatives: they could retire fully and receive a pre-retirement benefit or they could work part-time and receive 70 per cent income replacement. It was up to the employee to initiate the reduction in work hours and up to the employer to offer one of the two options available. Until 1986, 8 per cent of men eligible for early retirement and 13 per cent of women applied for part-time work. At that time employers had consented to 22 per cent of the applications by men and 33 per cent of those by women. When part-time work was rejected employers usually offered full early retirement. Companies stated that they often had to reject applications for part-time work because they had problems in organising the flow of work and in splitting workplaces. In evaluating the alternatives to full and partial early retirement enterprises voted clearly for complete exit from the labour force. Thus far, in the opinion of employers, full retirement is a better way of reducing personnel and adjusting staff structures.

In addition, certain companies also established gadual retirement agreements. Table 5.9 gives an overview over the best-known models operating during the eighties.

Age discrimination

In social sciences the comparison of incomes of different groups of employees is often used as an indicator of discrimination against certain categories of staff. Seniority wages are empirically well documented, therefore income discrimination against older employees is not significant. The higher wages of older workers, however, bear risks, because wages above real or expected work productivity are an important incentive for companies to lay-off older workers. The decreasing labour force participation of older workers and the early retirement strategies of enterprises seem to confirm this hypothesis. Some studies on early retirement regard older workers as victims of the externalisation strategies of companies. Other research – especially on the effects of the Pre-Retirement Act – indicates that older employees have themselves a strong preference for early retirement and that they attempt to speed up their own withdrawal from the work force (see Kohli, 1993, p. 191).

Table 5.9
Company models of gradual retirement in Germany

Company	Start and duration of grad. retirement	Working hours	Income	Further conditions
Daimler Benz AG	from 60 for the last three years of employment	half-time	full income for 6 months, then gradual reducing to 80% of the last gross income	10 years work in 3 shifts
Deutsche BP	from 55 during the last year of employment	reduction of 2 hours daily during the first 6 months, then reduction of 4 hours	full income	
IBM	from 56	half-time	50% of the last gross income plus occupational pension	
Pieroth Weingut-Kellerei GmbH	(1) from 60 to 63 (2) from 63 to 65	(1) 35 hours weekly (2) 30 hours weekly	(1) income for 37.5 hours weekly (2) income for 35 hours weekly	10 years tenure
Siemens AG	from 56 to 63 at most 4 years	half-time	75% of the last gross income	20 years tenure

Sources: Schüle, 1987; Schusser, 1988; Stitzel, 1985 and Viebrok, 1993.

Early retirement is as a rule carried out with the agreement of older employees, because there is strong protection of older workers against dismissals, so they cannot easily be laid off. But 'social pressure' especially in times of high unemployment of younger people can be an important factor affecting an older worker's decision to retire. Companies control the labour force participation of older workers by using different retirement incentives. The range of methods runs from indirect measures like bad conditions at the workplace without any offer of retirement options to direct measures which offer concrete plans for retirement (see Rosenow and Naschold, 1994, p. 220 or Naschold *et al.*, 1994, p. 130).

Older employees face serious problems when they are laid off and do not want to enter full retirement, because, for example, their pension would be too low. Because of existing protection against dismissals the risk of getting laid off is not extremely high for older workers. The problem of unemployment of older people is its long duration: two thirds of about 474,000 long-term unemployed are 45 or older (see Bogai *et al.*, 1994, p. 74). A survey of long-term unemployed over 45 showed that 64 per cent had a stable employment biography before becoming unemployed (see Bogai *et al.*, 1994, p. 74). Bogai *et al.* supposed that age itself makes it difficult to find a new job and proved this hypothesis empirically. This underlines the hypothesis that with the spread of early retirement not only does its (average) age decrease, but also the age at which a worker is looked upon as becoming 'old' resulting in lower hiring probabilities. Another survey carried out with data from the employment administration confirmed the link between old age and the duration of unemployment and stressed the relevance of health status to reemployment (see Cramer and Karr, 1992). Also according to Bogai *et al.* (1994), health problems play an important role: two thirds of the long-term unemployed stated that they are suffering from bad health and more than 30 per cent had official status as disabled persons.

New company policies

Personnel policy

The need for better integration of older people into the work force is increasingly admitted in publications on personnel management and by employers in their statements. Demographic development is influencing not only the financing of social security but also the age structure of company staff. The provision of human resources of the right quality and in the quantity desired is a key task of personnel management (see Nienhüser, 1989, p. 13). However, demographic changes will, it seems, make fulfilment of this task difficult in the future. Although there is enormous pressure to produce new personnel policies for the future, there is as yet no evidence of significant change in companies' behaviour.

Flexible work and pay policy

Although there are flexible work arrangements in some companies or branches (in the metal and chemical industries in West Germany), which make possible reduction of weekly work hours and longer vacation for older workers also (see Weidinger and Kutscher, 1992), the main difference between such arrangements and former models of part-time work in old age is that the employers no longer substitute income loss due to reduction of work hours. It is up to the employee to save work hours during prior periods on a 'time account' basis so as to enable him to reduce work activity in the period leading up to full retirement.

Partial pension

Implementing partial pensions according to the 1992 Pension Reform Act raises several problems. The result is, as mentioned already, that the partial pension is hardly used as an opportunity for gradual retirement. Older employers still have a preference for early retirement, the expected shortage, for demographic reasons, of younger workers has as yet not occurred and many firms still want to cut down their staff so as to reduce labour costs.

Further problems relate to regulation of the partial pension itself. The calculation of work hours according to an earnings ceiling is a complicated exercise which requires flexible organisation of the work force by companies. Every change in the hourly wage, for example through collective bargaining, demands fresh calculation of working hours and perhaps a changed work schedule. This involves high transaction costs for employers.

The introduction of partial pensions was accompanied by the abolition of mandatory retirement[6], with the result, in particular, that provisions in collective agreements which stipulate that work contracts automatically end at 65 are no longer valid. This caused an unintended effect: some employees abused the regulation by negotiating a golden handshake from their employer in exchange for withdrawing from the labour force. These incidents stirred up a discussion about mandatory retirement which ended with the restitution of its former legal status (see Schmähl and Gatter, 1994).

Occupational pension schemes can be an obstacle to gradual retirement when occupational pensions are paid only to workers who retire completely. Adapting entitlement to occupational pensions to payments from the statutory pension scheme will have a positive impact on the use of gradual retirement. Moreover, if the occupational pension is based on the last gross earnings, then workers choosing gradual retirement will be able to reduce their occupational pension claims.

Training

Development of the qualification structure of the work force demands increased training efforts in most occupations. In workplaces in almost all sectors of the economy, the call for lower qualifications is fading while the number of higher qualified employees is increasing constantly. This trend, it is thought, will continue at least for the next decade (see Buttler and Tessaring, 1993).

Nevertheless, older employees seldom take part in further vocational training even in branches which provide many training opportunities. A study of the German insurance industry (see Schmähl and Gatter, 1994) confirms the prejudices against the learning abilities of older workers and the rejection of further training by older employees themselves. Thus the participation of older employees in extended training declines dramatically at the age of 50. The example of the insurance industry shows that there is a strong need for new personnel policies in companies in order to prepare for the changing age structure of the labour force.

Reliable data on age structure of extended vocational training on a broader base are only available for public measures financed by the Federal Labour Office. The labour administration carries out further training when people are faced with serious problems on the labour market. On account of the weak labour market position of older workers we can assume that they are in principle an important target group for public-financed vocational training. Nevertheless, not even 10 per cent of all participants of such training measures are 44 and older (see Buttler, 1994, p. 35). If we make the reasonable assumption that vocational training of older workers is widely neglected in the private sector, then it can be said that an essential condition for changing the employment behaviour of older workers is lacking. Only by providing qualification facilities for older workers will the use of delayed models of gradual retirement like the partial pension under the 1992 Pension Reform Act become more common.

5.3 Potential for gradual retirement and recommendations

Our analysis of the transition to retirement in Germany has shown that there is still a strong tendency to early as well as full retirement. This is in line with the current preference of many employees and in accord with the strategy of many firms to solve their firm-specific problems by externalising older workers and rejuvenating staff. Now, however, some firms are beginning to complain that reduction and rejuvenating of staff has gone too far.

Recently, there has been a public debate in Germany about the fact that the early-exit strategies of firms are shifting costs to social insurance, especially to the pension system, and are increasing contribution rates and thereby labour costs, at a time when firms are precisely demanding a reduction in those labour costs. A reform of the Act on Employment Promotion is announced for the near future and will contain measures to reduce early exit.

Regarding the rapid aging of the German population, a delay in exit from the labour force and longer periods of contribution payments to social security will be necessary for financing social insurance, especially statutory pension insurance. Gradual retirement could be a way of achieving this aim especially if, in the light of future labour market trends, it is combined with other social policy measures as well. Part-time work is likely to increase the productivity of work per hour. This holds true for older employees, and would meet the interest of employers in reducing unit labour costs.

In 1995 labour unions proposed a gradual reduction of work time for older workers prior to being able to claim an old age pension. There should be a right to a part-time job for older workers and earnings should be combined with benefits from unemployment insurance. However, employers may be expected strongly to contest any rule whereby employees and not employers decide upon working time arrangements. From the point of view of firms, controllability and reversibility seem to be of great importance (see Staehle, 1989).

There is also an increasing debate about changing retirement ages for civil servants aimed at reducing early exit and introducing gradual retirement options, the purpose of both these measures being to lengthen working life and reduce (tax-financed) pension costs for households.

It is obvious from past experience that institutional rules matter a lot and influence behaviour and expectations. Acceptance of changes in institutional rules can be assumed to be quicker if the rules are accompanied by favourable environmental conditions as well as attractive incentives. Now however, rules are changed although environmental (e.g. labour market) conditions remain unfavourable: in the future there will be less incentive to retire earlier.

How firms and employees react within the new legal framework will be influenced above all by labour market conditions. Labour market projections (e.g. Prognos, 1995; Enquete-Kommission, 1994) point to a radical change on the labour market (mostly influenced by demographic change) after 2010. So, among other things, firms must decide whether they want to employ older workers with high qualifications longer (beyond even the reference retirement age of the statutory pension system) and on a part-time basis (women and men), or try to make up for the lack of manpower by using immigrants. Preparing for the future, then, means increased training for workers commencing in mid work-life at the very latest, as a necessary prerequisite for extending the employment of older workers in a world where the demand for highly qualified manpower is on the increase.

Given this situation, given also the growing interest among employees in flexible work-time arrangements, gradual retirement options could well give firms a competitive edge in the future struggle for a share in the limited pool of employees of qualification and experience. With life expectancy set to increase further, gradual retirement could give those able and willing to work longer an opportunity to do so, and those workers with health impairments a reprieve from untimely full retirement in the form of part-time employment.

To date, the German experience of gradual retirement has not been particularly promising. The indications are, however, that the situation is about to change.

Notes

1 For their assistance in preparing this overview we are grateful to Jutta Gatter and Holger Viebrok, who are – of course – not responsible for any remaining errors.

2 This pathway became known as the '59-Regulation' because workers in the past could draw unemployment benefits at the age of 59. Meanwhile, this bridge to pension starts at 57 years and 4 months, taking into account 32 months of unemployment benefits before 60.

3 For a detailed overview concerning the regulations on earnings ceilings see Reimann (1991) and Schmähl (1992a, p. 94).

4 For possible future effects of these changes see Schmähl (1992a).

5 The German Socio-economic Panel (SOEP) is a longitudinal survey of a representative sample of about 5,000 households, which started in 1984.

6 According to § 41 Abs. 4 S. 3 Sozialgesetzbuch VI.

References

Bellmann, L. (1989), 'Seniority-Based Wage Systems and Postponed Retirement' in Schmähl, W. (ed.), *Redefining the Process of Retirement*, (pp. 150-162), Springer, Berlin, Heidelberg.

Bellmann, L. and F. Buttler (1989), 'Lohnstrukturflexibilität – Theorie und Empirie der Transaktionskosten und Effizienzlöhne', *Mitteilungen aus der Arbeitsmarkt- und Berufsforschung*, 22, pp. 202-217.

Blaschke, D., H. Hofbauer and E. Hoffmann (1986), 'Einstellungen älterer Arbeitnehmer zum Übergang in den Ruhestand' in Institut für Arbeitsmarkt- und Berufsforschung (ed.), *Arbeitszeit und flexible Altersgrenze. Beiträge zur Arbeitsmarkt- und Berufsforschung* no. 75, 2nd ed., (pp. 272-290), Institut für Arbeitsmarkt- und Berufsforschung, Nürnberg.

Börsch-Supan, A. (1992), 'Population Ageing, Social Security Design and Early Retirement', *Journal of Institutional and Theoretical Economics*, 148, pp. 533-557.

Bogai, D. *et al.* (1994), 'Binnenstruktur der Langzeitarbeitslosigkeit älterer Menschen und Frauen', *Mitteilungen aus der Arbeitsmarkt- und Berufsforschung*, 27, pp. 73-93.

Buttler, F. and M. Tessaring (1993), 'Humankapital als Standortfaktor', *Mitteilungen aus der Arbeitsmarkt- und Berufsforschung*, 26, pp. 467-476.

Cramer, U. and W. Karr (1992), 'Lebensalter und Dauer der Arbeitslosigkeit' in C. Brinkmann and K. Schober (eds.), *Erwerbsarbeit und Arbeitslosigkeit im Zeichen des Struktur-*

wandels. Beiträge zur Arbeitsmarkt- und Berufsforschung no. 163, (pp. 189-206), Institut für Arbeitsmarkt- und Berufsforschung der Bundesanstalt für Arbeit, Nürnberg.

Deters, J., W.H. Staehle and U. Stirn (1989), *Die Praxis des gleitenden Übergangs in den Ruhestand. Geht eine sozialpolitische Idee in Rente?*, Edition Sigma, Berlin.

Dohse, K., U. Jürgens and H. Russig (1982), 'Die gegenwärtige Situation älterer Arbeitnehmer im Beschäftigungssystem. Einführung in die Probleme' in Dohse, K., U. Jürgens and H. Russig (eds.), *Ältere Arbeitnehmer zwischen Unternehmensinteressen und Sozialpolitik*, (pp. 9-60), Campus, Frankfurt, New York.

DIW (1988), Deutsches Institut für Wirtschaftsforschung, *Verteilungs-, sozial- und arbeitsmarktpolitische Bedeutung eines Teilrentensystems, Gutachten im Auftrage des Ministers für Arbeit, Gesundheit und Soziales des Landes Nordrhein-Westfalen*, Berlin.

Drumm, H.J. (1992), *Personalwirtschaftslehre*, 2nd. ed., Springer, Heidelberg.

Emnid (1993), *Nachberufliche Tätigkeit älterer Menschen. Bericht* in Bundesministerium für Arbeit und Sozialordnung (ed.), Forschungsbericht no. 226, Bonn.

Engfer, U., K. Hinrichs, C. Offe and H. Wiesenthal (1983), 'Arbeitszeitsituation und Arbeitszeitverkürzung in der Sicht der Beschäftigten', *Mitteilungen aus der Arbeitsmarkt- und Berufsforschung*, 16, pp. 91-105.

Enquete-Kommission Demographischer Wandel (1994), *Zwischenbericht – Herausforderungen unserer älter werdenden Gesellschaft an den einzelnen und die Politik*, Deutscher Bundestag, Referat Öffentlichkeitsarbeit, Bonn.

Göbel, D. (1983), *Lebenseinkommen und Erwerbsbiographie*, Campus, Frankfurt.

Hentze, H. (1994), 'Motivation älterer Mitarbeiter. Ergebnisse einer empirischen Untersuchung', *Personalführung*, pp. 150-157.

Hoffmann, E. (1993), 'Zur Beschäftigung älterer Arbeitnehmer in Westdeutschland – Qualitative und quantitative Aspekte', *Mitteilungen aus der Arbeitsmarkt- und Berufsforschung*, 26, pp. 313-327.

Jacobs, K. and W. Schmähl (1989), 'The Process of Retirement in Germany: Trends, Public Discussion and Options for its Redefinition', in Schmähl, W. (ed.), *Redefining the Process of Retirement*, (pp. 13-38), Springer, Berlin, Heidelberg.

Knoll, L. (1994), *Intertemporale Entlohnung und ökonomische Effizienz – ein Beitrag zur Theorie und Empirie von Alters-Verdienst-Profilen*, VVF, München.

Kohli, M. (1993), 'Altersgrenzen als Manövriermasse? Das Verhältnis von Erwerbsleben und Ruhestand in einer alternden Gesellschaft' in Strümpel, B. and M. Dierkes (eds), *Innovation und Beharrung in der Arbeitspolitik*, (pp. 177-208), Stuttgart.

Kohli, M. *et al.* (1989), *Je früher – desto besser? Die Verkürzung des Erwerbslebens am Beispiel des Vorruhestands in der chemischen Industrie*, Edition Sigma, Berlin.

Landenberger, M. (1983), *Arbeitszeitwünsche. Vergleichende Analyse vorliegender Befragungsergebnisse*, discussion paper IIM/LMP 83-17 des Wissenschaftszentrum Berlin.

Naschold, F. *et al.* (1994), 'Germany: The Concerted Transition from Work to Welfare' in Naschold, F. and B. de Vroom (eds.), *Regulating Employment and Welfare*, (pp. 117-182), de Gruyter, Berlin, New York.

Prognos (1986), *Bestandsaufnahme und Bewertung praktizierter Modelle zu vorgezogenen Ruhestandsregelungen* in Bundesministerium für Arbeit und Sozialordnung (ed.), Forschungsbericht no. 152, Bonn.

Prognos (1995), *Perspektiven der gesetzlichen Rentenversicherung für Gesamtdeutschland vor dem Hintergrund veränderter politischer und ökonomischer Rahmenbedingungen* in Verband Deutscher Rentenversicherungsträger (ed.), DRV-Schriften, Band 4, VDR, Frankfurt.

Reimann, A. (1991), 'Teilrente ab 1992 in der gesetzlichen Rentenversicherung', *Betriebliche Altersversorgung*, 3, pp. 61-66.

Rosenow, J. and F. Naschold (1994), *Die Regulierung von Altersgrenzen. Strategien von Unternehmen und die Politik des Staates*, Edition Sigma, Berlin.

Schmähl, W. (1992a), 'Changing the Retirement Age in Germany', *The Geneva Papers on Risk and Insurance*, 17, pp. 81-104.

Schmähl, W. (1992b), *Transformation and Integration of Public Pension Schemes – Lessons from the process of the German Unification*, Centre for Social Policy Research, University of Bremen, Working Paper 3/92.

Schmähl, W. (1993), 'The 1992 Reform of Public Pensions in Germany: Main Elements and Some Effects', *Journal of European Social Policy*, 3, pp. 39-51.

Schmähl, W. and J. Gatter (1994), 'Options for Extending the Working Period and Flexibilising the Transition to Retirement in the German Insurance Industry – the Current Situation and Assesment for the Future', *The Geneva Papers on Risk and Insurance*, 19, pp. 433-471.

Schüle, U. (1987), *Der gleitende Übergang in den Ruhestand als Instrument der Sozial- und Beschäftigungspolitik*, Lang, Frankfurt, Bern, New York, Paris.

Schusser, W.H. (1988), 'Stufenweiser Übergang in den Ruhestand aus Sicht der betrieblichen Praxis' in Schmähl, W. (ed.), *Verkürzung oder Verlängerung der Erwerbsphase.* (pp. 213-224), Mohr, Tübingen.

Schwahn, J. (1988), 'Erfahrungen mit dem Vorruhestand und betrieblichen Modellen des Übergangs in den Ruhestand aus Arbeitgebersicht: Das Beispiel der Zigarettenindustrie' in W. Schmähl (ed.), *Verkürzung oder Verlängerung der Erwerbsphase*, (pp. 88-95), Mohr, Tübingen.

Staehle, W.H. (1989), 'Employment of Older Persons from a Management Point of View' in Schmähl, W. (ed.), *Redefining the Process of Retirement*, (pp. 163-173), Springer, Berlin, Heidelberg.

Stitzel, M. (1985), 'Der gleitende Übergang in den Ruhestand – eine Pensionierungsform der Zukunft?', *Mitteilungen aus der Arbeitsmarkt- und Berufsforschung*, 18, pp. 116-123.

Thomae, H. and U. Lehr (1973), *Berufliche Leistungsfähigkeit im mittleren und höheren Erwachsenenalter*, Verlag Otto Schwartz, Göttingen.

VDR (1994), Verband Deutscher Rentenversicherungsträger, *VDR Statistik Rentenzugang des Jahres 1993*, Frankfurt.

Viebrok, H. (1993), 'Rentner auf Raten. Betriebliche Gestaltungsmöglichkeiten des Übergangs vom Erwerbsleben in den Ruhestand' in Angestelltenkammer Bremen and A. Mittelstädt (ed.), *Betriebliche Sozialpolitik. Relikt vergangener Zeiten oder Gestaltungsebene mit Zukunft?* (pp. 80-106), VSA-Verlag, Hamburg.

6 Gradual retirement in the United Kingdom

Philip Taylor and Alan Walker

The aging of the work force and the organisation of the public pension system are currently high on the political agenda in the UK. In recent years government policy on older workers has changed from one of encouraging their early retirement to one of trying to increase the supply of older workers and of encouraging employers to utilise this source of labour. In addition, the age at which women can draw a state pension is to be increased in stages to equal that for men (65 years) by the year 2020.

The purpose of this chapter is to assess the extent of prospects for gradual retirement in the UK. We begin with an examination of the position of older workers in the UK labour market. Trends in the employment of older workers are discussed and explanations offered. A particular focus is the impact of government policy on the labour market experiences of older workers. The second part of the chapter examines recent changes in government policies on retirement and policies which have an impact on the employment prospects of older workers. The third part of the chapter examines attitudes and policies towards older workers among employers and how these affect the employment of older workers and the potential for gradual retirement. The fourth part of this chapter looks at examples of company policies which facilitate gradual retirement among older workers.

6.1 Macro issues and policies

Recent trends

Labour market position of older workers

In the UK approximately 21 per cent of people aged over 50 are in the labour force (Taylor *et al.*, 1993). Agriculture has by far the highest proportion of older workers in the labour force (32 per cent of people aged over 50) although the proportion of all older workers employed in that sector is relatively small (3.5 per cent). However, it is the service sector that has the highest concentration (Taylor *et al.*, 1993). According to Tillsley's (1995) analysis of Labour Force Survey (LFS) data, 66.8 per cent of workers aged between 50 and the state pension age work in the service sector.

There are also important gender differences among older employees. There are the expected higher concentrations of older men in primary industries but also in finance and insurance and other services (as a proportion of all men in those sectors) (Taylor *et al.*, 1993). Women workers aged between 50 and the state pension age are considerably more likely to be employed in service sector industries than men (84.3 per cent compared with 55.2 per cent), whereas men aged between 50 and the state pension age are more prominent in manufacturing and construction (Tillsley, 1995).

Additionally, there are differences between older age-groups in the number of hours worked. Taking men in the age-group 55-59 first, the vast majority (roughly 95 per cent) work for more than 30 hours per week. Fewer men in the age-group 60-64 (89 per cent) work for more than 30 hours per week. But the picture is considerably different for men in the 65-69 age range: only 42 per cent of those employed work for more than 30 hours a week. The hours worked by women in the UK show a similar pattern to that for men. Taking the 55-59 age-group first, 50 per cent of women in this age-group work for 30 or more hours per week. In the 60-64 age range, 34 per cent of women work for 30 or more hours per week and only 21 per cent in the 65-69 age-group (Taylor *et al.*, 1993).

Among older workers, part-time employment has been increasing since the 1980s (Taylor *et al.*, 1993). Recent data (Tillsley, 1995) indicate that, in 1994, 52.7 per cent of women aged 50-59 years, 71.1 per cent of those aged 60-64 years, 85.2 per cent of those aged 65 and over were working part-time. Turning to working men, in 1994 5.7 per cent of those aged 50-59, 14.6 per cent aged 60-64 and 61.2 per cent of those aged 65 and over worked part-time.

Self employment among older workers is increasing for both men and women. The 65-69 age-group has the highest prevalence of self employed people. Within this age-group, in 1989, 37 per cent of male employment and 21 per cent of female employment was self employment. In the case of the 60-

64 age-group, the rates were 19 per cent and 10 per cent respectively (Casey and Laczko, 1992).

Turning to redundancy, figures for Spring 1994 (Employment Department, 1995) show that people in the 55 and over age-group had a redundancy rate of 10.9 per 1,000 employees compared to rates of 9.7, 9.1, and 8.8 for the 45-54, 35-44, and 25-34 age-groups respectively. Only the 16-24 age-group shows a comparable rate, of 10.8 per 1,000 redundancies.

Data obtained in 1992 indicate that only 59 per cent of unemployed men aged 50 and over were seeking full-time employment. Small but significant proportions of older unemployed men were looking for part-time jobs (13 per cent) or self employment (10 per cent). The majority of all unemployed women aged over 50 were seeking part-time employment but a substantial minority (28.8 per cent) were looking for full-time employment. Looking at married women only a larger majority were seeking part-time employment (61.3 per cent), with 19.8 per cent seeking full-time jobs (Taylor *et al.*, 1993).

Older people are considerably more likely to be found among the long-term unemployed. In 1989 the vast majority of unemployed men in the age range 55-64 were long-term unemployed (long-term unemployment defined in this instance as 12 months or more) (Taylor *et al.*, 1993). Older men were considerably more likely to be long-term unemployed in 1989 than they were in 1983. In 1983, 59 per cent of unemployed men in the age range 50-64 were long-term unemployed. By 1989 this figure had risen to almost 70 per cent. By contrast the incidence of long-term unemployment among the 25-54 age-group declined slightly between 1983 and 1989 from 59 per cent to 55 per cent. This suggests a widening gulf between older and younger workers in terms of the incidence of long-term unemployment. Long-term unemployment among unemployed women aged between 55 and 64 remained fairly stable between 1983 and 1989, at 55 per cent. However, long-term unemployment among the 25-54 age-group declined markedly over this period from 38 per cent to 29 per cent, leaving a wide gap in the incidence of long-term unemployment between older and younger women.

Older workers are also disadvantaged in terms of the amount of training they receive. Figures for Spring 1994 (Employment Department, 1994) show that 25 per cent of employed people in the 16-19 age-group had received job-related training in the last 4 weeks compared to 20.3 per cent in the 20-24 age-group, 17.4 per cent in the 25-34 age-group, 14.7 per cent in the 35-49 age-group and 8.4 per cent in the 50-59/64 age-group.

Trends in the employment of older people
The UK will see an increase in the percentage of people aged over 50 in the general population over the period 1990 to 2020 from 31.2 per cent to 38 per cent. As in other European countries the main factors explaining this change are declining fertility and mortality rates (Walker, Guillemard and Alber,

1991). This trend appears against a background of declining numbers of older people in the labour market. The UK has experienced a decline in the employment of older men since the 1950s. This accelerated in the 1970s and 1980s and, as table 6.1 shows, resulted in just over three quarters of men aged 55-59, just over half of men aged 60-64 and less than one tenth of men aged 65 and over being economically active in 1994.

The participation of women in the labour force has tended to increase slightly since the 1970s (Walker, 1984) though, looking at the cross-sectional series shown in table 6.1, it is important to bear in mind that the cohort effect of increased labour force participation of women in the post-war period is likely to coincide with many of the same factors influencing male participation rates in later life. Once the cohort effect of the post-war rise in female economic activity is disentangled from the cross-sectional picture shown in table 6.1, a similar trend has occurred among older women, although it is less steep than the male one (Guillemard, 1993). Research shows that, for women aged over 50, age is more strongly related to employment status than household characteristics. Ginn and Arber (1995) found that, for married women aged in their 50s, age was related to the probability of being in employment whereas this was not the case for women aged in their 40s. The probability of being in employment for women aged 58-59 was found to be half that for women aged 50-51.

Table 6.1
Economic activity rates of older women and men in Britain, 1951-1994

Age	1951	1961	1971	1975	1981	1985	1990	1994
Women								
55-59	29.1	39.2	50.9	52.4	53.4	52.2	55.0	55.7
60-64	14.1	19.7	28.8	28.6	23.3	18.9	22.7	25.6
65+	4.1	4.6	6.3	4.9	3.7	3.0	3.4	3.2
Men								
55-59	95.0	97.1	95.3	93.0	89.4	82.6	81.5	76.1
60-64	87.7	91.0	86.6	82.3	69.3	55.4	54.4	51.2
65+	31.1	25.0	23.5	19.2	10.3	8.5	8.7	7.5

Sources: 1951-71 Census of Population for England and Wales and for Scotland; 1975-81 Department of Employment, Gazette; UK Labour Force Survey (Spring).

Modes of labour exit
The main factors explaining the growth of early exit from the labour market among British people are demand-related, particularly the recessions of the mid-1970s and early 1980s (Walker, 1985; Trinder, 1989). Additionally, while

economic activity among older people declined only slightly between 1985 and 1989 when the UK economy was expanding rapidly, table 6.1 shows that, with the start of the UK recession in 1990, the decline in economic activity among older workers accelerated again. Trinder (1989) has identified three reasons for the decline in economic activity among older people. First, the share of older people in employment has fallen most in the older, declining industries and rather less in industries were there has been growth (Jacobs, Kohli and Rein, 1991). Second, older workers were more likely to be dismissed than younger ones and they were less likely to find employment if they were made redundant. In fact, research suggests that, whereas the prospects of younger people improved following the recession of the early 1980s, the work chances of older unemployed people were permanently impaired (Payne and Payne, 1994). Third, for organisations needing to shed staff quickly, it was relatively easy to negotiate early retirement for those close to retirement age. A study conducted by Casey and Wood (1994) shows that voluntary redundancies and, particularly, early retirement were used as a means of achieving staffing reductions in large organisations, in organisations with a trade union presence, in manufacturing and in the public sector. By contrast, in small firms, in service sector organisations, in the private sector, and in organisations with little or no trade union presence, compulsory redundancies are more frequently practised.

Non-employed older workers appear to hold an indeterminate position in the labour market. This issue was explored by Casey and Laczko (1989) who related declining economic activity rates among older workers to levels of unemployment. Using data for the years 1979 and 1986 they showed that, for men aged 55 to 64, there was a considerable increase in those classifying themselves as 'discouraged workers' whereas there was only a slight increase in those classifying themselves as retired among men in the 55-59 age-group, and a marked decline in those classifying themselves as retired among men in the 60-64 age-group. Thus, rather than demonstrating an increasing trend towards early retirement in order to enjoy a 'happier old age', this research suggests that the major factor in explaining falling levels of economic activity was a deterioration in the labour market.

During the recessions of the mid-1970s and early 1980s, when the UK experienced simultaneous contraction of full-time employment and historic high points in the numbers of young people entering the labour market, older people were actively encouraged to take early retirement (Walker, 1985). Youth unemployment was given a high priority by government: this led to the introduction of the Job Release Scheme in 1977, which was intended to be a temporary measure to alleviate unemployment among younger workers by providing allowances for men and women to retire one year prior to the state pension age if their employer replaced them with a previously unemployed person. Participants received a flat rate benefit paid directly by the state. The scheme reached its peak in 1984-85 when approximately 88,000 men, about one eighth of the number of non-working men in the 60-64 age-group, were receiving benefits. The programme was closed in 1988 when the Department of Employment judged that its resources could be better targeted elsewhere (Casey and Wood, 1994). From 1981 unemployed men in the age range 60-64 have been eligible for an additional income support (the UK's basic scheme) social assistance premium if they withdrew from the unemployment register (Walker and Taylor, 1993).

Pensions and social security

The UK operates a two-tier pension system. The first tier consists of a basic flat rate social insurance pension which is payable to everyone with a complete record of contributions. If contributions are incomplete the pension is reduced.

The second tier is the State Earnings Related Pension Scheme (SERPS) which provides an additional pension based on a person's lifetime earnings. Employers operating an approved defined benefit occupational pension scheme are allowed to opt out of the state scheme. In addition, since 1988, individuals making sufficient contributions to a personal pension plan are also allowed to opt out of the state scheme. Also since 1988, it has been possible to contract out of SERPS into money purchase (defined contribution) schemes.

In 1993 the replacement ratio of the basic and additional pensions combined, as a percentage of earnings, was 33 per cent for a person with average earnings (Government Actuary, 1994).

About 30 per cent of the UK work force are only members of the state pension scheme (basic and SERPS), 20 per cent are not only in the state scheme but have a private pension (and might or might not be opted out of SERPS), while 48 per cent are members of company schemes (the majority are opted out of SERPS and some may also have a personal pension) (Government Actuary, 1994). The majority of employees in this latter group are members of defined benefit schemes (Davis, 1993). Nearly 5 million people, or approximately a quarter of the work force, have a personal pension and the majority have opted out of SERPS (Davis, 1993; Government Actuary, 1994). Approximately 400,000 employees are thought to be members of contracted out defined contribution schemes (Government Actuary, 1994).

New public policies

With the rapid expansion of the UK economy in the late 1980s, coupled with the so-called demographic 'timebomb' of falling numbers of young labour market entrants, the government introduced a series of measures aimed at encouraging older people to remain in or to re-enter the labour market. These include the abolition, in 1989, of the earnings rule which penalised people who worked beyond the state pension age earning more than £75 per week. In 1986 the Sex Discrimination Act was amended to make it unlawful to compulsorily retire women at an earlier date than their male counterparts. Additionally, the 1990 European Court of Justice judgement in the 'Barber' case effectively requires that men and women receive the same pension benefits at the same age. The effect on employer policy seems to have been that the pension ages of men and women have been equalised at 65 in most cases (IDS, 1994). The UK government has also been keen to scale down the role of the state in pension provision. This led, in 1988, to an extension of the rights of individuals to opt out of SERPS into a personal pension scheme and allowing money purchase schemes to contract out (Walker, 1993).

In addition, in December 1993, the age limit for access to Training for Work, the main government training programme for long-term unemployed people, was raised from 59 years to 63 years. However, it should be pointed out that the impact of this measure on the employment of older workers has not been assessed. Moreover, there are other areas where discrimination against older workers remains. For example, legislation against unfair dismissal does not apply to workers aged over 65. In addition, the amount of a redundancy settlement is based on length of service and this acts as an incentive to target older workers on the basis that they are more cushioned against the impact of redundancy (Casey and Wood, 1994).

An ideological belief in the need for an unfettered labour market has meant that the current UK government has consistently expressed its opposition to legislation outlawing age discrimination in employment. Instead, the government favours an educative approach. In 1993 it launched the 'Getting-On' campaign with the aim of educating employers to the value of recruiting older people. This high profile campaign is ongoing and aims to make employers more aware of the issue and better informed about the qualities of older workers. The campaign has included the production of a booklet, sent to 165,000 employers of over 75 people in March 1994, advising them, with examples of good practice from major UK companies, how to avoid discriminating against older people. As with other policies in this area, the impact of this campaign has yet to be assessed.

Partly as a result of earlier research which showed that staff in official employment agencies (Jobcentres), where employers can place recruitment advertisements, discouraged older people from seeking employment (Taylor and Walker, 1991), staff received instructions to question employers about the need for age bars in advertisements (Casey and Wood, 1994). In addition, the Employment Service has recently produced a leaflet, 'What's age got to do with it?', which provides Jobcentre staff with information about age discrimination and advice on what they should do if they believe that an employer is discriminating unfairly. A study of advertisements placed in Jobcentres showed that, in 1990, 11 per cent of vacancies were not open to people aged 60 or over (Jones and Longstone, 1990). However, a recent report states that only

8 per cent of Jobcentre advertisements carried age bars (Personnel Management, 1994).

During the 1980s the idea of a 'flexible decade of retirement', between the ages of 60 and 70, achieved considerable exposure (Schuller and Walker, 1990) and became part of the Labour Party's policy. However, fears concerning the Exchequer cost implications of allowing men access to pensions at 60 led the Government to reject this proposal and the equalisation of pension ages at the cost neutral age of 63, and to opt instead for the phased increase in the female pension age to 65 by the year 2020.

6.2 Micro issues and policies

Recent trends

So far it has been shown that older workers occupy a disadvantaged position in the labour market. We have argued that demand-side factors have had a major impact on older workers' employment prospects. In this section, the issue is examined in more detail by reviewing research on employers attitudes and practices towards older workers.

In order to obtain information on employers' policies and attitudes towards the employment of older people, we carried out a national survey of 500 large organisations (with more than 500 employees) covering virtually the whole range of industrial sectors (apart from agriculture) between September 1991 and January 1992 (Taylor and Walker, 1994). This survey indicated that most employers were not developing any strategies geared to older workers although many of them held favourable attitudes towards this group. Less than a fifth of employers stated that they were seeking to recruit more older people, and less than a tenth of employers had in place a partial retirement scheme or were encouraging later retirement. These findings indicate that, despite displaying largely positive attitudes towards older workers, the employment of more older people, or attempting to retain them by encouraging later retirement or introducing partial retirement schemes, were not considered priorities by employers. Significant numbers of employers said they would consider the employment of older people as a means of overcoming labour shortages in the future but, equally, many said they would not consider later retirement or partial retirement schemes. In contrast to employers, older workers themselves have been found to be enthusiastic about the idea of flexibility in the age at which they retire (Taylor and Walker, forthcoming).

In fact, almost two fifths of respondents had in place early retirement schemes. Almost half the employers in the production and construction sectors operated early retirement schemes compared to just over a third of service sector employers. Service sector employers were more likely to be recruiting greater numbers of older workers although there were no sectoral differences in the likelihood of offering later or gradual retirement.

Data from our survey of employers, and from an earlier survey of older workers' experiences in the labour market (Taylor and Walker 1991; 1994), indicate that older people seeking work in the early 1990s face considerable ageism from employers. In our study, age restrictions in job advertisements were cited by older people as barriers to employment, and in our survey of major employers we found that 15 per cent specified age bars in jobs. Moreover, 43 per cent of employers stated that age was an important consideration in the recruitment of staff.

Employers were also asked about factors which might discourage them from recruiting older people. The overwhelming factor discouraging recruitment and employment of older workers in the eyes of employers was a lack of appropriate skills, 72 per cent regarding this as an important factor, while the payback period on training and maximum recruitment ages were rated as important discouraging factors by many employers. In addition, almost half the respondents thought that pension scheme rules acted to discourage the employment of older people.

A subsequent study of the employment of older workers in local government conducted by Itzin and Phillipson (1993) found that local authorities were only just beginning to introduce positive older worker policies. While authorities were beginning to make efforts to remove age bars in recruitment advertisements, and one third included age in their equal opportunities policies, early retirement was being actively used by the majority as an alternative to compulsory redundancy in the reduction of staffing numbers. Policies such as phased retirement and job-redesign to better accommodate older employees had seldom been implemented. In addition, line managers' attitudes towards, and beliefs about, older workers were identified by senior management respondents as being significant obstacles to the recruitment, training and promotion of older workers. Finally, Warr and Pennington (1993) have conducted a large scale postal survey of personnel managers and found ambivalence in their attitudes concerning older staff. Although this group were seen as being more 'effective' than average in terms of experience, loyalty, reliability, conscientiousness and team working, they were also seen on average as being less adaptable.

Research has demonstrated the existence of a number of myths about older people with respect to employment (Casey, Metcalf and Lakey, 1993). For example, it is held that older workers are not a worthwhile investment as regards training, their performance is lower and they are absent more often than younger workers. However, research suggests that, in general, rated job performance is unrelated to age, overall absenteeism tends to be greater among younger employees, accident rates are higher among younger workers, and staff turnover declines with age (Warr, 1993).

The research which has been summarised here indicates that age discrimination in the UK labour market is commonplace. The next section of this chapter focuses on examples of employer policies which have the effect of facilitating gradual retirement.

New company policies

The following examples of good practice towards older workers come from in-depth interviews conducted with 100 employers selected from among the employers who responded to our postal survey (Taylor and Walker, 1994).

Personnel policy

Among those employers in our survey who had developed policies on older workers, we encountered a variety of approaches which might encourage the recruitment or retention of older people. Policies aimed at enabling older workers to enter organisations included recruitment policies such as removing age bars from advertisements and checking them for language which might discourage older applicants. In one company, qualification specifications were excluded or were accompanied by the statement: 'or equivalent experience'. Positive statements, such as 'looking to return to work?', were sometimes used to encourage older people to apply. A retail company's literature, sent to candidates applying for posts, ensured that any pictorial material gave representation to different groups in the community (including age-groups). In addition, one employer stated that, if a private recruitment agency was used, then it was informed of the organisation's equal opportunities policy and asked to adhere to it or was asked for written evidence of its commitment to equal opportunities, where advertisements would be placed and what pool of labour would be used to recruit from.

In order to persuade management of the benefits of employing older workers, some personnel departments publicised examples of where the organisation had successfully deployed older people. The potential problem of a lack of receptiveness among some line managers to recruiting more older people had been anticipated by a personnel manager who had attempted to overcome this by trying it out in departments that he felt would be likely to be the most receptive. Then, in subsequent attempts to extend the implementation, this department was given as an example of success in recruiting older people. The Head of Personnel of an employer involved in pharmaceutical research and development stated that the company was in the process of educating its line managers about the issue of age discrimination; adding that, initially, management had not been good at getting the message across. One of the difficulties had been communicating to line managers, who made the final selection decision, that the company had a cogent set of business reasons for pursuing this policy as well as a desire for social equity in employment practices. Another problem acknowledged by the management of this company was what the Director of Human Resources described as the 'natural biases' he felt that line managers often had in terms of selection and promotion. In an attempt to counter this, the company had introduced training modules about equal opportunities in all supervisory and management training and retraining and refresher courses, so that the issue of equality and age was raised and debated regularly.

We found little evidence of monitoring of the impact of company policies on older workers. However, in one company annual reviews of the company's performance pay system include checks for bias by grade, sex, and age.

Turning to redundancy, unlike many employers in our survey, a manufacturer of starter motors and alternators for the motor industry eschewed the use of age as one of the criteria for selecting staff for redundancy. Management felt that, as such a practice would be likely to result in a loss of highly skilled people, such a practice could damage the productivity of the company and thus endanger the jobs of the remaining employees. Instead, management had introduced a policy of compulsory redundancy whereby staff reductions were targeted to make sure that the best employees were retained. The system the company developed was based on the ranking of employees in performance terms and a concept they called the 'zone of indifference'. The key issue was the relative and absolute distance between employees. For example, while three employees could be ranked (say) fourth, fifth and sixth, they could actually display widely different levels of performance. The two employees ranked fourth and fifth could be relatively close in performance terms but the performance of the employee ranked sixth could be considerably poorer. If two employees had a similar ranking and their performance levels were similar, then the company was 'indifferent' as to which of them left and if one volunteered, he or she would be allowed to go.

It is increasingly common for UK employers to have written equal opportunities statements. However, in only a small minority of cases had employers included age in their equal opportunities statement. The following statement on age was taken from an employer's equal opportunities statement:

> Ageism is a form of discrimination which is not specifically covered by the law, although from the earlier example it can be seen that when an age limit affects a greater proportion of one sex or the other it can amount to indirect discrimination. There are no barriers to any position and this should be borne in mind when recruiting, appraising and considering staff for promotion.

Redesign of work

In our study there was little evidence of job re-design specifically aimed at improving the work performance and environment of older workers. However, a manufacturing company had introduced a policy called 'easy working' which was an attempt to re-design the working environment to make work tasks easier to perform in order to reduce the possibility of injuries to staff and to maximise the working lives of employees. It involved, for example, reducing the gaps between machines where people have to lift things across, the height people have to lift things, and the amount of repetitive actions they had to take. The company was also promoting job changes to avoid repetitive strain, a problem which is common in light engineering because of the number of repetitive activities required. The company has negotiated flexibility agreements with the trade unions whereby job demarcation (strictly defined job boundaries) had been reduced significantly. Under the agreement, an employee with a health problem caused by carrying out particular repetitive actions could move to a job where such actions were minimal. Similarly in another organisation older employees could take a pension at the age of 60 and then be re-employed at a lower grade until the age of 65.

Flexible working arrangements

General human resource policies which also assisted older workers were more likely to be in operation than schemes specifically targeting older workers. Such policies were often aimed at encouraging greater employment of women workers, reflecting a greater emphasis among the employers in our sample on recruiting women workers. Over twice as many employers in our postal survey were trying to use more female labour than were trying to recruit greater numbers of older workers. Similarly, significantly more employers were operating flexible working hours and job-share schemes than were seeking to recruit more older workers. One such policy was that of annualised hours whereby employees were required to work a set number of hours in a year rather than per week. This gave all employees the option of building up a block of lieu time (time account). However, our research indicated that policies on older workers and encouraging flexible working practices were largely unrelated, although policies on the employment of women workers were related to the implementation of policies aimed at increasing flexibility (Taylor and Walker, 1994). These findings suggest that 'flexibility' is more associated in the minds of employers with the employment of women than older workers.

Training and development

In our survey of employers we came across several examples of employer training programmes targeting older workers. A company which provided insurance and re-insurance services had set up, in conjunction with three other local insurance companies, a returning to work course with a local college. The company was aware that the training needs of an older recruit might differ from those of a younger person. It was felt that, because insurance is a very computer-related sort of industry, older people, who might never have used a computer before, would need slightly more training. However, the company's policy of tailoring of training to an individual's need meant that this problem had been easily overcome. Confidence building was an important feature of the support which it had been necessary to provide for some older recruits who had not been employed for extended periods.

In terms of employee development, a company involved in food and related distribution actively encouraged employees to train to keep their skills up to date. Every employee in the company had a performance appraisal interview to look at what work they would be doing in the coming year and what skills they would need to be able to achieve their goals. If an employee felt they were short of skills then a programme of training would be devised. The review was mandatory for all employees, regardless of their age. The company's factories division was facing a shortage of skilled engineers, primarily because they were no longer getting the same volume of younger applicants. In addition, in response to technological advances, management wanted to improve the quality of the existing work force. As a solution they decided to offer older workers in the production area the opportunity to do an accelerated two year apprenticeship to enable them to work on skilled craft tasks.

Gradual retirement

Turning to retirement and retention we found only a limited amount of evidence of flexibility in the age of retirement. As noted earlier, only a very small number of respondents were encouraging later retirement and, similarly, very few offered gradual retirement schemes. One such company's policy is outlined below:

> We operate a scheme whereby 2 years prior to retirement you start off taking half a day off each week, and then in your last year it's a day per week, building up to 2 days a week in the last 3 months.

A few employers had also introduced more flexible arrangements whereby, for example, both male and female employees could retire at any age between the ages of 60 and 65, while one employer did not have a rigid policy on retirement and thought that the state pension ages should only be used as a guideline with each case being treated on its merits.

A major retail fashion department store had changed its retirement policy so that both men and women could retire at the age of 60 if they so wished. The company had a policy, set out in its personnel handbook, that when a staff member reached retirement age, management were happy to talk to them about staying with the company. Another policy change within this company which had assisted in the retention of older people had been with regard to contracts of employment. Previously, staff who had continued past the state pension age had been put on temporary contracts which had disadvantaged them in terms of sick and holiday pay. This policy has been changed so that these staff have the same conditions as other employees.

We only came across two instances where employers had adjusted pension arrangements in order to reduce barriers to recruiting older workers. One of these stated that pension arrangements in the company had acted as a barrier to the recruitment of older people, while the other felt that these could discourage older people from taking jobs. These companies had modified terms and conditions of employment to encourage more older people to join the company and to retain them for longer. In the words of the two personnel managers we spoke to:

> By changing our contracts of employment so all employees are contracted to 65; allowing entry into our pension scheme up until 58, we have sort of pushed out the barriers. Women's contracts were 60, men were 65, women's pensionable age was 60 and men 65, and 55 was the maximum age for entry into the pension scheme. We have eliminated all the bars, so that even somebody doing 4 hours a day could come into the pension scheme. Women can contribute to the pension scheme up to 65.

> We're putting the latest age of entry into our pension scheme up five years. It's currently 55 but, because we're taking on staff who are over 55, we've said to ourselves, well it is a discouragement to older staff to find that, yes they're being offered a job, but they have no opportunity to join the pension scheme when, potentially, and you might be a 56-year-old, you've got nine years employment ahead of you.

Other employer policies

Another area where we found evidence of policy innovation was with regard to employees with caring responsibilities. In most cases this was an informal arrangement between the manager and the staff member, although a small minority of employers had written policies to which managers, employees and trade unions could refer. One such policy is outlined below:

> Responsibility Break allows staff with personal responsibility for elderly, sick or disabled relatives to take a complete break from work or to work on a temporary part-time basis for up to six months if longer term care suddenly becomes necessary. Open to both men and women, Responsibility Break gives staff with a minimum of two years' service the opportunity to negotiate a temporary working pattern to suit both their needs and the needs of the company. Part-time work can last between one and six months and, where possible, will continue at the existing workplace. During this period existing staff benefits are retained. Alternatively, staff can choose to take an unpaid full break from work for a similar period of time whilst retaining existing staff benefits. Staff return to work after that period at the same grade. Those who

are unable to return to full-time work after six months will be given the opportunity to work on a permanent part-time basis at the same grade. If a member of staff finds it necessary to resign however, their name can be placed on a reserve list for a period of two years, giving them priority consideration for vacancies if a return to work becomes possible during this time.

6.3 Potential for gradual retirement and recommendations

What are the prospects for gradual retirement in the UK? The research presented in this chapter indicates that, at the present time, the prospects for gradual retirement are limited. Significant numbers of employers cite pension rules as being a barrier to the employment of older workers and there seems to be little enthusiasm among employers for later or phased retirement, even among service sector employers who seem to have done most to encourage the greater recruitment of older workers. Moreover, a culture of gradual retirement would run counter to the culture of early exit in British industry which, with the support of government, trade unions and employers, developed in the 1980s to the point where today, early retirement has become a feature of the majority of programmes of redundancies (IRS, 1995).

What needs to be done in order to reverse this trend and improve the prospects for gradual retirement? While present efforts being made by government to increase the supply of older workers and to encourage employers to recruit from this labour pool have been important, evidence of a continuing decline in economic activity rates among older workers would suggest that this approach has not yet been successful (although it is accepted that some changes may take a long time to have an effect). If ultimately, the present approach is found to have been unsuccessful, more radical steps may have to be considered. In particular, government may need to amend existing employment legislation and change its policy concerning social assistance payments to older workers in order to make clear its commitment to improving the prospects for this group and to tip the scales in their favour. First, it will be necessary to remove the incentive to target older workers when decisions about redundancy are being made by employers and trade unions. This will mean amending the UK Redundancy Payments Act which links compensation to age (Casey and Wood, 1994). Second, government will need to end the practice of awarding men in the 60-64 age range an additional social assistance premium if they withdraw from the unemployment register. Additionally, it is unlikely that significant progress towards gradual retirement will be achieved without a move away from defined benefit occupational pension schemes which provide benefits based on salary at or near to retirement and, as such, contain a built-in incentive to retire abruptly (Casey, 1994). However, even if the government is forced into introducing legislation to outlaw age discrimination in employment the experiences of other disadvantaged groups would suggest that this would not necessarily result in immediate gains for older workers.

References

Casey, B., H. Metcalf and J. Lakey (1993), 'Human resource strategies and the third age' in Taylor, P. *et al.*, pp. 43-74.

Casey, B. and F. Laczko (1989), 'Early retired or long-term unemployed? The situation of non-working men aged 55-64 from 1976 to 1986', *Work, Employment and Society*, 1, 4, pp. 509-526.

Casey, B. and F. Laczko (1992), 'Older worker employment: change and continuity in the 1980s' in Gilbert, C.N. and R. Burrows (eds.), *Fordism and flexibility: Social Divisions and Social Change*, Macmillan, London.

Casey, B. and S. Wood (1994), 'Great Britain: firm policy, state policy and the employment of older workers' in Naschold, F. and B. de Vroom (eds.), *Regulating employment and welfare: company and national policies of labour force participation at the end of worklife in industrial countries*, Walter de Gruyter, Berlin.

Davis, E.P. (1993), *The structure, regulation, and performance of pension funds in nine industrial countries*, World Bank, Washington.

Employment Department (1994), *Labour Force Survey quarterly bulletin*, 9, September.

Employment Department (1995), *Employment gazette*, March.

Ginn, J. and A. Arber (1995), 'Exploring mid-life women's employment', *Sociology*, 29, 1, pp. 73-94.

Government Actuary (1994), *Pension provision in Britain*, HMSO, London.

Guillemard, A-M. (1993), 'Travailleurs vieillessants et marche de travail en Europe', *Travail et Emploi*, 57, pp. 60-79.

Income Data Services (1994), *Pensions manual*, London.

Industrial Relations Services (1995), 'Managing redundancy', *IRS Employment Trends*, March, pp. 5-16.

Itzin, C. and C. Phillipson (1993), *Age barriers at work*, METRA, London.

Jacobs, K., M. Kohli and M. Rein (1991), 'Testing the industry mix hypothesis of early exit' in Kohli, M., M. Rein, A.M. Guillemard and H. Gunsteren (eds.), *Time for retirement – comparative studies of early exit from the labor force*, University Press, Cambridge.

Jones, A. and L. Longstone (1990), *A survey of restrictions on Jobcentre vacancies*, Research and Evaluation Branch Report 44, Employment Service, Sheffield.

Payne, J. and C. Payne (1994), 'Recession, restructuring and the fate of the unemployed: evidence in the underclass debate', *Sociology*, 28, 1, pp. 1-19.

Personnel Management (1994), 26, 12, p. 20.

Schuller, T. and A. Walker (1990), *The time of our life*, IPPR, London.

Taylor, P. and A. Walker (1991), *Too old at 50*, Campaign for Work, London.

Taylor, P. and A. Walker (1994), 'The aging work force: employers' attitudes towards older workers', *Work, Employment and Society*, 8, 4, pp. 569-591.

Taylor, P. and A. Walker (forthcoming), 'Intergenerational relations in employment: the attitudes of employers and older workers' in Walker, A. (ed.), *The new generational contract*, UCL Press.

Taylor, P., A. Walker, B. Casey, H. Metcalf, J. Lakey, P. Warr and J. Pennington (eds.) (1993), *Age and employment: policies attitudes and practices*, Institute of Personnel Management, London.

Tillsley, C. (1995), 'Older workers: findings from the 1994 Labour Force Survey', *Employment Gazette*, 103, 4, pp. 133-140.

Trinder, C. (1989), *Employment after 55*, National Institute for Economic and Social Research, London.

Walker, A. (1984), *Older workers and early retirement in the Sheffield steel industry*, report to the ESRC (Ref. G 01250004).

Walker, A. (1985), 'Early retirement: release or refuge from the labour market?', *The Quarterly Journal of Social Affairs*, 1, 3, pp. 211-229.

Walker, A. (1993), *Social and economic policies and older people in the United Kingdom*, prepared for the EC Observatory on Aging and Older People, EC, Brussels.

Walker, A., A-M. Guillemard and J. Alber (1991), *Social and economic policies and older people*, EC, Brussels.

Walker, A. and P. Taylor (1993), 'Ageism versus productive aging: the challenge of age discrimination in the labour market' in Bass, S., F. Caro and Y. Chen (eds.), *Achieving a productive aging society*, Auburn House, London.

Warr, P. and J. Pennington (1993), 'Views about age discrimination and older workers' in Taylor, P. *et al.*, pp. 75-106.

Warr, P. (1993), 'In what circumstances does job performance vary with age?', *European Work and Organizational Psychologist*, 3, 3, pp. 237-249.

7 Gradual retirement in the Netherlands

Lei Delsen

The Dutch experience of employment for older workers differs significantly from that of other industrialised countries. Relative to most other OECD countries, the Netherlands are becoming a country of early retirement. Over the period 1960-1990, the drop (42 per cent) in the Netherlands in the male activity rate for the 55-64 age-group has been the sharpest in the OECD. The activity rate of older persons (over 50 years) more generally (42 per cent in 1990) is still one of the lowest in the EU where the average was about 50 per cent in 1990, and that of men 55-64 (46 per cent in 1990) is one of the lowest in the OECD. This chapter attempts to explain these divergencies by looking at the Dutch macro and micro policies on employment of older workers. The aging process in the Netherlands is more marked than in other countries, as also are its financial consequences. Future policy options including gradual retirement to cope with these problems are discussed.

7.1 Macro issues and policies

Recent trends

Labour market position of older workers

The proportion of the service sector in total employment (70.1 per cent in 1991) in the Netherlands is the highest in the EU, while the share of industrial employment in the same total is one of the lowest. Over the 1983-1990 period, employment (full-time equivalent) growth in the Netherlands was strong: 1.4 per cent per annum, which compares with 0.9 per cent in the EU, 1.0 per cent in OECD Europe, and 1.5 per cent in the OECD as a whole. Between 1983 and 1989 service employment growth was 3.9 per cent per annum and that of industrial employment 2.5 per cent. New jobs were mainly filled by new entrants to the labour market, which is why unemployment rates as well as the proportion of long-term unemployment show only a moderate decrease. Most of these new jobs were part-time and occupied by women. Since the beginning of the 1980s also the volume of temporary employment has increased, the volume of atypical employment in the Netherlands being high, relative to other European countries (Delsen, 1993).

Table 7.1
Labour market position of older work force in the Netherlands, 1989

| Age | Dependent employment | | Self employed | Unemployed | Ex-labour force | Total |
	Full-time	Part-time				
55-59	43.1	7.7	10.8	3.7	34.7	100.0
60-64	11.0	3.9	8.7	0.9	75.5	100.0

Source: Trommel, 1993.

Age of retirement
The pension age in the Netherlands is 65 years. However, the effective retirement age is much lower and has decreased over the past years from 64.2 in 1960 and 62.2 in 1980, to 60.3 in 1990 (Besseling, 1994). The Netherlands stand out as having a particularly high proportion of male part-time workers in the age-group between 55 and 64. The high proportion of part-time employment among older male workers aged 60-64 (17.8 per cent in 1985) can partly be attributed to the sectoral gradual retirement schemes and, for those aged 55-59 (10.4 per cent in 1985), to the reduction under collective agreements of work hours for older workers. But for males of 65 years and over the part-time rate is also high (51.7 per cent in 1985), as also is the proportion of part-time worked by older (55+) women in the Netherlands, relative to other OECD countries. In 1985 it was 70.9 per cent for females aged 55-59 years, 70.8 per cent for those aged 60-64 and 64.5 per cent for women of 65 years and over. From table 7.1 it can be deduced that in 1989 the proportion of part-time employment was 26.2 per cent for employees aged 60-64 and 15.2 per cent for those aged 55-59. The proportion of involuntary part-time employment among men aged 55 and over is below average and for women aged 55 and over above average, although lower than for other age-groups. In general there is a significant positive correlation between the level of both female and male labour force participation rates and

the proportion of part-time employment. In this respect the Netherlands are an outlayer (see WRR, 1990; Delsen, 1995).

Modes of labour exit
The most important exit routes from the labour process for older persons in the Netherlands are the General Disability Benefit Act (AAW) and the Disability Security Act (WAO) on the one hand, and the branched-based Voluntary Early Retirement (VUT) schemes and the Unemployment Act (WW) on the other. In 1989, 55 per cent of older workers (55-64 years) used VUT to end employment and 32 per cent left for other reasons, mostly disability, with only 13 per cent working until retirement age. The situation varies considerably from one activity sector to the next (see table 7.2). In building, the low outflow to disability can be explained by the fact that such outflow takes place at relatively young ages. But, in any case, in this sector only 3.2 per cent of employees are 55 years or older. In the industrial sector and road transport, older workers are present in relatively large numbers. The low proportion of VUT in the trade and retail sector is related to low VUT provision. The banking and commercial services sector is a more complex case, there being no obvious reason for the situation that prevails there.

Table 7.2
Labour market position of older people (55-64 years) by economic sector in the Netherlands, 1989

Economic sector	Proportion 55+	VUT-potential	Exit route from firm (%)		
			VUT	Pension	Other
Industry	6.1	95	54	15	31
Building	3.2	96	90	1	9
Trade and retail	4.9	65	45	27	28
Road transport	6.0	99	66	9	25
Banks and commercial services	4.8	83	48	8	44
Other services	5.0	92	53	15	33
Total	5.0	84	55	13	32

Source: SZW, *Rapportage Arbeidsmarkt*, Den Haag, 1991.
Proportion 55+: number of employees aged 55-64 years as a percentage of total number of employees.
VUT potential: percentage of employees in a sector able to benefit from a Voluntary Early Retirement (VUT) scheme.
Exit route: VUT – number of persons 55+ that retire early (VUT) as a percentage of the total number of employees.
Exit route: 'Pension' includes death.
Exit route: 'Other' – almost exclusively exit to disability (WAO); leaving for another job almost never occurs.

The extent of unemployment as a labour exit route is more limited. However, table 7.3 shows clear differences between the age classes 50-54, 55-59 and 60-64 years. The percentage of unemployment among older workers is relatively high. In 1991, of those aged 60-64 over 22 per cent were unemployed, compared with only 8 per cent of the total work force. Moreover, the duration of unemployment is longer. In 1990, of the older persons in this age class 90 per cent were long-term (>12 months) unemployed, compared with 50 per cent of the total work force. This is partly because the Unemployment Act (ww) is used as an exit route, and the duration of ww benefits depends on the number of years worked. But it is in part also attributable to the 57.5 year-rule. Persons aged 57.5 years or older, when they become unemployed, retain their right to a follow-up benefit until the first day of the month in which they reach the age of 65. As was seen in the respective chapters, similar regulations apply in Germany and Sweden. These workers are exempted from the obligation to apply for another job. In the Netherlands, perhaps more than in other OECD countries, it is difficult for older workers to find work once they have become unemployed. Recently the tripartite Board of the Public Employment Service (PES) has decided to remove the age criterion from all its training and placement measures. In 1994, the Minister of Social Affairs and Employment repealed existing age discrimination in redundancies (de ouderenrichtlijn) used to support the Government's policy for increasing the labour market participation rate. This directive on dismissal of older workers had implied that in cases of dismissal on economic grounds, subject to certain conditions, workers of 55 and older could be shedded first.

Table 7.3

Distribution of unemployment (1991) and long-term unemployment (1990) by age in the Netherlands

Age	Unemployed work force (% of work force) (1991)	Proportion of long-term unemployed (% of all registered unemployed) (1990)
<25 years	11.6	28
25-49 years	7.2	55
50-64 years	10.7	76
50-54 years	7.8	73
55-59 years	10.6	80
60-64 years	22.6	90
Total	8.6	49

Source: SZW, *Kwartaalbericht Arbeidsmarkt*, Derde Kwartaal 1993, Den Haag, 1993.

In the Netherlands, the proportion of disability benefit recipients in the work force (12.6 per cent in 1992) is the highest in the OECD. Among older workers aged 55-64 this proportion is about one third. Unemployment benefits and (full) disability benefits, for various reasons, have acted and continue to act as substitutes (Delsen and Klosse, 1992). In assessing the degree of disability, the prevailing labour market situation was taken into account. This was also true of Sweden and Finland. The partially disabled were treated as if they were fully disabled, so that almost 85 per cent of all WAO beneficiaries received full benefits. In particular, in respect of older workers who have grown less productive, disability insurance has provided a convenient way of masking lay-offs. Indeed, employers cannot off-load workers without complying with redundancy procedures, and employees can count on receiving until their 65th year a benefit equal to 70 per cent of their last wage while the duration of wage-related unemployment benefit is limited. In 1986 over 50 per cent of original beneficiaries in the 55 to 65 age-group were receiving a disability benefit, illustrating the fact that the WAO functions as a form of early retirement. Estimates of the size of the hidden unemployment component in disability insurance in the Netherlands vary from 15 to 50 per cent of all beneficiaries. Eligibility for disability programmes was made more stringent from the middle of the 1980s onwards, and in 1985 benefits were substantially reduced. This resulted in a slight increase in the unemployment benefit scheme. In 1987 the 'labour market consideration' was removed from disability insurance leading to an increase in the volume of partially disabled. However, the overall impact of this policy change has been very limited, and chances on the labour market are still taken into account (WRR, 1990; Bolweg and Dijkstra, 1993).

In 1987 also the generosity of the unemployment scheme was reduced and its eligibility requirements tightened. As a result VUT became more popular as an alternative to disability and unemployment benefits (Trommel and de Vroom, 1994). Originally the *temporary* VUT schemes were aimed at promoting employment for youngsters and improving the well-being of older workers, with about one in every three jobs released by the scheme being refilled. However, by the end of the 1980s hardly any youngsters were being taken up. Not refilling positions opened by VUT is clearly a saving for enterprise and, as an employer, for the Government. However, for society as a whole the policy is an expensive one. In the Netherlands, in actual fact, there is no national early retirement scheme. The country's numerous sectoral schemes are based on collective agreements. Most of these sectoral VUT schemes have the following characteristics (Delsen, 1993): the average exit age is 60 years; the benefit, which is income tested, is 75 to 80 per cent of the gross final wage irrespective of the number of years of service; there is a 10-year service minimum for elegibility and the schemes operate on a pay-as-you-go basis. Over 85 per cent of all employees in the sectors in question are covered by a VUT scheme.

Between 1983 and 1990, the number of VUT beneficiaries tripled, resulting in more than 119,000 participants at the end of 1992. This growth was mainly due to a drop in the age-thresholds and to an increase in the number of schemes. The average VUT age decreased from 60.2 years in 1986 to 59.8 in 1993. However, in the last two years of that period, some collective agreements provided for an increase in the VUT age. Moreover, in 1994, in three such agreements, the VUT benefit was reduced by 5 per cent-points (DCA, 1994). Earlier in 1991 and 1992, in a number of agreements, eligibility for VUT was extended to include part-timers which as a category had previously been excluded. In 1986 total VUT premium was 2.4 per cent of wages, and by 1993 it had risen to about 3.6 per cent. The premium varied from less than 1 per cent in hairdressing, to over 8 per cent in textiles, and 10.5 per cent in the dairy industry. Over the same seven-year period, employees' contributions increased from 0.6 per cent to 1.2 per cent. Extrapolations of existing trends in the number of VUT participants would suggest the following increase: 147,000 in the year 2000; 213,000 in 2010 and 240,000 in 2020. VUT is popular because of the relatively small income loss, the voluntary nature of the scheme and the absence of the stigma attached to disability and unemployment benefits.

Until recently, employees had to choose between full exit or full-time employment. The provision of part-time employment may reduce the extent of the hidden unemployment in the exit routes. It reduces by about one half the risk of becoming disabled, and, moreover, contributes to reintegration (Delsen and Klosse, 1992; Aarts and De Jong, 1992; Delsen, 1995). In order to make early retirement more flexible, sectoral part-time VUT schemes have recently been introduced in the metal sector (SUM; SVUM) and for employees in architects' bureaus (SUA) as well as in banking (RABO), retail sector (KBB) and care sector (PGGM-OBU). Under the RABO and KBB schemes, benefits increase with the age of retirement, thus providing an incentive to postpone retirement. In the metal sector work time can be reduced and reinstated. OBU and SUA have two-step part-time VUT schemes, the latter being upstream of the full VUT schemes (Ten Brink and Delsen, 1993). But most of these schemes, set up in 1988 or subsequently, were experimental in nature and have since been discontinued, and/or replaced by flexible pension schemes (see below). Initiated by employers, the main aims of these part-time schemes were to reduce total early retirement costs, retain within the firm the knowledge and experience of older workers and redistribute employment between young and older workers. Conditions are similar to those of the full VUT schemes. However, in contrast to the latter, employees have no automatic right to part-time early retirement, since the employer must agree. Moreover, in the public sector, part-time VUT for civil servants is used to reduce staff costs and unemployment and to rejuvenate personnel. About one half of potential participants actually take up this option. The effective take-up rate of part-time VUT schemes in the private sector is lower: about 10 to 15 per cent (Delsen, 1989; Heemskerk, 1994). In 1992 and 1993 part-time VUT schemes were introduced into carpentry factories, the textile industry and contract catering. In 1994 a number of new schemes were set up under collective agreements, concluded *inter alia* in various wholesale and retail trade branches.

Attitudes to work and retirement

Approximately one quarter of older workers in the Netherlands would be willing to leave work at the age of 60, even if this meant a 30 per cent drop in net income. There is also considerable supply-side potential for gradual retirement. Of those already retired, 27 per cent would have taken part-time early retirement (i.e. have reduced their normal work hours by half), 51 per cent would have refused, and 22 per cent did not know. Of pre-early retirees, 38 per cent would have taken up part-time early retirement, 46 per cent would not have and 16 per cent did not know (Henkens and Siegers, 1992).

Pensions and social security

Social security benefits and finance

The General Disability Benefit Act (AAW) entitles all disabled persons previously gainfully employed up to the age of 65, to a basic flat-rate benefit derived from the net social minimum. Costs are charged to the Government. The Disability Security Act (WAO) covers all privately employed up to the age of 65 and, from the end of the first year of illness until, if need be, the age of 65, and provides for a benefit which depends on the previous earnings and the degree of disability. Benefits under the WAO supplement AAW benefits. The maximum benefit, paid monthly, is 70 per cent of the previous wage, where 80-100 per cent disability is established. Conversely, that benefit can never fall below the legal net minimum wage. In 1993 the marginal WAO premium paid by employees was 11.75 per cent. Partially disabled persons who are unsuccessful in finding employment commensurate with their ability are entitled under the WW to supplementary unemployment benefit. After lapse of the WW entitlement period, the partially disabled would revert to wealth-tested national assistance if their household incomes failed to reach the social minimum. In order to mitigate the effects of wealth-testing, considered unduly harsh for partially disabled or unemployed workers, the Act on Income Provision for Older and Partially Disabled Workers (IOAW) was introduced. It provides financial assistance to older long-term unemployed for whom the maximum period of entitlement to WW and follow-up benefits has expired. The IOAW is primarily intended for persons who, at the time of becoming unemployed, are between 50 and 57.5 years old. It, in addition, applies to those employees aged 57.5 and older who meet the '26 weeks requirement' but not the '3 out of 5 requirement' stipulated by the WW (see below). The IOAW is a publicly financed facility.

Following a change in 1990 in the Unemployment Act (ww), persons who have worked for at least 26 weeks in the 12 months prior to unemployment are entitled to ww benefits (70 per cent of the daily wage) for six months. In order to claim benefit for longer than 6 months, those concerned must have received a salary for at least 52 weeks during three of the five calendar years prior to the year in which unemployment occurred (the '3 out of 5 requirement'). The duration of the benefit (to a maximum of 5 years) moreover depends on the number of years worked. At the end of the period for which the benefit can be drawn, persons who are still unemployed receive a follow-up benefit for a further year. Unemployment insurance is financed on a tripartite basis.

Pension system
The Dutch pension system consists of three pillars (Besseling, 1994; Dekkers *et al.*, 1994). The *first pillar* is the state-run General Old Age Act (AOW) under which a pay-as-you-go financed scheme has been established. Contributions (14 per cent in 1993) are levied up to a ceiling on taxable income. For two partners it provides a flat-rate pension benefit approximately equal to the legal net minimum wage from the age of 65 (for a single person 70 per cent of that wage). This is a compulsory old age pension for all residents. In principle the gross minimum wage follows the index of average negotiated wages. But because elements of the wage drift (incidental wage increase) are not included in this index, the adjustment mechanism plays an important role in limiting the future burden of statutory pensions. Moreover, this linkage has to some extent been abolished. Between 1980 and 1994 growth in the net AOW pension lagged 19 per cent behind that of the gross wage. Furthermore, the fact that pensions and the minimum wage are linked on a net basis, has contributed to controlled expansion of pension expenditure.

The *second pillar* is made up of quasi-private pension schemes. These schemes supplement AOW provision and are the responsibility of the social partners. However, the state provides both a legal framework and fiscal support. The law stipulates that supplementary pension schemes must be funded. In general, employers contribute 50 per cent or more. There are 82 branch pension funds in industry and 1,058 company pension funds. These 82 funds are members of the Association of branch pension funds. In addition, over 20,000 companies provide insured pension plans for (some of) their employees and 9 professional occupational pension schemes for self employed such as doctors and chemists (Pierik, 1991). The Insurance Board, a private agency, is vested with the authority to supervise pension funds. A separate law makes participation in the branch pension fund compulsory for all businesses. A company can opt-out only if it establishes a company scheme with a level of provision that exceeds that of the branch funds.

Of employees aged 24-64 years 82 per cent are covered by a supplementary pension scheme; 72 per cent of these participate in a final-pay scheme; 15 per cent in an average (median) pay scheme, 5 per cent in a modified final-pay scheme (combination of the first two) and 7 per cent in a scheme providing a flat-rate benefit. Only 0.6 per cent participate in a defined contribution (available premium) scheme (Bezemer, 1991; Besseling, 1994). The AOW benefit included, the final pay schemes promise a maximum gross benefit equal to 70 per cent of the last gross income earned, provided contributions have been paid in full over 40 years (1.75 per cent per year is tax-exempt). Employees who have enjoyed only temporary employment and those who have frequently changed jobs suffer pension loss. Because the benefit itself is not related to the size of the contribution payments these pension rights are not fully portable. External labour mobility is thus hampered. Privately operated funds may refuse to take over obligations from each other, when a worker leaves one job and begins to contribute to another fund. As a result, mobility of workers is penalised with considerable loss of future income and accumulated pension rights. However, since mobility within a given branch is the norm, the branch-wise organisation of pension funds tends not to affect mobility adversely. Moreover, as of 8 July 1994, employees who switch jobs are entitled to have their accrued pension claims transferred to the pension fund of the new employer. From that date also, part-timers may no longer be excluded from pension provision, a measure which is of importance to almost all working women in the Netherlands, since most work part-time. Previously, over one third were excluded from the coverage of private pension arrangements. Should a minimum-wage threshold exist, the wage of the part-timer is recalculated to the full-time wage. There is, moreover, the condition that the pension claims of the part-timer are *pro rata* those of the full-timer.

Internal labour mobility is also hampered. Many supplementary schemes simply do not allow older workers to step back in their careers. The ABP, however, the biggest Dutch pension fund, is an exception. A cut (knip) in the workload may be requested when the salary goes down by more than 5 per cent, because of demotion or change in function. The building up of pension rights is divided into two parts. Given the defined benefits structure, i.e. the final pay base of most semi-private pension schemes, a relative decrease in AOW benefits results in an increase in supplementary pension benefits. Thus AOW is gradually being privatised. There is a trade-off (about one half) between AOW premiums and premiums for supplementary pensions (Petersen, 1989).

Pension benefits only are taxed, supplementary pension contributions and interest income from pension funds being tax-exempt. The latter is not the case for contributions to the basic pension. A gradual privatisation of the AOW implies a loss of tax revenues. Pensioners enjoy a special low rate of income tax and are not required to contribute to the pension scheme. The wedge on labour income has increased steadily, while that on retirement income has risen only very little. Consequently, a 70 per cent final-pay scheme yields a net pension of approximately 85 per cent of the net final pay. The latter could be a reason for limiting the coverage of supplementary schemes. Another reason could be the growing individualisation of Dutch society. For example, regarding to household types, the Central Planning Bureau (CPB) sees the following trends between 1990 and 2015. The proportion of singles without children will increase from 31 to 43 per cent, partly due to aging; the proportion of households with a partner and a child will decrease from 37 to 26 per cent. The uniform 70 per cent-final pay system for all employees has obviously been designed for the standard breadwinner with a house-keeping spouse. In an individualistic society there will be a greater call for flexible supplementary pension schemes suited to an individual's circumstances. An average pay scheme would be more appropriate. Contributions under the present system are a function of current wages, and benefits of last earned wages. This results in uncertainty about the reserves necessary to cover pension claims, excessive reserves being almost inevitable for most pension funds. Reducing costs means abolishing the final-pay system (Pierik, 1991; Besseling, 1994).

Demographic developments in the Netherlands would seem to indicate that by the year 2035 a doubling of the contribution rate is to be expected. In its advice to the Government, the Drees Commission (1987) proposed the following main changes: reduction of the AOW benefit for singles from 70 per cent to 50 per cent of the net minimum wage; raising the retirement age to 66 years and increasing AOW premiums paid by those 65 years and older. The Commission concluded that either the purchasing power of pension benefits will be reduced by half or that the premiums will have to be raised (doubled) after 2000. The Government concluded that the finance of the AOW is guaranteed and therefore no action is necessary!

The *third pillar* consists of the voluntary pension arrangements individuals have organised for themselves. The premiums paid are not part of the wedge; personal provision has a neutral effect on the labour market. Individual pension schemes are financed by definition on a funding basis (Besseling, 1994; Gosling, 1994) and enable individuals to create their own additions to the first two pillars.

Conclusions

Unemployment, early retirement and disability are significant causes of early termination of active careers by older workers (aged 55 and over) in the Netherlands. These three phenomena function as communicating vessels. At present Dutch employer organisations are in favour of abolishing the VUT scheme, while trade unions favour extending it, for example, making it available to workers with 40 or more years of service. Abolishing VUT will inevitably increase the pressure on disability and/or unemployment benefits. In a number of sectors, in attempts to remove full VUT altogether so as to make early retirement more flexible and thereby more affordable, part-time VUT and partial and flexible pensions have recently been introduced. However, the take-up rate has been low because of the continuing existence of generous full early retirement options. On the supply side, there is, indeed, considerable potential for gradual retirement.

With a view to increasing the labour market position of older workers, the Dutch Government has taken various measures, including the removal of age discrimination from redundancy settlements and the PES policy. As the AOW gradually becomes privatised, supplementary pensions, and hence funding, will become increasingly important. The latter will act as a stimulus to gradual retirement. The replacement of the final-pay by an average-pay system will promote gradual retirement, and thus the participation rates of older workers, control the costs of the supplementary pension schemes and favour age-specific personnel management. Moreover the linkage with prices instead of with wages is more in line with the trend towards individualisation in pension provision.

New public policies

Pension reform

In consultation with employer and employee organisations the Kok-van Mierlo Government is searching for ways to encourage greater flexibility and variety in work patterns, including changes in work hours, through the entire professional life-cycle (SZW, 1994). Based on reports by the Drees Commission (1987) and the Netherlands Scientific Council for Government Policy (WRR, 1990; 1993), the Government is examining ways of broadening the basis of AOW financing. The AOW will remain the basic pension since for some elderly it is the only source of income. In 1995 income-related tax-relief will be introduced for the latter category. As of 1996, in order to be able to guarantee AOW provision over the long term, in cases where one of the partners is younger than 65 years, the Government feels it will be reasonable to provide the AOW supplement only when the family income is below the social minimum. The fact that part of the AOW benefit is to be made conditional on, for example, a supplementary pension, implies that the AOW will take on a supplementary role, while the supplementary pension becomes the basis. Other measures to be taken are: a higher threshold for WW, privatisation of the Sickness Act and the introduction of the market process into its operation through opting out, and premiums differentiation in the WAO.

According to the Government, gradual exit from work is more in accord with individual freedom of choice and societal development. In so far as is possible, obstacles to work after 65 years will be removed, and this will require 'customising' social security in some measure and giving greater flexibility to pensioning. Gradually, there will be less room for VUT arrangements, because of the too low level of labour participation of older employees (szw, 1994). Although flexible pensioning has been cited as an alternative to VUT, there has been no research into the cost consequences of such a scheme, and one may wonder whether such a scheme will promote the labour participation of older workers. It seems that the Government is seeking an alternative to VUT, in order to check the shift to ww and WAO benefits. Current exit routes and practice have to change to make remaining in employment relatively attractive (see Trommel, 1993). It should be noted, however, that the supplementary pension and the VUT schemes are the responsibility of the social partners, and that the Government has no direct control over them.

In response to the WRR's 1993 report, the Government has stated its conviction that, in view of the changes in the age structure of the work force, a different wage profile is needed. For instance, a higher wage at the beginning of a career, when productivity is highest, and a relatively lower wage at the end. However, the notion that productivity decreases with age remains no more than a prejudice since it has not been empirically established (see below). This change would also entail a change in the pension accruing. In the matter of supplementary pensions, the Dutch government is in favour of average-pay to replace final-pay schemes, because of the digressive intergenerational redistribution of income. It, moreover, advocates that consumer price indexation replace wage indexation (Tweede Kamer, 1991). The legal frame work for supplementary pensions has recently been adopted in order to make pensions more flexible and to ease the replacement of the expensive VUT by pre-pension schemes. Full and partial drawing of pensions is possible between the age of 55 and 70. Tax exemption is raised from 1.75 per cent to 2 per cent per year. The absolute benefit maximum of 70 per cent is abolished; the new maximum is 100 per cent of gross final pay. As of the year 2000 the partner pension can be exchanged for a higher individual pension.

Collective agreements on older workers

As far as collective agreements on older workers are concerned, the latter confine themselves to age of ending the work contract, early retirement, extra days off and exemption from overtime or shift work. On the issues of employment and labour market position, recruitment and selection, personnel and job policy, training and social-medical prevention, most collective agreements to date are silent as far as older workers are concerned and focus mainly on corrective measures. In trade union policy since 1990 there has been a shift towards preventive measures, including training, gradual early retirement, task reduction and improvement of working conditions. Some trade unions, however, are against policies specific to the older worker (LTD, 1991; FNV, 1992).

7.2 Micro issues and policies

Recent trends

Work performance

Dutch research on age and productivity is limited. Van Heeringen (1983) found the notion that the productivity of researchers decreases with age not to be based on empirical grounds, but on – largely implicit – supposition. It is impossible to estimate the influence of age on the level of productivity; although one could, at the very outside, test to what extent age influences changes in productivity. The growth rate of productivity is higher before 30 than after that age. Based on cross-sectional data, Gelderblom and de Koning (1992) found that productivity is highest for those between 40 and 45 years. The productivity of employees aged 60 and over with the same level of formal education is 45 per cent lower.

Company pension regulations

Part-time VUT schemes have recently been introduced at Ahold (a retail corporation) and the Dutch Railways (NS). The Ahold scheme links age with the level of the benefit and the extent of the work time reduction. NS has a two step part-time VUT scheme, placed upstream of its full VUT scheme. Several other bigger Dutch enterprises (Buehrmann Tetterode; DSM; ESSO; KLM) have recently introduced a flexible pension age. At Akzo Nobel, Heidemij and Wavin the current VUT schemes will gradually be replaced by pension schemes. At Akzo Nobel, this operation has to be completed by the year 2005. Early retirement is financed from an individual's personal savings or by an early drawing of the supplementary pension. One third of the saving on VUT expenditure is used to introduce an activating elderly policy and two thirds go straight to the employees. Employees have the right to partial retirement between 60 and 65 years but for pension purposes, in order to supplement their wage, must draw upon their own supplementary schemes. At Heidemij (starting in 1997) flexible and partial pensioning will be possible from 55 years onwards. The net benefit is 85 per cent of the last salary for those completing 40 years of service. The savings on VUT are used to finance the new scheme, additional premiums being paid by the employer. At Wavin (1994), employees may retire fully or partially as of the age of 55, depending on the pension rights accrued. The schemes at Buehrmann Tetterode and Wavin are tailor-made 'cafeteria' systems. The menu includes the following options: supplementary leave, overtime pay, profit shares, changing yearly benefit and the choice of the retirement age (Ten Brink and Delsen, 1993; Heemskerk, 1994). All these schemes guarantee a benefit equal to a given percentage of the final pay. In none of these schemes is the option to retire after the pension age (between 65 and 70 years) explicitly mentioned.

Age discrimination

Not only does age discrimination occur in the recruitment of personnel, but there is also age-based selectivity in cases of dismissal. Dutch employers apply age ceilings for personnel recruitment purposes (De Vroom and Blomsma, 1991). When firms reorganise, the reduction of personnel follows a certain pattern (LTD, 1992). Older workers (55 years and over) are the first to go in line with existing legal regulations and with specific provisions at the enterprise or branch levels. Redundancy or dismissal is, in most cases, based on age, number of years in service, pension and early retirement rights and the nature of the contract. In at least 70 per cent of enterprises the legal social benefit for unemployment as well as disability is supplemented up to 100 per cent of the last wage. The level and duration of the supplement almost always depend on age and seniority. In one half of cases the pension is supplemented, and in about 25 per cent of enterprises the VUT benefit is supplemented (see also Bolweg and Dijkstra, 1993; Trommel and de Vroom, 1994). Kerkhoff (1981) concludes that Dutch firms seldom recognise the specific problems of older workers, and rarely develop strategies to integrate them. In fact, it was the existence of VUT and the WAO as exit routes that stimulated firms to implement an exit strategy rather than devise new age-specific social policies. Dutch employers seek to reduce personnel at least possible cost. But employees have proved well able to defend their cause and this has resulted in high costs with WAO still a major exit route. Dutch employers are not in any hurry to abolish VUT, because they view it as an integral part of a broader strategy for downsizing their organisation (Bolweg and Dijkstra, 1993). Nevertheless, it should be noted that these exit routes are mainly used for or by unskilled blue-collar workers and middle white-collar workers, with top-level employees normally opting to stay on (WRR, 1990; De Vroom and Blomsma, 1991). For employees with relatively little qualification the major exit route is disability, while for the more highly educated early retirement is the preferred route. Abolishing VUT will thus mean different things for different categories of worker (Henkes and Siegers, 1992; Gelderblom and de Koning, 1992).

New company policies

Personnel policy

A survey of 760 firms in 1990 (LTD, 1991) shows that 9 per cent of firms with older (55+) workers on the payroll take the physical loadability of such workers into account. In building 25 per cent of firms, in industry 12 per cent and in road transport 18 per cent do this. Only 2 per cent of enterprises with older people on the payroll apply a deliberate policy for the task loading of older workers. The larger the firm the greater the likelihood that age-management policies will exist: 28 per cent indicated an *ad hoc* policy, 70 per cent stated that older workers are not considered because of the nature of the firm or because of function requirements, 29 per cent of those surveyed indicated that they use the knowledge and experience of older workers. This was particularly true of the building sector (50 per cent) and to a lesser extent of trade and hotel and catering (16 per cent). There is an age-limit (on average 56 years) on shift work and irregular shifts in one fifth of the enterprises. This does not apply in the building sector, while it does in 42 per cent of the firms surveyed in the banking sector. In 23 per cent of enterprises there is also an age limit on overtime. But more recent experience in the Netherlands in the matter of age-specific personnel management would suggest a new trend: a tempering of existing policy instruments on age and more generally a change in thinking about the employment of older workers. Van der Kloet *et al.* (1994) found that employer-employee talks about job functions play an important role in age-specific personnel management. Such discussions are deemed valuable in the reallocation of functions to suit the loadability of end-of-career workers. Information gleaned from such talks also serves as a basis for the formulation of careers and training policy.

Pay policy

In addition to prejudice about senior employees generally, the pay system is itself an obstacle to labour participation of older workers. Wages increase with age. Before 45 years wages are below productivity, and after 45 years above (Gelderblom and de Koning, 1992). Young workers are, in fact, subsidising the higher wages of older workers. In one sense there is nothing wrong with such a system. It acts as an incentive to higher productivity and to greater loyalty to the firm. However, the system begins to cause problems when, due to greying, the average age of the work force increases. The expensive older worker is then off-loaded. Gelderblom *et al.* (1994) also found that the productivity/wage ratio is unfavourable to older workers. Jacobs (1985) concluded that, for young employees, wages increase relatively fast. As the worker grows older, first the rate of wage increase diminishes, then the wage is static and finally shows a slight decline.

Demotion, redesign of work and job rotation

Age is often considered an independent cause of employment situation problems. However, wastage and exhaustion may also result from inappropriate loading and from monotonous and repetitive work. Kerkhoff (1981) argues that a more dynamic placement and allocation policy, in combination with training and schooling opportunities, will certainly increase costs, such costs, however, will in time be repaid by an increase in willingness to change and a broader skills package. Recent research in the Netherlands seems to confirm this. Function adjustment, through a reshuffling of tasks within a given job or function to include less burdensome ones, is a crucial part of the individual career policies that can be used to prevent drop-out and reduce sick leave. Employees value this as positive, and organisations have found it a useful source of knowledge and experience. Social motives also play a role. If stigmatisation is to be avoided, changes in tasks and functions should not be presented as career alternatives for older workers only; length of the service should be the initial criterion. In addition, collective function readjustment may be used to achieve a more favourable balance between work-load and load-ability at the department level, and may include rotation of functions and the broadening of personnel deployment. Both the latter have proved successful in reducing sick leave and in promoting change and enrichment in the work place. The broader deployment of staff can also contribute to a more effective organisation of work. Change and improvement in work conditions is one important way of keeping employees healthily active until the normal retirement age. Work conditions include safety, health and wellbeing but also how these are perceived by older workers. Giving proper attention to these factors improves motivation and the self confidence of employees (Van der Kloet *et al.*, 1994). Gelderblom *et al.* (1994) conclude that regular function adjustment as well as job-changing (job-hopping) in a career will preserve the productivity of employees. The decreasing mobility of older employees within a company leads to static behaviour in which they increasingly regard their function as a final stage rather than a springboard for keeping up with change in the organisation (Kamstra and Van de Craats, 1992). It may be concluded that it is not age, but performing the same task year in year out that is the main cause of diminished productivity.

Part-time work

In the Netherlands, all sectors of industry practice what are known as 'seniors' days: an increase in the number of holidays for older workers (LTD, 1991). For those aged 55 years, 3 days (in commerce 2 days and in building 6 days), for those aged 64, almost 5 days (in building 9 days and in road transport 3 days). Part-time employment is also practiced, i.e. an individual reduction in work time at one's own expense is used for older workers as of a certain age (see table 7.4). In the building sector part-time employment for older workers does not exist. In road transport a tiny number of enterprises (1 per cent) offer gradual retirement. Even so, in such firms 9 per cent of employees use this option. This may be explained by the fact that part-time is used in certain large

Table 7.4

Reduction in working time of older workers by sector of activity
in enterprises with older workers on the payroll

Sector of activity	Enterprises with favourable working conditions	Average age ceiling for working time reduction	Older employees with reduced working time
Industry	7%	60.3	3%
Building	0%	–	0%
Trade/hotel and catering	7%	59.1	10%
Road transport	1%	56.9	9%
Banking/commercial services	35%	60.7	8%
Other services	22%	58.2	10%
Average	11%	59.5	7%

Source: LTD, 1991.

enterprises employing many older workers. The reverse is true of banking and commerce and of other service sectors. In many enterprises, even though such part-time options are on offer, few older employees make use of them. In small (<10 employees) businesses, 10 per cent of older workers retire gradually.

Table 7.5

Participation of employees in internal and external courses by age,
1988-1992, in the Netherlands

Age	1988-1990		1990-1992	
	Internal	External	Internal	External
16-29	22	29	25	36
30-44	21	20	25	21
45-64	16	10	19	9

Source: OSA, *Trendrapport*, 1993.

Training

There is evidence that training contributes to labour mobility and productivity. Table 7.5 shows an increase in the participation of employees in courses since 1990 and reveals that older employees, relative to their younger colleagues, are less likely to be considered for supplementary training. However, participation in internal courses by older workers has increased over recent years. Other

Dutch research shows, nonetheless, that participation in training by older employees is still low, notably by the less educated and those employed in smaller units (Kamstra and Van der Craats, 1991; Gelderblom and de Koning, 1992). The LTD (1991) survey also shows that, relative to younger employees (11 per cent), older employees are underrepresented (7 per cent) in courses and training. Most of the training is aimed at skills preservation so as better to be able to execute current functions and only a small part at retraining for new functions.

Gelderblom and de Koning (1992) and Gelderblom *et al.* (1994) found that training has a greater positive impact on productivity than on wages. This confirms the view that training can be an important way of improving the functioning of senior workers, i.e. the productivity-wage ratio. There appears to be no difference in the productivity-enhancing effect of training courses as between seniors and other categories of worker. This is in line with other investigations into the relationship between age and 'learning capacity'. The latter does not decline with age, so long as the design of the training is suited to the needs of the senior citizen. Hence, form and content will influence its effectiveness. The 1992 study also shows that external courses have a greater effect on both wages and productivity than internal ones. They conclude that there exists a real potential for enhanced productivity, since, physical and notably mental faculties decline less with age than many people believe. Training within the company reduces the number of people dropping out on grounds of disability. Other recent research (Van der Kloet *et al.*, 1994) shows that training is seen as a means of raising the quality of an employee's skills and hence the quality of the product. It increases the self confidence, motivation, flexibility and mobility of older workers. Recurring schooling and training promote the activity rate of older people and can avoid knowledge aging.

Best practice in gradual retirement

Of special interest is the funded gradual retirement scheme that has recently been agreed upon for the Harbours of Rotterdam and Amsterdam, and which by 2010 will replace the present pay-as-you-go VUT scheme (Delsen, 1994). The harbours apply an average pay pension system, facilitating gradual retirement. Resolution of the dilemma between flexibility and solidarity has been found in the co-existence of obligatory and voluntary modes of financing the basic supplementary pension and in a partial plugging of the AOW hole with early retirement, i.e. before the age 65. In this way, gradual retirement becomes a feasible option for all employees, including the lower paid. Two bridge options are available: additional finance through a temporary bridge pension split into a compulsory collective part (for those aged 63-65), employers paying 2/3, employees 1/3 of the premium, and a voluntary individual part (for those aged 60-62) borne fully by the individual worker. The annual premium for the collective bridge pension is 1 per cent from age 21 to age 62;

for the individual bridge pension 3.6 per cent from 45 year to 60 years. The second option is partial pensioning to plug the AOW hole. The establishment of fully funded retirement provision takes 15 years, since for each benefit, prior to the first disbursement, the total present value has to be accumulated. A transitional scheme has been agreed upon to cover the period until effective introduction of the new system. Because both current VUT benefits have to be paid and future pension claims to be built up, there is a double premium burden. Over this period the VUT system will be progressively transformed into a gradual early retirement scheme, with the VUT benefit depending on the years of service, the age of exit and the number of hours of work-time reduction (full or partial retirement). In order to link up with the pension system the VUT benefit will be reduced to 70 per cent (now 90 per cent) of gross final pay. Over this transition period also, part-time employment is to be promoted by these financial incentives so as to keep income at a certain level should the years of service be too few. In order to safeguard the VUT, funds can be created to which both employee and employer contribute. Flanking policies for older workers, including function content, work time and periods of work, and training and retraining are to be an integral part of the reform towards a gradual retirement scheme. The aim of this policy is to keep the employee motivated until retirement age. Lightening the mental and physical burden on the individual worker is also expected to reduce disability leave.

7.3 Potential for gradual retirement and recommendations

A flexible retirement age contributes more to postponing retirement than does increasing the AOW age. The latter will result in savings on AOW and supplementary pensions, but recourse to VUT and WAO will increase. And since WAO and VUT benefits are higher, an adverse effect may be expected. This measure will only be effective if at the same time early exit routes are drastically reduced. In addition, those without supplementary benefits will lean more on other collective services. Flexible pensioning may, moreover, take into account differences between individuals and sectors. Judgements about the present linkage, levying premium on income above AOW (basic pension) and increasing the AOW age, are political ones (WRR, 1993). However, most believe that it is in the field of supplementary pensions that the real problems will occur.

Previous sections have suggested a considerable potential for gradual retirement in the Netherlands. For current older workers it is too late to introduce individual early retirement saving schemes and training programmes. For the short term, then, two options remain open: partial VUT and the possibility of changing function within the firm, the idea being in both instances that more appropriate use be made of the experience and capacities of the older employees.

A more permanent solution can be found in an individualised gradual retirement scheme enabling full and partial early as well as full and partial deferred retirement – by integrating the VUT and pension schemes and by introducing funding to replace the pay-as-you-go system (Delsen, forthcoming). In the Netherlands, supplementary pensions are financed by funding. Moreover, bearing in mind the 'greying' of the labour force, funding is desirable as a means of financing the various sectoral VUT schemes. A shift from pay-as-you-go towards funding will make it possible to retain the present pension level and pension age, and at the same time avoid a too high burden on the future active labour force due to the aging process. The link between premiums paid and entitlements will be tighter, creating an incentive to work more years, meaning that an early pension will imply an actuarial reduction, while working more years will imply a higher pension. It will, moreover, make the labour market more flexible, because, with funding, pension rights are portable, while pay-as-you-go financed VUT rights are not. The job mobility of older workers will increase, and the future unpaid bill will be avoided. Such a link will also be better suited to a labour force that is becoming increasingly heterogeneous and where variety in employment contracts, reflecting, in particular, part-time employment and other atypical employment relations, is rapidly becoming the norm in the Netherlands. The impact of recent changes in the pension system and the fiscal support on gradual retirement is still unclear. If the full benefit of the potential advantages is to be enjoyed, final-pay pension schemes will need to be replaced by average-pay schemes. Only in this way will older workers avoid the otherwise detrimental consequences of gradual retirement from the labour process. Net savings on pension expenditure will be the result. Indexation based on consumer prices instead of on wages will afford additional future savings. Moreover, the discrepancy between pay and performance of older workers could be narrowed by flexible pay systems and training facilities, with the latter being partly financed from savings on VUT benefits. An age-related personnel policy could offset the changing capacities of age-groups through investment in permanent education, to keep the human capital intact throughout working life. Such steps have yet to be taken in the Netherlands. The gradual greying of the work force will ensure that taken they are.

References

Aarts, L.J.M. and Ph.R. de Jong (1992), *Economic Aspects of Disability Behaviour*, North Holland, Amsterdam.

Besseling, P.J. (1994), 'Pensions, Savings and the Labour Market in the Netherlands' in Bovenberg, A.L. (ed.), pp. 41-66.

Bezemer, P.J. (1991), 'Protecting One's Pension Rights when Changing or Losing One's Job' in Schmähl, W. (ed.), pp. 227-234.

Bolweg, J.F. and J.H. Dijkstra (1993), *Vervroegd Uittreden of Ouderenbeleid*, OSA-werkdocument W 112, Organisatie voor Strategisch Arbeidsmarktonderzoek, Den Haag.

Bovenberg, A.L. (ed.) (1994), *The Economics of Pensions: The Case of the Netherlands*, Papers and Proceedings 9401, Research Centre for Economic Policy, Rotterdam.

Brink, N. ten, and L. Delsen (1993), *Inventarisatie van flexibele pensioen- en VUTregelingen*, Vakgroep Toegepaste Economie, Katholieke Universiteit Nijmegen, Nijmegen.

DCA (1992-1994), *CAO-afspraken 1992-1994*, Dienst Collectieve Arbeidsvoorwaarden, Ministerie van Sociale Zaken en Werkgelegenheid, Den Haag.

Dekkers, G.J.M. *et al.* (1994), 'Reform in the Dutch Pension System' in Bovenberg, A.L. (ed.), pp. 67-80.

Delsen, L. (1989), *Deeltijd-VUT in Europa*, OSA-werkdocument W 60, Organisatie voor Strategisch Arbeidsmarktonderzoek, Den Haag.

Delsen, L. (1993), *Managing Redundancies in the Netherlands*. National Economic and Labour Council, CNEL Rome.

Delsen, L. (1994), 'Geleidelijke uittreding uit het Arbeidsproces', *Sociaal Maandblad Arbeid*, 49, pp. 609-617.

Delsen, L. (1995), *Atypical Employment: An International Perspective. Causes, Consequences and Policy*, Wolters-Noordhoff, Groningen.

Delsen, L. (forthcoming), 'Gradual Retirement: Lessons from the Nordic Countries and the Netherlands', *European Journal of Industrial Relations*.

Delsen, L. and S. Klosse (1992), 'Integration of the Disabled in the Work Process: The Dutch Policy', *The Geneva Papers on Risk and Insurance*, 17, pp. 119-142.

Drees Commission (1987), *Gespiegeld in de tijd, de AOW in de toekomst*, Ministerie van Sociale Zaken en Werkgelegenheid, Den Haag.

FNV (1992), *Werk en ouder worden. 50 Plus en arbeidsvoorwaarden*, Federatie Nederlandse Vakbeweging, Amsterdam.

Gelderblom, A. and J. de Koning (1992), *Meerjarig, minderjarig, een onderzoek naar de invloed van leeftijd op produktiviteit en beloning*, OSA Voorstudie 39, Organisatie voor Strategisch Arbeidsmarktonderzoek, Den Haag.

Gelderblom, A., N.B.J.G. 't Hoen and J. de Koning (1994), *Beloning en produktiviteit*, OSA Voorstudie 120, Organisatie voor Strategisch Arbeidsmarktonderzoek, Den Haag.

Goslings, J.H.W. (1994), 'The Structure of Pension Benefits and Investment Behaviour' in Bovenberg, A.L. (ed.), pp. 25-39.

Heemskerk, C.A.M. (1994), *Flexibel en geleidelijk met pensioen: een onderzoek naar de mogelijkheden*, Voorlopige Raad voor het Ouderenbeleid, Rijswijk.

Heeringen, A. Van (1983), *Relaties tussen leeftijd, mobiliteit en produktiviteit van wetenschappelijke onderzoekers*, Den Haag.

Henkens, K. and J. Siegers (1992), *Vrijwillige vervroegde uittreding*, OSA-werkdocument W 102, Organisatie voor Strategisch Arbeidsmarktonderzoek, Den Haag.

Jacobs, H. (1985), *De loonstructuur, analyse van verschillen in beloning tussen werknemers in het bedrijfsleven*, Groningen.

Kamstra, E. and W. van der Craats (1991), *Eenrichtingsverkeer op de arbeidsmarkt*, OSA-werkdocument W 91, Organisatie voor Strategisch Arbeidsmarktonderzoek, Den Haag.

Kerkhoffs, W.H.C. (1981), *Ouder worden, verouderen en het personeelsbeleid*, Universiteit van Amsterdam, Amsterdam.

Kloet, H.T. van der, A. Sikkema and R.Ch. Boom (1994), *Leeftijdsbewust personeelsbeleid in bedrijf. Praktijkervaringen van tien bedrijven en organisaties*, Commissie Ontwikkeling Bedrijven, Sociaal-Economische Raad, Den Haag.

LTD (1991), *Ouderenbeleid in arbeidsorganisaties*, Ministerie van Sociale Zaken en Werkgelegenheid, Den Haag.

132   Lei Delsen

LTD (1992), *Sociale plannen bij reorganisaties*, Loontechnische Dienst, Ministerie van Sociale Zaken en Werkgelegenheid, Den Haag.

Petersen, C. (1989), *Economie en pensioenen*, Stenfert Kroese, Leiden.

Pierik, J.B.M. (1991), 'The Dutch Perspective' in Schmähl, W. (ed.), pp. 152-160.

Schmähl, W. (ed.) (1991), *The Future of Basic and Supplementary Pension Schemes in the European Community – 1992 and beyond*, Nomos Verlagsgesellschaft, Baden-Baden.

SZW (1994), *Sociale Nota 1994, 1995*, Ministerie van Sociale Zaken en Werkgelegenheid, Den Haag.

Trommel, W. (1993), *Eigentijds met pensioen*, Ministerie van Sociale Zaken en Werkgelegenheid, Den Haag.

Trommel, W. and B. de Vroom (1994), 'The Netherlands: The Loreley-Effect of Early Retirement' in Naschold, F. and B. de Vroom (eds.), *Regulating Employment and Welfare. Company and National Policies of Labour Force Participation at the End of Worklife in Industrial Countries* (pp. 51-115), Walter de Gruyter, Berlin.

Tweede Kamer (1991), *Pensioennota*, Vergaderjaar 1990-1991, 22167, no. 1, Den Haag.

Vroom, B. de, and M. Blomsma (1991), 'The Netherlands: An Extreme Case' in Kohli, M., M. Rein, A. Guillemard and H. van Gunsteren (eds.), *Time for Retirement. Comparative Studies of Early Exit from the Labor Force*, (pp. 97-126) Cambridge University Press, Cambridge.

WRR (1990), *Een werkend perspectief. Arbeidsparticipatie in de jaren '90*, Rapporten aan de Regering 38, Wetenschappelijke Raad voor het Regeringsbeleid, Den Haag.

WRR (1993), *Ouderen voor ouderen. Demografische ontwikkelingen en beleid*, Rapporten aan de Regering 43, Wetenschappelijke Raad voor het Regeringsbeleid, Den Haag.

PART III

GRADUAL RETIREMENT
IN JAPAN
AND THE UNITED STATES

8 Gradual retirement in Japan: macro issues and policies

Noriyuki Takayama

It is well known that Japan's population is aging very rapidly. By 1994 about 14 per cent of the population were elderly (65 years or older). Projections suggest large increases in the number of the elderly over the next fifty years, so that by 2040 more than 30 per cent of the population will probably be 65 or above. Japan will then have one of the oldest populations in the world.

Meanwhile, around 2000, the working population will begin to diminish. Growth in productivity will to some extent offset the decline in the size of the working population, but if people work more after 60 years, Japan is more likely to maintain her economic vitality into the twenty-first century. This, in turn, will make it easier for Japan to support its growing elderly population.

In this chapter we attempt to describe the current labour market situation of the elderly in Japan, and to explain why a move towards early retirement has been taking place. We also examine what kind of policy measures have been adopted to encourage later retirement and whether or not they are effective in achieving this. Finally, we consider what kind of policies will be needed to promote gradual retirement and to reduce the future financial burden of social expenditure.

8.1 Recent trends

Labour market position of older workers

The labour market positions of older workers in Japan have been very severe. The mandatory[1] retirement age used to be 55. As of April 1998, a mandatory age for retirement under 60 will no longer be permitted by law. In 1994, most companies in Japan (84 per cent) were mandating their employees to retire at 60 years or above.

Currently only 20 per cent of companies in Japan re-employ all employees wishing to continue to work until the age of 65. Those employees mandated to retire when they reach the age of 60, if they are highly skilled or possess some special expertise, are usually given an opportunity to be re-employed by their former company or a closely related one. However, their salaries are very likely to decline sharply after the age of 60. The effective demand/supply ratio for those re-entering the external labour market in their early sixties was just 0.08 in November 1994. The likelihood of their securing a new job in the external labour market after mandatory retirement is negligeable.

On the other hand, a fair proportion of retired employees become self employed after the age of 60. Among highly industrialised countries Japan is perhaps rather special in this respect.

In 1992 nearly 60 per cent of Japanese workers said they wished to continue working in labour market employment over the age of 65, the majority of them wishing to be in part-time jobs after the age of 60. Their main reasons for wishing to continue working after 60 were in order to maintain good health and to remain active in society, but not primarily in order to get money.

Pensions and social security

Currently Japan has a *first pillar* system comprising six public pension programmes covering different sectors of the population. The earliest plan was established in 1890; the most recent, in 1961. All sectors of the population receive a basic minimum benefit. Five employee systems provide a contributions-related supplement on top of the minimum. Although each system has its own particular contribution and benefit structure, all systems are similar, for the most part operating on a pay-as-you-go basis (see Takayama, 1992).

The monthly minimum benefit was 65,000 yen[2] per person in 1994 while monthly earnings-related benefits are typically about 30 per cent of average past monthly real earnings. Equal percentage contributions are required of employers and their employees. The total percentage currently in effect from November 1994 is 16.5 for the principal programme for private sector employees (the Kosei Nenkin Hoken; KNH). This contribution rate is applied to monthly earnings. From April 1995 contributions are for the first time to be taken out of bonuses, which are usually paid twice each year and account for a substantial portion of many employees' income. A special 1 per cent contribution rate split equally between employees and employers will apply to bonuses without any ceiling.

At present, KNH old age benefits for a new 'model' retiree (based on average earnings over 37 contribution years) and his dependent spouse (full-time housewife) were about 231,000 yen per month in 1994, replacing 68 per cent of the average monthly earnings of currently active male workers.

In Japan, employees usually receive semi-annual bonuses which typically amount to from four to five months salary, although in small companies they are often more modest. Since they are not included in the earnings base for public pension benefits, the replacement rate for the above-mentioned 'model' retiree will be considerably lower, about 50 per cent of the average annual earnings.

To put it another way, the 68 per cent replacement is the rate for gross salary. Active workers pay income tax and make social security contributions, and their deductions currently average 16 per cent of their monthly earnings. For retirees the deduction from their pension benefits is zero or quite small. Consequently the current replacement rate to monthly take-home pay or net income is about 80 per cent.

As for the *second pillar*, Japan has occupational pensions and/or lump sum retirement benefits. Currently the coverage of occupational retirement benefits is close on 90 per cent, although the coverage of occupational pension plans is nearer 50 per cent.

The average lump sum retirement benefits paid to mandated career male retirees were 20 to 24 million yen in large firms and 10 to 13 million yen in smaller firms in 1989. For employers, the main attraction of their type of occupational pension plan is that instead of paying out annuities, they can accumulate funds on favourable tax terms. In actual fact, more often than not, almost all retiring employees choose their retirement benefits as a lump sum, although their employers operate annuity-based formal pension plans.

There are three major schemes whereby employers can prepare provision for retirement benefits. One is to fund plans on a pay-as-you-go-basis with book-reserve accounting (started in 1952, and similar to West Germany's). Book reserves are tax deductible within certain limits: namely 40 per cent of the benefit liability can be deducted from income tax-calculations as a corporate expense. Originally a deduction was permitted on 100 per cent of the liability. Another scheme is a tax-qualified plan (TQP started in 1962). Plans of this kind must be funded externally through a group-annuity contract or a trust agreement. An employer's contributions to a tax-qualified plan are 100 per cent tax deductible as a business expense. A special 1.173 per cent corporate tax is levied annually on fund assets. Such plans must contain provision for annuity payments, though a lump sum option is permitted. The third scheme is for contracted-out plans (started in 1966) through the Kosei-Nenkin-Kikin (KNK, Employees' Pension Fund). KNK benefits comprise two components: an equivalent benefit of the earnings-related portion of social security (excluding the benefit resulting from indexing), and a supplementary benefit. The latter is financed primarily by the employer. It can be received in a lump sum at the discretion of the employee, although in principle it should be in the form of a life annuity. The plan must be funded through a trust fund or an insurance contract. Tax treatment of the contracted-out plan is substantially the same as that of the tax-qualified plan, except that the KNK does not pay taxes on accrued benefit liabilities equal to 2.7 times the benefit equivalent of the fixed earnings-related portion of the state scheme.

By the end of March 1993 the number of persons insured under company pension schemes (KNK and TQP) was 11.57 million for the KNK and 10.4 million for the TQP. In spite of the fact that some companies have adopted both systems, overall about one third of employees is covered by KNK and another third by TQP. The number of companies with a TQP pension age of 60 years has increased steadily and by 1992 60 had been adopted by 57.2 per cent of those offering TQP schemes (JILI, 1993, p. 122).

Book reserves are not funded outside, but are in fact retained as profits inside, contributing to the further investment of firms. The funded reserves of tax-qualified and contracted-out plans have been growing rapidly and are helping to augment national savings in Japan.

And what of the *third pillar* in Japan? The accumulation of private savings is among the highest in the world. But the distribution of monetary asset holding is very skewed. Those elderly, whose monetary asset holdings remain small, are not a few even in Japan today.[3] In the past, the role of individual pension plans was not so great. But more recently it has been growing fast, so the household coverage of individual pension plans stood at about 35 per cent in 1994.

In April 1991 a special type of individual pension account, called the Kokumin-Nenkin-Kikin, became available for non-employees and their spouses (ages 20 to 59). A contribution up to 68,000 yen per month per person is now tax exempt, which is very generous compared with only 50,000 yen per year for all individual 'pension' insurance policy premiums in respect of salaried workers together with their dependent spouses.

The recent move towards early retirement

Since the early 1970s, early retirement has become very popular in OECD member countries, and Japan is no exception.[4] Recently a growing number of males in younger cohorts has been earning wages and salaries, with the proportion of salaried men in their late forties, for example, reaching nearly 80 per cent of the work force. Meanwhile, the proportion of salaried men in their early sixties has been gradually decreasing. It was less than 40 per cent in 1988.

And what of the average retirement age of salaried men in Japan recently? Figure 8.1 presents the employment status in 1986 for men aged 59-64 years who had once been, or continued to be, wage and salary earners. By the time they were 61, a majority of these people were moving into full retirement or had become self employed. In Japan, then, the average age of exit from employment for salaried men would have been just before 61 years.

Figure 8.1 Employment status of men by age in Japan in 1986

Source: The 1986 Basic Survey of Japanese Living Conditions.

Why, then, do the majority of salaried men in Japan today cease to be salary and wage earners around the age of 60? The main reason is, undoubtedly, that at that age they begin to draw public pension benefits. The normal pensionable age for men in the KNH is still 60 years, and currently their average amount of public pension benefits is 200,000 yen per month, fairly high by international standards. Indeed, the above amount is currently a little more than the average monthly salary initially paid to college and university graduates in Japan.

Moreover, by the time they are 60 the majority of wage earners in Japan today have 35 years or more of work experience. At this stage in their professional life, in a Japan where firms are competing fiercely for rapid, refined and innovative technological advantage, it is very understandable that many elderly workers, especially non-office workers, are 'burnt-out', that some have a sense of fulfillment, but that most are weary and ready for retirement.

Furthermore, the mandatory retirement age for most of firms in Japan is currently 60 years.[5] Employers are more likely to dismiss their employees at the age of 60 or even earlier. As going concerns, firms must struggle to survive. Productivity growth is the top priority, and new technologies will be built into corporate practice by younger, and not by elderly, workers. Promotions are as a general rule useful incentives to harder work, so that ordinary managers and directors in Japan are generally asked to retire when they reach 55.

Figure 8.2 shows the age distribution for men who started drawing KNH old age benefits in fiscal 1990. It reveals that nearly two thirds of them began receiving their old age benefits as of 60 years, although their average starting age was 62.1.

Figure 8.2   Age distribution of men in Japan who started to receive old age pensions of the KNH in fiscal 1990

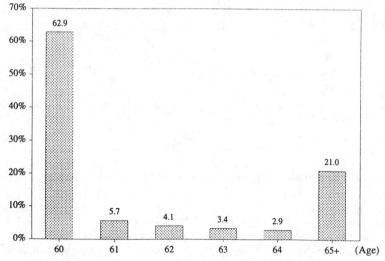

Source: Social Security Agency, Japan, Annual Report.

Why exactly did a majority of them start receiving KNH old age benefits at 60? First, prior to 65 years postponing the start of KNH old age benefits increases the sum of the benefits to a very limited extent only; the first-tier flat-rate benefits of the KNH have a 37-year ceiling in the benefit formula, so that postponing start-up before the age of 65 produces no actuarial increment in the level of the monthly benefit.

Second, employers in general have little or no incentive to hire elderly people. Supporting retired workers aged 60 years or more has been socialised by the KNH, meaning that all employers have to contribute to the KNH in support of retired workers regardless of their efforts to continue to employ the latter. On the other hand, hiring workers including elderly ones is essentially on a private basis, so that employers who *continue* to employ workers aged 60 years or more are effectively paying the wages out of their own pocket. A 'free rider' problem arises, and employers are thereby more inclined to dismiss their employees by the time they reach 60.

In short, the KNH has its own built-in inducement causing people to start drawing old age benefits as soon as they reach 60.

There are other incentives, too. It was often said that the past earnings test of the KNH was inducing early retirement around the age of 60. It was indeed the case that the marginal 'tax' rate through the KNH earnings test would be about 100 per cent, but that was only half the story. In point of fact the KNH had, and continues to have, loopholes. First, the earnings test depends on monthly wages and salaries which do not include semi-annual bonuses. Employers and their employees can negotiate the fixing of monthly salaries at a fairly low level (for example, a little under 95,000 yen), while promising abnormal bonuses amounting to, say, 20 months salary per year. With such negotiated arrangements, the employees can 'sponge' on the KNH, while, at the same time, the employers can continue to re-employ the more able among them after they reach 60 years.

Second, the KNH earnings test is applied to those working 33 hours or more per week (three fourths of ordinary hours). If the elderly limit their work time to less than 33 hours per week, then they can enjoy KNH old age benefits in full, while still earning a substantial portion of their salaries.

In the past, a Japanese employee when reaching 60 could draw both an old age pension and unemployment benefits (up to 300 days). Should the employee decide to cease working altogether, he or she could enjoy both benefits totalling about 400,000 yen or so per month. This was another great incentive to retiring early.[6]

8.2 New public policies

In 1994 the Japanese public pension and employment insurance systems were reformed with a view to promoting later retirement. In this section we indicate what those reforms were and attempt to assess to what extent they have been effective in generating jobs for the elderly.

Incentives in public pension schemes

The 1994 reform in public pension schemes includes a raising of the pension age and a change in the earnings test. Both measures were adopted so as to promote employment of the elderly.

Two pension ages will be applied to salaried workers. While the start of basic benefits will be gradually shifted to the age of 65, earnings-related benefits will continue to be available at 60 years. This arrangement corresponds basically to a system once envisaged in Britain.[7]

Figure 8.3 shows the new payout configuration for men both in 2001, the first year of their shift, and in 2013, at the shift's end. From 2001 through 2003, men will have to wait until they are 61 before they can receive the full amounts of basic benefits. This will affect those males born between 2 April 1941 and 1 April 1943 (see table 8.1). The phasing out of basic benefits for female employees will be delayed five years behind the schedule for male employees, starting only in 2006. Eventually, retired workers under the age of 65 will not receive any of the special benefits now available for enrollees in the 60-64 age bracket, though they will still be eligible for full amounts of the earnings-related 1st pillar benefits (tier 1).

Figure 8.3   Adjustment in the commencement age of pension benefits for men in Japan

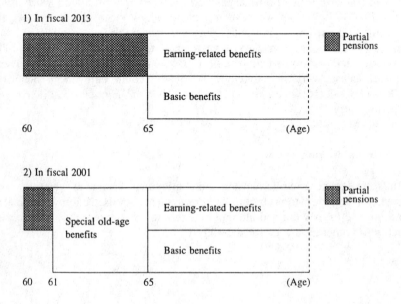

Table 8.1
Start of full basic benefits for male employees in Japan

Date of birth	Age
Before 1 April 1941	60
Between 2 April 1941 and 1 April 1943	61
Between 2 April 1943 and 1 April 1945	62
Between 2 April 1945 and 1 April 1947	63
Between 2 April 1947 and 1 April 1949	64
After 2 April 1949	65

Those in this age bracket can also receive advance payments at a reduced rate from the Basic Pension on tier 1 (1st pillar). At present non-salaried workers can already take advantage of this system, and at the start of the twenty-first century salaried workers will gain the same right. Advance payments are to be handled by paying out Basic Pension benefits at a reduced rate until the end of the pensioner's life. The size of the reduction now being applied rises from 11 per cent for one year of advance payments to 20 per cent for two years, 28 per cent for three years, 35 per cent for four years, and 42 per cent for five years. As some people feel that the current rates of reduction are too steep, their appropriateness is to be reviewed in 2001 using the latest data on life expectancy. Meanwhile, 60-year-old retired wage earners will continue to receive earnings-related benefits without any reduction in their amounts.

When we add these factors together, we find that in the standard case of a long-term enrollee who fully retires at the age of 60, the total benefits including advance payments from the Basic Pension will probably amount to from 60 to 70 per cent of the active worker's take-home pay. This level is in no way inferior to that in the West's industrially advanced countries. When the income of the pensioner is set at 100, the after-tax wages of the active worker lie between 143 and 167. If one takes into account the differences between the households they typically have – one with an old aged couple, the other with four household members – this does not seem an unreasonable balance.

The second measure is a change in the earnings test from April 1995. First a 20 per cent cut in benefits is mandated for anyone who, upon reaching the age of 60, continues to work and to bring home wage income. Then the remaining 80 per cent of the benefits is added to the worker's monthly pay. If the total is under 220,000 yen, the worker receives these benefits in full. If the total exceeds that level, the benefits are reduced by 10,000 yen for each 20,000 yen increment in wages. After monthly wages reach 340,000 yen – a level more or less in line with the current average pay of male employees – each additional step up the wage scale causes benefits to step down by the same amount.

What sets this arrangement apart from the existing system, making it an incentive to later retirement, is that salaried workers can increase their total income by earning more money. With each hike in wages, the combined sum of their benefits and wages moves up. The 2:1 ratio between wage increments and benefit reductions happens to be one that used to be employed by the United States.

Incentives in employment insurance schemes

In the employment insurance system, old age employment benefits are to be introduced for those who continue to work from April 1995. The purpose of this measure is to plug a hole in unemployment compensation, which in some cases gives people who have passed the retirement age more money if they stop working than if they stay employed. The measure is designed to motivate those with the will and the ability to work to remain employed during their early 60s.

Figure 8.4   Earnings and old age employment benefits in Japan

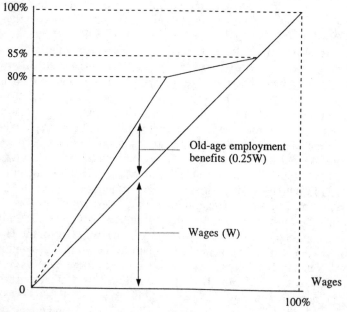

Note: The 100 per cent line of wages means the wage level just before the mandatory retirement age.

In the normal Japanese company, employees reach the mandatory retirement age at or around 60. Some people do indeed retire then, but many go on working, at least for a while. What, instead, generally happens at 60 is that employees, whether they stay with the same employer or switch jobs, suffer a large salary cut, and at that point the unemployment compensation they are entitled to may be larger than their new wages. The newly introduced measure rectifies this problem by hereafter treating those who have a sharp decline in wages as quasi-unemployed; specifically, these people are to be provided benefits amounting to 25 per cent of their new wages. These benefits, when combined with wage income, will give many of those in the 60-64 age-group more money than they could receive from employment insurance alone. The 25 per cent benefit rate begins to drop at the point where workers are still receiving 64 per cent of their former salary, and for those who receive 85 per cent or more, the rate reaches zero and no benefits are provided (see figure 8.4).

Figure 8.5 Wages and benefits for employees in their early sixties in Japan (Unit: yen 10,000)

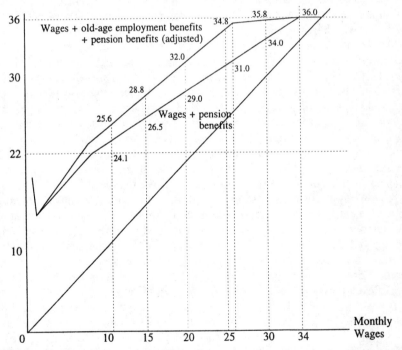

Note: The amount of monthly wages just before mandatory retirement is assumed to be ¥400,000. The full amount of monthly pension benefits is assumed to be ¥200,000.

Shown in figure 8.5 is the net income of a worker receiving both these old age employment benefits and the old age benefits paid by the pension system. To balance the employment benefits, the pensions of such workers are to be cut by an amount equivalent to 10 per cent of their new monthly salary.

Moreover, from April 1998 people will no longer be able to draw both unemployment compensation and old age pension benefits.

Future prospects

Stated above are the new policies the Japanese Government has introduced recently. Will they be really effective in promoting later retirement?

As has already been demonstrated in other OECD countries, legislation on increasing the normal age of retirement alone is not enough to reverse the trend towards early retirement. Indeed, on reaching the age of 60, a long-term enrollee can still enjoy very generous pension benefits if he or she receives advance payments from the Basic Pension even after 2013. The elasticity of employment with respect to pension benefits is rather limited in Japan (see Takayama, 1992). The labour market situation for those in their early 60s will not be much different from the current situation. Rather, increasing the normal retirement age will be effective in cutting down the amount of pension benefits for those who begin to draw them before the age of 65.

Turning to the new incentives created by the change in the earnings test and the introduction of old age employment benefits; they seem, at first sight, to be effective. But on closer examination, our findings turn out to be rather different. The absolute sum of pension and old age employment benefits paid to employees in their early sixties will be highest if monthly wages and salaries are kept at a level slightly below 95,000 yen. Introduction of the new measures described above will not alter this situation. Employers and their employees are likely to make a joint decision to seek from the Government the highest level of benefits (subsidies) available. In this sense, no significant changes will occur on the labour market to affect the elderly.

A number of issues have yet to be dealt with. For instance, thus far bonuses have not been considered in the earnings test. Again, the reform will not affect the practice of awarding full benefits to those who continue to receive wage income but work fewer than 33 hours per week, as in the case of part-time advisors and people working on commission. Furthermore, once a private-sector wage earner reaches the age of 65, the full pension becomes payable regardless of whether he or she is earning a high salary.

If we really want the elderly to be employed more, we should have incentives directly influencing the demand side of the labour force, rather than the supply side. As already stated, current legislation is not cost-neutral as to the decision of employers to employ people in their early sixties. If employment neutrality of public pensions for those in their early sixties is desirable, public pension benefits paid to those in the 60-64 age bracket should come from their former employers (and/or employees). The so-called merit system in contribution rates will require them to be set lower for those businesses that actively employ older people.

If later retirement is to be promoted, it is essential that older workers achieve higher productivity. Increased incentives for higher productivity training must be created. Job re-designing to include more part- and flexible-time work patterns is also required.

As far as reducing the future financial burden of social security is concerned, a switch from a gross- to a net-wage basis for setting benefit levels will yield substantial results, as is shown in table 8.2. It is true that the primary purpose of the switch is to preserve a stable balance between the net income of the two groups (actively working generations and retired ones), bringing about a much fairer distribution of income between generations, but it will also prove effective in reducing the future cost of public pensions (see Takayama, 1994; 1995). Japan made this switch in 1994.[8]

Table 8.2

Net income of actively working generations in Japan under population aging

Year	Annual growth rate of gross salary	Actively working generations			Retired generations
		Gross salary[a]	T&SSC[b]	Net salary	Public pension benefits[c]
1995	–	100	16	84	68
2030	2.0%	200	64	136	110
	1.0%	142	45	97	78
	0.6%	123	39	84	68

a The amount of gross salary in 1995 is assumed to be 100.
b Tax burdens and social security contributions (T&SSC) are assumed to equal 16 per cent in 1995 and they will double in 2030.
c Public pension benefits in net terms are set to equal 80 per cent of net salary of actively working generations.

Continued growth of the economy will be necessary if net indexation is to function successfully.[9] Table 8.2 tells us that more than 0.6 per cent real annual growth of gross wages and salaries may be required for members of the active population to be richer than their parents.

The issue of funding becomes important, therefore, if only from the standpoint of avoiding constraints on economic growth. If we ask, as we must, which of the three main revenue sources available – income tax, social security contributions, and consumption tax – is least likely to slow down growth, the answer is consumption tax. Over the long term, accordingly, it will make sense to fund part of the increased cost of our society's 'greying' by raising the rate of consumption tax, which will have the effect of obviating an increase in social security contribution rates.

A shift from a pay-as-you-go to a funded system is often proposed as a way of encouraging savings and, thereby, of stimulating the economy to higher growth. It should be borne in mind, however, that the transition from a pay-as-you-go to a funded system is a rather delicate matter, since the transitional generation has to participate in both systems, paying for pensions twice. This is likely to constitute a political hot-potato especially in societies where population aging continues. Besides, in the Japan of today, it is by no means clear that the public sector will be more effective than the private in stimulating economic growth through investing the funded reserve. For Japan at least, then, a continued lowering of the generous level of the old age benefits operating on a pay-as-you-go basis together with giving much more incentives to private pensions on a funded basis seems to be the advisable course.

Notes

1 It is neither the official/legal age, nor the age at which one is entitled to draw a state pension. Mandatory retirement age is the age at which retirement is compulsory for anyone who has benefitted from lifetime employment. In some cases there is an option to be re-employed by the same company after that age. The mandatory age is set within each company by management-union negociation or by the employer.
2 ¥10,000 = us$112.0 = £70.10 = DM157.7 as at 27 March 1995.
3 See Takayama-Kitamura (1994).
4 The labour force participation rate for those in their early sixties stopped declining in 1989 and began to increase thereafter. This change might be due to favourable labour market conditions in the asset price 'bubble'.
5 Actually, the majority of employees in large firms are leaving long before age 60. However, in these firms, the monthly salaries of non-executive workers are often forced downwards after the age of 55, and, as a general rule, the mandatory retirement age for executive workers is 55. In other words, the spirit of the earlier mandatory age of 55 is still preserved in large firms. Outplacement of employment after the age of 45 is quite popular in these firms. Substantial lump sum retirement benefits are paid to those mandated to retire.
6 The eligibility requirements for disability pensions in Japan are very severe, causing the latter to be a route seldom used by early retirees.
7 See Takayama (1995) and Secretary of State for Social Security, UK (1991).
8 Other ways of reducing the cost of social security pensions would be to raise the normal retirement age from 65 to 67 and to increase the number of contribution years required for full benefit from 40 to 45.
9 Continued growth of the economy will be also necessary if the elderly are to be employed more.

References

Secretary of State for Social Security, UK (1991), *Options for Equality in State Pension Age*, HMSO, London.

Takayama, N. (1992), *The Greying of Japan: an Economic Perspective on Public pensions*, Kinokuniya and Oxford, Oxford University Press, Tokyo.

Takayama, N. (1993), *A Recent Move Toward Early Retirement and the Fourth Pillar in Japan*, a paper presented at the SASE conference, New York, March.

Takayama, N. (1994), 'Preparing Public Pensions for an Old aged Society', *Japan Echo*, 21 (Special Issue), pp. 67-71.

Takayama, N. (1995), 'The 1994 Reform Bill for Public Pensions in Japan: its Main Contents and Related Discussion', *International Social Security Review*, vol. 48, no. 1, pp. 45-65.

Takayama, N. and Y. Kitamura (1994), 'Household Saving Behavior in Japan' in Poterba, J.M. (ed.), *International Comparisons of Household Saving* (pp. 125-167), The University of Chicago Press, Chicago.

9 Gradual retirement in Japan: micro issues and policies

Isao Shimowada

High economic growth in Japan during the years 1960 to 1975 was achieved with a remarkably young work force. This situation, however, has now reversed so that, over the coming decades due to a serious labour market shortage of younger workers, many firms in Japan will be obliged to employ elderly and women workers in increasing numbers. Bigger companies, which until recently had either laid off older workers or assisted them in finding alternative employment elsewhere in their group or in affiliated companies, will shortly be left with no choice in the matter of whom they employ – older workers will soon have become an indispensible part of the labour force. As a matter of urgency, employment policies in Japan will have to adjust to the reality of limited manpower and to the task of achieving a productive aging society. At the microeconomic or company level, this will mean more efficient deployment of older workers. As Mr Takayama has shown, the Government, in taking up this challenge, has begun to promote policies for effecting the necessary changes in employment practice and pension provision. In this way it hopes to create an environment conducive to gradual retirement and to the transition from, as the catchphrase has it, 'a society which retires at 60 to one that works until 65'.

9.1 Recent trends

The Law on the Stabilisation of Employment for Older Workers (LSEOW) came into force in 1986. It is designed to encourage and to stabilise employment for older workers. To this end, it empowers the Government to sanction companies which fail to implement retirement policies with a mandatory retirement age at 60 years, and it provides incentives and assistance to companies seeking to employ workers aged 60 and over (Shimowada, 1992, p. 49). This law was amended as recently as 1994 to promote continued employment until 65 concurrent with the retirement schemes now uniformly mandatory at 60; the idea being to encourage, after they have entered mandatory retirement, early re-deployment of older workers and to ensure that temporary and part-time employment become an option for them.

As things stand in Japan, many companies have already set the mandatory age for retirement at 60 years and a few have even adopted age-limits at over 60. The drive to achieve a 'society that works until 65', however, does not mean that all companies will be expected to retain all employees until 65. What it does mean, rather, is that Japan will strive to achieve a society that offers its older people a friendly work environment where they are able and encouraged to work beyond the age of 60 in consonance with their abilities and state of health. The 1994 amendment to the LSEOW was accordingly shaped not only to encourage employers to retain or re-employ workers until 65 but also to provide the Minister of Labour with the power to put pressure on employers to devise re-employment schemes for workers in their early 60s. Specifically, under this amendment, starting in 1994, the Government has introduced various subsidy schemes to provide aid and incentives to companies wishing to employ workers after 60 or willing to introduce 10-day paid-leave periods for middle- and old aged workers desirous of preparing for a future job. Moreover, from April 1995 onwards, the unemployment benefit system will be launching a new scheme for promoting continued and re-employment after retirement, whereby beneficiaries of 60 years or over whose wage is lower than 15 per cent of their income at 60 years can continue, between the age of 60 and 65, to draw an additional 25 per cent of the 60-year income in the form of what is called a 'continued employment benefit'.

Since the oil shock, and especially during the 1980s, the share of services in Japan's overall economy has been expanding rapidly and with it the number of employees in service industries. Employees in secondary industries tend to work the same hours in the same place, i.e. the factory. Work patterns in the service sector, however, are by comparison variegated, with employees working in different ways, according to different schedules and in different locations. The growing place of services in the economy will, therefore, be a spur to increased diversity and flexibility in work styles in general, doubtless over time favourable to the employment of older workers in particular. Indeed, year on year, there is already substantial growth in the employment of part- and short-time workers. And yet, for the older worker specifically, the prevailing economic situation in Japan with its mismatch of supply and demand on the labour market means that this trend towards greater flexibility and diversity will remain largely without effect unless the current eligibility requirements for State employee pension insurance (Kosei Nenkin Hoken – 1st pillar), which are still severe for part-time workers, can be loosened.

Success with employment systems for older workers until 65 and beyond will obviously in large measure depend as much upon how attractive the prospect of employment after retirement can be made as upon their willingness to work after retirement. Numerous studies show the participation rate for elderly workers in Japan to be very high by comparison with that of other countries. A survey by the Prime Minister's Office of 1992 of the willingness to work had 17 per cent of respondents in all categories stating their desire 'to continue working until about 65'. The same figure for respondents in the 'elderly people' category, however, was over 30 per cent: specifically, 31.3 per cent in the 50 to 59 age-group and 31.9 per cent in the 60 to 64 age-group. When asked 'did they wish to work until 70 years or as long as they possibly could?', 68.8 per cent of the 50 to 59 year-olds and 91.2 per cent of the 60 to 64 year-olds said they did. In other words, almost all employees in their early 60s would wish to continue working after retirement until 70.

The Japanese Government's recent reform of social security and employment policies for older workers, referred to above, concerned, among other things, improvement of 1st pillar pension payments to employees continuing work after 60, the suspension of simultaneous payment of pension and unemployment benefits and a number of essential amendments to the LSEOW. All these reforms have served to remove some of the institutional disincentives to those willing to work after retirement age and thus to promote their employment. Furthermore, changes ushered in by the Pension Reform Act of November 1994 will contribute to raising the labour participation rate of elderly people and their effective age of retirement, because of improved pension payments to those remaining in work and because, starting in the year 2001, it progressively raises the official pension age from 60 to 65.

The performance of elderly workers

There is substantial research evidence in Japan to suggest that productivity does not always decrease with age, but that it is influenced by variations in ability. With the exception of a small number of functions, most jobs can be performed satisfactorily by older people especially where tools like eye-glasses and hearing-aids are readily available. In older workers what has been lost in physical strength and stamina is often more than offset by increased skill and experience. Their productivity, it is suggested, is almost identical to that of younger workers.

In smaller firms, 20 per cent of elderly workers have had problems with physical strength. In almost all cases, however, the firms concerned had no difficulty in devising appropriate shift-schedules or assigning the workers in question to tasks like product inspection which require sustained concentration and, in this instance, eye-work. Differences in performance and productivity, as was found in firms in France, tend to be greater from worker to worker than from one age-group to the next.

As to the rapid advance of technology, which is often held to be the cause of disqualification of the middle-aged and older worker who frequently has no more training than that received in compulsory education, two things need to be said. First, that self-same technological progress is helping to produce precisely the easy-to-work environment the older worker needs and, secondly, cohort-related knowledge obsolescence will cease to be a significant factor for the generations reaching occupational maturity in the near future, for they, and the 'baby-boomers' are an example, will be more mechanically inclined and less technologically shy than their predecessors. Indeed, the proportion of school-leavers going on to undergraduate studies (university or college) has been rising since 1960 and by the mid-1970s had exceeded 30 per cent. With this rising trend, the quality of older workers will also improve. According to Economic Planning Agency projections, supply of blue-collar labour exceeds demand by about 3 million. But with technical employees with special skills, the projections suggest, supply falls short of demand by about 2.8 million as a result of changes in industrial and employment structures due to the expanding share of the tertiary service sector within the economy as a whole (see figure 9.1). It can safely be said, then, that the early middle-aged or maturer graduates of tomorrow entering the labour market after a prolonged period of study will not always be occupying managerial posts in factory and firm but, more often than not, involved in flexible, part-time employment patterns as visiting workers and consultants, that is, as independent professionals with specialised experience and skills to offer.

Company pension schemes

Since their introduction in the 1960s, the company pension schemes (Employee Pension Fund or Kosei-Nenkin-Kikin and Qualified Retirement Pension or Teki-Kaku-Nenkin) spread rapidly in the 1970s and 1980s spurred on by tax benefits and the reforms to the State pension schemes.

This trend has been successfully encouraged by the LSEOW of 1986 which rewarded companies adopting a pension age of 60 years. Consequently, according to the JILI survey of 1992, in 1986 when the LSEOW came into force only 38.6 per cent of companies with a Qualified Retirement Pension (QRP) mandatory retirement age had opted for a pension age at 60. By 1992 this proportion had gone up to 57.2 per cent, and today the 60 year pension age applies in almost all Japanese companies (JILI, 1993, p. 122).

Figure 9.1 Projection of mismatch of supply and demand on the Japanese labour market in 2000

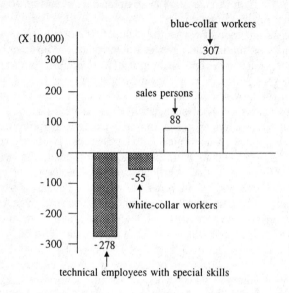

Source: Economic Planning Agency, Human Resource Development in the Period of Fundamental Social Change of Occupational Structure, 1987.

For many reasons, some already alluded to, labour mobility is set to expand steadily. However, company pension regulations, whose effect has hitherto been to restrain that mobility, must now adjust to the changing labour market situation and allow for greater portability of pension benefits. Many company schemes are of the 'corporate type', i.e. function vertically within a single company, group of companies or industrial conglomerate. If employee mobility between companies is to be possible in the medium and long terms, company pension schemes will need to adapt to allow employees to select benefits from horizontally-organised schemes established on a regional, branch or industry-wide basis.

Over the decade between 1982 and 1992 the number of joint contracts under the QRP (Qualified Retirement Pension) system almost doubled, climbing from 4,462 to 9,224. A 'joint contract' is offered simultaneously by all companies within a group and this means that benefits can easily be transferred should an employee decide to change company or a parent company to 'shukko' one of its employees, i.e. transfer him or her to an affiliated company. This type of contract also makes it possible for smaller-sized companies with from 1 to 14 employees to adopt the QRP system and, from the standpoint of pension entitlements, for employees to move from big companies to smaller ones.

With the EPF (Employee Pension Fund) system, the same tendency has been observed recently with so-called 'joint' or 'general' multi-employer schemes, as opposed to single-establishment big-company ones, on the increase (JILI, 1993, p. 135). The combined effect of these trends within the QRP and EPF systems will be to enhance the portability of company pensions in general.

Retirement options

According to a 1991 Ministry of Labour survey into work force management, only 5.1 per cent of companies overall offer middle-aged and older employees a range of options for future working life. But this proportion does increase with size of company so that, of big companies with a work force of more than 5,000, no less than 47.2 per cent operate programmes of this kind. The most popular option, available in 3.3 per cent of companies overall and in 42.5 per cent of big companies (again with a work force of more than 5,000), is early retirement. Even so, the take-up rate of this option as an exit route into full retirement is extremely low. A far greater number of employees are 'shukkoed'. One big company in ten runs a 'shukko' system of this sort (Seike, 1992, p. 87).

Amendment of the worker leasing law

The Worker Leasing Law (WLL) came into force in 1986 and provides for the establishment of employee-leasing firms which send staff registered on their books to contracting companies. However, in order to protect workers the Law limited the number of occupations where employee-leasing was permitted to 16, among others, softwear and machine design, certain special office functions like translation and interpretation, and other more general ones like shorthand, filing and secretarial work. The number of employees registering with such schemes, even so, increased rapidly, women and retired older workers being attracted by the flexible work hours and employment styles, with the result that over the 7 or so years following legal recognition, the employee-leasing business has expanded enormously. But in 1993, with the number of workers registered in leasing schemes at 570,000, this trend had bottomed out and began to show a slight decline influenced by the depression following the collapse of the 'bubble economy'. In November 1994 work began on revising the WLL with a view to expanding the list of permitted occupations.

In 1994 also the LSEOW was amended to facilitate employment of older workers and to loosen up the rules on permitted occupations where workers aged 60 and over are concerned. This means that the latter can now be employed as visiting workers in almost all occupations: management, office work and service functions excluding, however, harbour transportation, construction, work as guards and manufacturing. However, by law, the leasing of older employees on the relaxed terms referred to above is permitted only to those employee-leasing companies which set up special firms for the purpose. In one employee-leasing company operating the new rules in January 1995, 15 per cent of all employees registered were workers aged 60 and over and their leasings accounted for 26 per cent of total supply-contracts serviced by the company. From the customer's standpoint, many appreciate the high skill and experience levels of these visiting older workers and many, especially the smaller customers, are hoping to make increasing use of the know-how that retirees from bigger companies have to offer. The Tokyo branch of an electrical manufacturing firm with a work force of 360 already employs 11 of these older visiting workers and plans to develop the practice. It feels that their know-how, expertise, skills and personal connections will prove a valuable additon to the firm's resources.

9.2 New company policies

Personnel policy

Personnel policy in Japanese firms is typified by the following features:
1 incentive systems are based exclusively on promotion to managerial posts;
2 assessments contained in service records are not normally disclosed to the employees concerned; and
3 personnel departments are answerable to the company rather than to the work force, their status and management is not independent.

All of these features create problems, all of which are exacerbated by a rapidly aging work force and a declining young population and will accordingly now need to be addressed by firms.

The Labour Administration Institute's survey of 1993 reveals that the number of companies disclosing personnel-assessment information to employees is on the increase. Of the companies studied, 47.6 per cent have established an interview procedure which includes examining with the interviewee the results of the latter's service record assessment; 13.8 per cent have introduced open recruitment procedures and 69.5 per cent operate employee self-assessment schemes. The increased transparency and flexibility in personnel management policies, of which the above procedures are examples, will help to rectify the imbalance between performance and wages which is thought to constitute a major obstacle to more widespread employment of older people (Fujimura, 1994, pp. 34-35).

In the early 1970s the proportion of companies which had adopted a mandatory retirement age was less than 70 per cent. Since then, however, this proportion has grown rapidly to its current level of around 90 per cent. While big companies, almost without exception, have always had a mandatory retirement age, in smaller companies employing between 30 and 99 workers such an arrangement obtains in roughly only half. Major economic disruption triggered by the oil shock has forced these smaller companies to reduce their work force and to limit wherever possible the cost burden of the seniority-based wage system. Many have chosen to address these constraints – by 1990 84 per cent had done so – by introducing an age-limit rule thus obviating the costly rigmarole of dismissal and lay-off.

In the mid-1970s, 55 years was the mandatory retirement age in the majority of Japanese companies, only 30 per cent having set that age at 60 years. Since that time, however, egged on by Government subsidies and administrative pressure and to a remarkable extent by the entry into force of the LSEOW in 1986, the proportion of companies with a 60-year age-limit steadily increased to around 64 per cent in 1990 and 80 per cent in 1993. But the LSEOW amendment of 1994 left the remaining 20 per cent or so no choice in the matter. It prescribed a legal minimum age for retirement at 60 years making anything less illegal. For medium- and small-sized firms, however, given their special situation, this stipulation will not come into force until April 1998.

A survey of work force management made in 1993 reveals that, of companies with a mandatory retirement age after 60 years, 71.7 per cent run extended employment and re-employment schemes, and 70 to 80 per cent of that number have set a maximum age-limit on eligibility for such schemes at 65 years. But the survey also reveals that only 28.6 per cent of companies running such schemes make them systematically available to 'all comers'. As table 9.1 shows, of the big companies studied with a work force of more than 5,000 employees, 40.1 per cent have adopted a mandatory termination date for managerial staff and 41.1 per cent have an early retirement scheme. Of big companies also, 47 per cent run optional future-job schemes – the 'shukko' transfer schemes to affiliated companies being an example – designed to assist their older employees find other jobs or transfer to more specialised functions. This percentage declines rapidly with size of company (Takada, 1994, p. 15).

Wage policy

As the mandatory retirement age has climbed from 55 to 60 years, so have the bigger companies attempted to level-out the seniority-based wage curve and reduce other employment costs. Ministry of Labour statistics for 1987 showed that 52.6 per cent of companies overall operated a basic wage decrease at a given age (frequently 50 years), and that this proportion rose to 85 per cent for companies with a work force of more than 1,000.

Table 9.1
Readjustment of treatment for older workers in Japan (January 1991)
(Percentage of companies with schemes)

Size of companies	Mandatory termination date for managerial staff	Early retirement schemes	Optional future-job schemes to select future working life at the certain age for older employees			
			Adopted*	'Shukko' transfer schemes to the affiliated companies	'Assist employees in finding new jobs' schemes	'Transfer employees to more specialised functions' schemes
Total	11.5	3.1	3.9	0.3	0.1	0.3
5,000-	40.1	41.1	47.0	10.1	8.0	2.4
1,000-4,999	34.1	28.8	30.7	2.6	2.3	1.7
300-999	24.3	13.7	14.7	0.4	0.5	1.0

* These figures include the early retirement schemes of the left column.
Source: The Ministry of Labour, Survey on Employment Management, 1991.

Rapid structural change in industry and increasing labour market competition tend to foment labour mobility and diversification of work styles and occupational modes. Big companies, accustomed thus far to renewing their work force with an intake of new labour market entrants every April, are now beginning to look to the veteran worker instead as a regular source of immediately useable and useful manpower. If, however, this trend is to continue, the wage curve will need to flatten out and the strict seniority-based wage system abandoned. Such changes, it goes without saying, will greatly facilitate the taking-on and re-employment of older workers and will in time combine with pressure from an expanding service industry and information network to diversify the structure of employment making part-time, flexible, visiting and temporary work patterns commonplace.

Redesign of work

Other reasons for modifying the seniority-based wage system in Japan are the overall rise in income levels across the labour market and the fact that raised higher-education standards are tending to push starting wages up. Companies operating seniority wage systems on traditional lines are now in a minority. Many are turning to merit-based systems instead, using personnel management techniques for the redesign of work and in the reallocation of workload levels. Indeed, personnel management of young and middle-aged white-collar workers in firms in Japan will concentrate on diversification with an emphasis in big companies being placed on the training of white-collar specialists rather than generalists. A similar trend – a call for special skills and abilities – may be observed in the labour market demand for older workers.

Flexible work arrangements and part-time work

As has been said, the growing share of services in the economy and the increased demand for white-collar workers on the labour market will diversify employment and so increase the opportunities and need for older workers. Much the same applies to the participation rate for women which the current labour shortage has forced upwards and which will add to existing pressure to diversify employment since women, like older workers, will need flexible and part-time work arrangements if quality employees are to remain in the labour force in sufficient numbers.

Diversification will affect employment in three ways; new arrangements regarding, first, how work is done, second, where it is done, and third, on what contractual terms. According to a survey of the Japan Productivity Organisation of 1990, many top managers are beginning to evaluate employee productivity not, as in the past, in terms of the number of hours worked but purely in terms of output and performance (Seike, 1992, p. 189). Work force diversification, made possible by progress with information technology, is already to be observed in the growing number of experiments in telecommuting and the use of satellite offices by white-collar specialists. Diversification of contractual arrangements can be seen in the growing use of part-time work, consultancy services, day-labour and fixed-term appointments of varying durations.

Vocational training

Older people are, generally speaking, not as physically strong as younger people. Yet physical strength and fitness can be maintained late in life with appropriate training and health management. High skill levels and competent judgement can be maintained through many years and rich experience garnered. The training and retraining of older workers should, therefore, take account of such potential strengths and not merely be designed to meet their more obvious needs and shortcomings.

For the small company, older workers are invaluable, for much of their knowledge and ability has been acquired naturally: it is the distillation of years spent at the same kind of task or tasks. In a small company, a single worker will often be responsible for a range of functions which in a larger company would be allocated to different divisions. In a smaller company also, the older employee, because of his or her wide-ranging experience, is frequently made to work harder and in ways more crucial to the company than the younger colleague. The older worker is, therefore, suited to the small and medium-sized firm and, because of his or her independence, to the self employment situation.

The ability to manage and pace oneself under such circumstances in the workplace becomes indispensible as also does the ability outside the workplace to strike a satisfactory balance between one's professional and expanding private life, to increase one's involvement in the community and to recycle one's social skills. But from the standpoint of the person employing the older worker, the real problem is to be able to make systematic and efficient use of the latter's rich experience and know-how. In this connection, the 1994 amendment of the Unemployment Insurance Law was epoch-making (Yamaguchi, 1994, pp. 22-25). Firstly, the Law provided for the founding of a centre for research into improved use of the experience of older workers and for the provision of support or 'silver-centre' desks for older workers in local job centres. The purpose of the latter is to assist middle-aged and older employees to acquire the necessary skills and knowledge for future jobs after retirement. Secondly, the Law sets up a subsidies system for companies which helps workers to prepare for employment after retirement by providing them with paid vacations (ten days or more) for this purpose.

The move to gradual retirement

IBM Japan got into managerial difficulties following far-reaching structural changes in the computer market and had to downsize its work force. This company, however, was reported to have turned the situation to good account when, through its Second-Career Support Programme which it operated until June 1993, it promoted the retirement of many of its employees and assisted them in finding new jobs. The case clearly demonstrates that, in spite of Japan's deep-rooted tradition of lifetime employment, employees welcome early retirement or changing company provided the latter options are designed to meet their expectations.

In actual fact, Japanese companies, especially the big ones, frequently re-employ retired former employees at their former workplace or in an affiliated company, or assist them in finding a new job. This practice is one of the reasons for the remarkably high participation rate for older workers at present. Japan's biggest travel agent, the JTB or Japan Tourist Bureau with a registered capital of 1.92 billion yen, a work force of 10,000 employees, and around 120 affiliated companies is a case in point (LDI, 1989, pp. 64-67). In 1946 it introduced a retirement system with a mandatory age-limit at 60 and in 1958 provision for flexible pension plans. In 1971 it set up the JTB Traveland Co whose main vocation was to be the re-employment of JTB's retired employees. Further, in 1975 it brought in its converter scheme whereby employees reaching 55 years would be encouraged to transfer to a job in one of the JTB's affiliates. Employees who agreed to convert could continue in the affiliate until 65 years, while those who refused to leave the parent company could continue working until 60 years only. The company uses its pension plan to supplement any wage reduction converters may sustain. From the company's point of view there are a number of advantages to this system. First, it allows considerable scope for reshuffling staff for personnel management purposes. Second, it can use an employee's career-path as a means of strengthening its own sales network across its group companies, and, third, it can use the system to contain and flatten retirement-related costs. Year on year, JTB's retirees will be increasing – by 1996 the annual cohort will be 300. In this connection, in 1992 JTB completely overhauled its wage policy, improved the quality of its work organisation, and widened the range of options open to its employees by creating the following schemes:

1 a scheme whereby employees entering full retirement at 55 years receive the same benefit as converters;
2 a support scheme whereby JTB pays employees aged between 45 and 47 years increased lump sum retirement pay or invests capital for them so that they are able to open up JTB agencies where none exist already; and
3 specialists who do not take up the travel-agency option or do not join a converter scheme may be offered the alternative of long-term 'shukko' in an affiliate.

To come now to retirement practice in smaller and medium-sized companies, we shall take the example of a metal-working firm with a work force of about 180 employees full-time and 40 part-time. It is located in a town near Kyoto and manufactures metal working-parts and frames (Fujimura, 1994, p. 38). It has adopted a mandatory retirement age at 60 years and over the next 20 years roughly 60 employees will be retiring at that age. Six retiree-workers are with the company at present and the latter hopes to be able to offer re-employment to all retirees desirous of working on. When workers are in their late 40s, the firm reviews their situation and decides on the best mix of functions which will carry them through without transferring from the workplace until they are 65. Thus a smooth transition from working-life to retirement is achieved through prospective end-of-career planning for older workers based on the following three principles:

1 that the workplace of older workers be approached from the standpoint of its long-term suitability over a period of from 10 to 20 years;
2 that no worker should normally be moved from a workplace after the age of 55; and
3 that all members of the firm community should be encouraged to create an atmosphere within the workplace conducive to the occupational well-being of older workers.

9.3 Potential for gradual retirement and recommendations

One can hardly overstress the importance of properly integrating public and company policies for promoting the employment of older people and gradual retirement. In Japan the prospects in this area look rather bright, and the reason for such optimism is success in the recent past in switching over from a 55 to a 60 year age-limit for retirement, something which, thanks to the combined impact of legislation, administrative guidance and company efforts, has been achieved in most firms over a relatively short 20-year period. The Japanese Government has pursued an active policy for promoting the employment of older workers and gradual retirement through recent reforms of social insurance, especially of pension and unemployment insurance. In general, companies are now offering a range of work options to older employees, the big ones, as we have seen, through their networks of affiliates and in companies with whom they have strong business connections; the smaller and middle-sized ones, because of their need for the skills older workers can supply and through function adjustment and intelligent use of information networks and of the 'silvercentre' desks in employment agencies and the like. Finally workplace transfer, i.e. employment flexibility, between similar kinds of job obviates to some extent the costs of retraining and seems to have merits for company and employee alike.

At the macroeconomic level, the Government has taken important steps by designing policies to promote environmental and infrastructural improvements facilitating the employment of elderly workers. Of note among these measures have been:

1 support with adjustment costs for older workers, for example, of vocational retraining inside and outside the firm;
2 expansion of the information on employment for older workers available in public networks and facilities;
3 promotion of policies for shortening work hours;
4 expansion of the subsidy policy for employment for older workers;
5 extension of State pension coverage to include a variety of work styles; and
6 establishment of social acceptance of, and a qualifications system for, the skills of older workers.

These measures will need to be reinforced in the years to come.

At the microeconomic level, the following company measures and approaches have proved important but will also need to be extended in the future:

1 a willingness and growing need to make jobs available to older people, to develop technology which is older worker 'friendly', and to provide workplaces where efficient use can be made of the older worker's high skills;
2 creation of a flexible system of employment allowing for shorter work hours and atypical schedules;

3 provision of an adjusted environment for older workers;
4 provision of retraining and skills development programmes;
5 design of wage and pension allowance schemes to encourage employment of older workers; and
6 production of appropriate personnel management policies and techniques.

And last, but by no means least, at the inter-company level, improvement of the portability of pension benefits.

References

Fujimura, H. (1994), 'A New Concept of Personnel Management in Japanese Firms', *Nihon Rôdô Kenkyû Zasshi* (The Monthly Journal of the Japan Institute of Labour), no. 414, pp. 30-41.

Japan Institute of Life Insurance (JILI) (1993), *Survey on Employees' Benefit Plan*, JILI, Tokyo.

Life Design Institute (LDI) (1994), *Kigyô Nenkin Hakusho 1994* (White Paper on Corporate Pension 1994), Nihon Keizai Shinbun, Tokyo.

Shimowada, I. (1992), 'Aging and the Four Pillars in Japan', *The Geneva Papers on Risk and Insurance*, vol. 17 (62), pp. 40-80.

Takada, K. (1994), 'What is the Future of Employment for Older People', *The Monthly Journal of the Japan Institute of Labour*, no. 414, pp. 13-21.

Yamaguchi, K. (1994), *Kôreisha no Koyô-Shûgyô Taisaku* (Recent Reforms of Employment Policy for Older People), *Shûkan Shakai Hoshô* (Weekly Social Security), no. 1814, pp. 22-25.

10 Gradual retirement in the United States: macro issues and policies

Yung-Ping Chen[1]

A three-legged stool, comprising social security, occupational pensions, and individual savings, has been the metaphor widely used to symbolise the sources of income to older people in the United States. Social security is designed to provide an income protection floor, and pensions and income from assets are meant to be important supplements to it. In fact, however, employment is another major source of income.

According to the latest available statistics, the proportions of those aged 65 and over who received income from these major sources in 1992 were (table 10.1 and Grad, 1994):
- social security 92 per cent;
- asset income 67 per cent;
- occupational pensions 45 per cent
  (private pensions 31 per cent);
- employment income 20 per cent.

The above sources of income did not contribute equally to the total income of the elderly, however. The relative shares of those sources in the total income in 1992 were (table 10.2 and Grad, 1994):
- social security 40 per cent;
- asset income 21 per cent;
- occupational pensions 20 per cent
  (private pensions 10 per cent);
- employment income 17 per cent.

These sources of income essentially reflect what has been proposed by the International Association for the Study of Insurance Economics (the Geneva Association) in its research programme on work and retirement, called 'Four Pillars' (Reday-Mulvey, 1990; Giarini and Stahel, 1993).

This chapter reviews the changing importance of these sources in the past and discusses some of the more significant factors affecting these income-generating mechanisms in the future. It then considers the long-range financial problem of social security, describes the labour market situation of older people, and points to some of the preconditions for implementing gradual retirement.

10.1 Relative roles of income sources

During the last three decades, important developments have occurred in the relative contributions of the various sources from which older persons derive income.

Table 10.1
Sources of income of those aged 65 and over in the United States, 1962-1992, selected years

Years	Social security (%)	Asset income (%)	Occupational pensions* (%)	Employment income (%)	Public assistance (%)
1962	69	54	18	36	14
1967	86	50	22	27	12
1971	87	49	23	31	10
1976	89	56	31	25	11
1978	90	62	32	25	9
1980	90	66	34	23	10
1982	90	68	35	22	8
1984	91	68	38	21	9
1986	91	67	40	20	7
1988	92	68	42	22	7
1990	92	69	44	22	7
1992	92	67	45	20	7

* Includes private pensions or annuities, government employee pensions, Railroad Retirement, and Individual Retirement Accounts, Keogh plans, and 401(k) accounts.
Source: SSA 1994, p. 20.

Social security (1st pillar)

Passed in 1935, the original social security programme was expanded to include survivors insurance in 1939 and disability insurance in 1956. These three components – old age, survivors, and disability insurance (OASDI) – are most often what is meant by social security.

During the last 30 years, social security has continued to gain in importance. Whereas in 1962, 69 per cent of the aged received income from it, in 1992, 92 per cent of them did (table 10.1). As regards social security's role in the total income of the older population, its contribution has also risen, from 31 per cent in 1962 to 40 per cent in 1992 (table 10.2).

Table 10.2
Shares of income of those aged 65 and over in the United States from various sources, 1962-1992, selected years

Years	Social security (%)	Asset income (%)	Occupational pensions* (%)	Employment income (%)	Public assistance (%)
1962	31	16	9	28	16
1967	34	15	12	29	10
1976	39	18	16	23	4
1978	38	19	16	23	4
1980	39	22	16	19	4
1982	39	25	15	18	3
1984	38	28	15	16	3
1986	38	26	16	17	3
1988	38	25	17	17	3
1990	36	24	18	18	3
1992	40	21	20	17	3

* Includes private pensions or annuities, government employee pensions, Railroad Retirement, and Individual Retirement Accounts, Keogh plans, and 401(k) accounts.
Source: SSA, 1994, p. 22.

Since the 1983 amendments, a portion of OASDI benefits has been included in taxable income for higher-income taxpayers, which reduces the relative importance of this income source to them. In addition, under current laws, the normal retirement age for full benefits will be gradually raised to 66 by 2009 and to 67 by 2027. After it has reached age 67, early retirement benefits commencing at 62 will be reduced to 70 per cent of full benefits, as compared to 80 per cent at present. These provisions will combine to reduce social security benefits in the future below what they would have been if the normal retirement age had remained unchanged.

Occupational pensions (2nd pillar)

Occupational pensions include private pension plans as well as federal, state and local government employee pension systems. As an income source, occupational pensions' relative importance has increased: from 18 per cent of older persons receiving them in 1962 to some 45 per cent in 1992 (table 10.1). These pensions accounted for 9 per cent of the total income of the elderly in 1962 and 20 per cent in 1992 (table 10.2).

In the future, government employee pensions as an income source will be reduced by the social security amendments of 1983, which mandated social security coverage for new federal employees beginning in 1984; the resulting supplementary civil service retirement plan naturally provides lower benefits than the plan applicable to 'old' employees. This legislation also prohibits state and local governments, which had previously elected coverage, from terminating coverage under social security for their employees and allows state and local governments that had withdrawn from social security to rejoin.

A major portion of occupational pensions consists of private pension plans. These have also gained in relative importance in the last three decades. Whereas in 1962 only 9 per cent of older people had private pension income, 31 per cent had such income in 1992. The relative importance of this income source has likewise increased, accounting for 5 per cent of total income of all aged units in 1962 and for 10 per cent in 1992 (Grad, 1994).

Private pension plans grew throughout the 1970s, but future growth in coverage for workers not yet covered is expected to be slower for several reasons:
1 the most accessible groups of workers (such as those in manufacturing, mining, and the transportation industry, and in large establishments) have already been covered;
2 industries with traditionally high pension coverage are expected to employ a declining share of workers, whereas industries with traditionally low pension coverage are expected to increase their share of workers; and
3 the large proportion of workers, primarily in small- and medium-sized businesses, will continue to find it difficult to obtain coverage (Andrews and Mitchell, 1986; Chen, 1985).

Although there has been a trend in recent years toward greater pension-receipt rates for women and minorities, a confluence of developments in the economy and the labour market does not bode well for the future of private pensions as a source of retirement income for many (Chen, 1995).

First, the decrease in the proportion of workers in manufacturing and the rising percentage of workers in low-paying service jobs implies less pension participation, because pensions are less prevalent in service fields than in industry.

Second, the growing importance of (voluntary) part-time employment and the movement toward 'contracting out' of work suggest that a lower percentage of the work force will be eligible for the retirement benefits earned by full-time employees.

Third, the movement from defined-benefit to defined-contribution pension plans will result in less predictable retirement income. With defined-contribution plans, investment risk shifts to the employee, making future benefit levels more uncertain.

And fourth, the downsizing of corporate America in recent years has compressed the ranks of middle management, just as women and minorities were making their way to that tier of business. All of this points to a future in which the role of pensions in providing retirement income may be even less dependable than it is at present.

Asset income (3rd pillar)

Over the past three decades, income from assets has comprised a growing proportion of older persons' total income, increasing from 16 per cent in 1962 to 21 per cent in 1992 (table 10.2). Fifty-four per cent of the elderly received income from this source in 1962, while in 1992 as many as 67 per cent of them did (table 10.1). In addition, asset income is the most important source for the highest income group.

Even though asset income represented an important percentage of the total income of the high-income aged, and even though a large proportion of the aged derived income from this source, the median amounts of asset income were quite low. One major reason is the typically small or modest value of their liquid or financial assets (Radner, 1988). Another problem is the non-liquid nature of home equity.

There now exist some tax-induced mechanisms to encourage retirement savings, such as the individual retirement account (IRA). Authorised in the Employee Retirement Income Security Act of 1974 (ERISA) and effective as of 1975, IRAs were created as tax incentives for generating retirement income to supplement social security and pension benefits. Although IRAs had been rather popular, the Tax Reform Act of 1986, which imposed restrictions on their use, dampened interest in and reduced the use of this savings vehicle for retirement.

Employment income (4th pillar)

Employment as a source of income for the elderly has clearly declined during the past three decades. Whereas 36 per cent of the older population had earnings in 1962, only 20 per cent of them did in 1992 (table 10.1). While earnings represented 28 per cent of total income of all older persons in 1962, they accounted for only 17 per cent of their total income in 1992 (table 10.2).

Earnings may contribute less to the total income of the aged in the future if participation of older persons in the labour force continues to decline and the early retirement trend continues to accelerate. However, it is also possible that earnings may become a more important income source if the elderly remain in the work force longer as a means of enhancing their income position during inflationary times. In addition, if the health status of older persons improves with the decline in the mortality rate, then they may wish to work longer. Finally, low birth rates in recent years and the low rates projected for the future will result in a smaller labour force (as defined by conventional ages) in the future. The aged may well be called on to work longer. Whether or not older people would continue to be labour force participants depends on a number of factors affecting the supply of and demand for older workers, a subject to be discussed later in this chapter.

However, it appears appropriate to note here one of the key similarities and differences between employment as an income source for older persons in the United States and employment as the fourth pillar of income. They are similar since employment is in both cases a source of income in old age. But they are also different. The fourth pillar concept envisions income from part-time employment with partial pensions, while employment income in the USA comes from both full-time and part-time work, with social security benefits withheld from some people for earnings exceeding a certain level per year, but not under a system of part-time employment with partial pensions.

The enduring importance of social security

The preceding review of income sources suggests that, under existing institutional arrangements and people's behavioural responses to them, much uncertainty surrounds individual savings, employer pensions, and employment as major contributors to the income of the elderly. Despite taxability of its benefits to some recipients and postponement of the normal retirement age, social security will continue to play a significant role in providing income to older persons. This would be especially true for many elders, particularly women and those within racial minorities, for whom, unfortunately, the pension leg and/or the saving leg are weak (Chen, 1995). For example, in 1992, while one in three whites (34 per cent) received private pensions, one in six blacks or Hispanics (17 per cent) received such income. Of whites, 17 per cent had income from government employee and railroad retirement programmes, compared to only 12 per cent of blacks and 7 per cent Hispanics.

Income received from assets was even more disparate: in 1992, 72 per cent of older whites had asset income, compared to 34 per cent of Hispanics and 26 per cent of blacks. Many fewer minority retirees than white retirees received income from individual savings because their generally low earnings when they were working hinder their ability to accumulate assets as a source of supplementary income in retirement.

Because of the singularly important role social security plays in the provision of income to older people, attention is now turned to its long-range financial problem.

10.2 Social security's long-range financing problem

A traditional pay-as-you-go social security programme entails intergenerational transfers. This works well when the population and economy are growing to the extent that, over a long period of time, taxes paid by workers and their employers are rising faster or at least keep pace with benefit payments to retirees and other beneficiaries. At this time, however, social security programmes in many countries are showing, or are projected to show, financial strain as a result of slow economic growth and population aging.

Scope of the financing problems

In its most recent (1995) report, the social security Board of Trustees indicates that, although the combined Old Age, Survivors, and Disability Insurance programme (OASDI) is actuarially sound in the short range (10 years), it is not in the long range (75 years). Under the intermediate assumptions, the long-range actuarial deficit for the period 1995 through 2069 is estimated at 2.17 per cent of taxable payroll. The Board also estimates that the OASDI trust funds will be exhausted in the year 2030. This does not mean that social security will cease to exist in 2030 and thereafter, however.

Because there will still be tax revenue based on the current 6.20 per cent rate on taxable payroll, paid at this rate by both employees and employers, benefits will continue to be paid; but the revenue will be insufficient to pay all the benefits on a timely basis as promised under present law. For example, the tax revenue in 2030 will amount to 75 per cent of what is required to pay benefits in full for that year if nothing is done to shore up the programme's finances. Mathematically, full social security benefits can be assured for the long range if the employee and employer payroll tax rates are each raised to 7.285 per cent from the present 6.20 per cent rate, for each year from 1995 through 2069. Many proposals have been advanced to deal with the deficit, most involving a combination of benefit reduction and tax increase. Among them, postponement of the normal retirement age for receiving full social security benefits is frequently suggested because of the role the demographic factor plays in financing these benefits.

Importance of the 'demographic load'

A large number of factors affect income and outgo under social security. One major factor is the 'demographic load,' the ratio of beneficiaries to workers/

taxpayers (Trowbridge, 1986). In 1955, this factor was about 0.077, indicating that benefits were being paid on 77 beneficiary accounts for every 1,000 taxpayer accounts. By 1984, the demographic load had increased to 0.255, meaning that benefits were being paid on 255 accounts for every 1,000 accounts on which taxes were being collected. The tripling of the programme costs during the 1955-1984 period resulted mostly from the fact that the rise in the number of beneficiaries was much more rapid than the increase in the number of workers covered (Bayo, Glanz, and Trowbridge 1986). In the past, the rapid rise in the number of beneficiaries resulted more from increases in the proportion of the aged becoming eligible for retirement benefits than from the expansion of the aged population.

The demographic load is projected to be at the 0.250 to 0.260 level until the turn of the century. After the turn of the century, the demographic load is projected to increase by over 80 per cent over the long range – to a level of about 0.450 to 0.460. For the future, the large estimated increases in the number of beneficiaries will be primarily the result of the rapid growth in the size of the aged population, despite the higher normal retirement age enacted in 1983. It follows then that keeping OASDI costs as a percentage of taxable payroll from increasing significantly will need to address the rapid growth in the number of beneficiaries relative to the number of workers. Raising the age of normal retirement further is one way to moderate the rise in benefit payments.

Raising normal retirement age

Before the 1983 amendments to the social security Act, the long-range actuarial deficit was estimated at 2.09 per cent of taxable payroll in 1982. The 1983 law enacted a large number of changes, which, in combination, removed the entire amount of the estimated shortfall for the long-range period, 1983 to 2057. Among the major changes was raising the normal retirement age gradually and eventually to age 67 by 2027, which removed one third of the projected actuarial deficit (U.S. House of Representatives, 1983).

Further increases in the normal retirement age have been explored. For example, the 1991 Advisory Council on social security staff entertained several possibilities for changing the normal retirement age (Goss, 1990). Several bills were introduced in the 103rd Congress, for example, by Representative Dan Rostenkowski and by Representative J.J. Pickle. The former would raise the normal retirement age from 65 to 67 in 2016 instead of 2027 as now scheduled. Under the latter, the normal retirement age would be gradually increased from 65 to 70 by 2037. In the current 104th Congress, Senator Bob Kerrey (Democrat of Nebraska) and Senator Alan K. Simpson (Republican of Wyoming) recently (May 1995) introduced legislation to reform social security, including raising the normal retirement age to 70 (from the scheduled increase to 67) which would not affect anyone over the age of 51 today (i.e. affecting only those born in 1944 or later).

Will more older people remain workers when the normal retirement age is postponed? Raising the normal retirement age might lead to a larger supply of workers at older ages. But are all able elderly workers willing workers? Further, supply alone does not a market make; the demand side of the labour force equation must also be examined. What is the labour market situation of older people?

10.3 Labour force situation of older people

Labour force participation rates

In 1993, more than 52 million Americans were older than age 55, 60 per cent of whom were age 65 or over (Leavitt and Crown, 1994). Most of them were labour force participants, defined as persons willing and able to work whether employed or unemployed currently. The average civilian labour force participation rate was 56.4 per cent for those aged 55-64 and 11.3 per cent for those in the 65 and over population (U.S. Department of Labor, 1994).

Labour force participation rates declined steadily from nearly 80 per cent for the age 50-54 group to just over 4 per cent for those over the age of 75. The most precipitous decline in labour force participation occurs during the age 55-64 group, but the drop continues after age 65. Some 20 per cent of the age 65-69 population continues to work, despite the fact that the normal retirement age under social security is 65.

Labour force participation rates for the age 65 and over population have declined steadily since 1950, from 28.1 per cent to 11.3 per cent in 1993. The decline among this population resulted from a steep drop in male participation. Male participation rates in 1993 were approximately one third the rates in 1950, with female participation rates remaining at 10 per cent or lower during 1950-1993 (U.S. Department of Labor, 1994; Leavitt and Crown, 1994).

In 1993, while 86 per cent of workers aged 45 to 64 worked full-time, 47 per cent of those aged 65 or older did (U.S. Department of Labor, 1994). Workers may be working part-time voluntarily or due to insufficient labour demand for full-time work. Nearly half of workers aged 65 and over worked part-time voluntarily, compared to less than 10 per cent of those aged 45-64. Among workers aged 65 and over, voluntary part-time work is common for both males (44 per cent) and females (54 per cent).

Reasons for working

Workers work for a variety of reasons and these reasons change as workers grow older. At ages 40-49, workers most often mention (in descending order) the need for income, enjoying work, feeling useful, being productive, work as an obligation, and maintaining health insurance. At ages 50-62, the most common reasons are enjoying work and feeling useful, followed by the need for income, being productive, work as an obligation, and maintaining health insurance. At age 63 and over, enjoying work is the most frequently cited reason, followed by feeling useful, being productive, work as an obligation, and maintaining health insurance, with the need for income least often mentioned (U.S. Department of Labor, 1989).

Potential older workers

In 1989 the Commonwealth Fund conducted a survey of plans and preferences on work and retirement of older Americans. A major conclusion was that many were willing and able to work longer than they currently did. It was estimated that between one and two million retirees would be willing to work longer, representing 13 to 23 per cent of all retired workers among men aged 50-64 and women aged 50-59. Of those not yet retired, approximately one million workers who expected to have to stop working before they wanted to represented about 12 per cent of those older employees. Additionally, five million who claimed they would work longer under hypothetical scenarios (including fewer hours and less responsibility) was over one half of this employed cohort (Quinn and Burkhauser, 1993).

Social security and older workers

Workers who want to retire gradually with an interim period of part-time employment face a number of obstacles. While pension plans rarely allow a beneficiary to continue working for the same firm, social security lowers benefits for those who earn beyond an allowable amount ($11,280 in 1995) – the earnings test. Older workers who lose some benefits (at the rate of $1 for every $3 of earnings) are being compensated with the delayed retirement credit (DRC). In other words, DRC increases their future benefits. The DRC rate is 4.5 per cent for persons born in 1929 or 1930. This is scheduled to rise to 8 per cent for those born in 1943 or later. When DRC is at the rate of 8 per cent per year, the compensation will become actuarially fair – what one doesn't receive today, one will receive tomorrow. However, for all those born before 1943 (thus attaining the normal retirement age before the year 2009), the compensation is actuarially unfair – future increases in benefits are less, in present value terms, than the current reductions in benefits. Therefore, the earnings test presents considerable work disincentives to persons with earnings beyond the annual exempt amount. These earnings not only result in a loss of some social security benefits, but also the payment of higher federal and state income taxes in addition to payroll taxes for social security and medicare (Myers, 1995).

10.4 Requisite conditions for gradual retirement

Slow economic growth and aging of the population have raised concerns about the ability of society to finance pensions (public and private) and health services for older Americans. In addition, projections of a slower growth in the labour force (in the traditional ages) resulting from population aging have led to concerns about labour force shortages in the future.

One way of resolving these problems may well be to prolong the working life of older people. Postponing the normal retirement age and the desire of older people to work part-time (as expressed in opinion surveys) would seem to provide a recipe for gradual retirement. And partial pensions for partial retirement may be a practicable approach.

Supply of and demand for older workers

For policies and programmes to expand employment opportunities, both supply and demand conditions in the labour market need to be considered. On the supply side, many complex factors, physical, psychological, and economic, determine the decision by individuals to continue working or to retire. Declining health, tiring of work, and sufficient financial incentives for retirement have led many to retire. On the other hand, the need for income, boredom with retirement, and an hospitable working environment may induce others to remain or re-enter the work force.

As far as the demand side of the labour force equation is concerned, many forces influence employers' decision to retain or retire older workers. The state of the economy and concern with productivity are important factors in determining the level of the demand for older workers.

Need for institutional and attitudinal changes

Assuming willingness of older workers to remain in the labour market, pension and social security provisions that offer early retirement incentives (or work disincentives) should be eliminated. For example, the delayed retirement credit under social security should be made actuarially fair. In order to accommodate workers in general and older workers in particular, flexible work schedules and retraining for improving existing skills or training for different skills should be made more widely and systematically available.

Since a larger supply of labour can only be accommodated by a greater demand for labour, strong and sustainable economic growth is essential. Moreover, the nature of the jobs available is very important. If indeed part-time jobs are what are needed to implement partial pensions, then willingness of employers to create such opportunities and cooperation of full-time workers to support them will be necessary.

Implementing gradual retirement by means of partial pensions will require major changes under social security and employer pension programmes. For example, a major incongruence exists in the retirement policies under social security and private pension plans. The US government attempts to encourage workers to postpone their retirement by raising the normal retirement age. But businesses continue to entice their employees to retire by early retirement incentive programmes (Schieber, 1993). Any major change requires time. In addition, partial pensions, at least as they are used in Sweden and other countries, require the creation of part-time jobs. This, too, will take time. However, since any journey begins with the first step, debate on how best to implement gradual retirement in the United States through a system of part-time work with partial pensions must now begin.

Note

1 Helpful discussions with Stephen C. Goss and Robert J. Myers are gratefully acknowledged.

References

Andrews, E.S. and O.S. Mitchell (1986), 'The Current and Future Role of Pensions in Old Age Economic Security', *Benefits Quarterly*, vol. 2, no. 2, pp. 27-35.

Bayo, F.R., M.P. Glanz and C.L. Trowbridge (1986), 'Components of Trends in Social Security Costs', *Transactions of the Society of Actuaries*, 38, pp. 7-42. (Preprinted in Chen, Y.P. and G.F. Rohrlich (eds.) *Checks and Balances in Social Security*, University Press of America, Lanham and London, pp. 320-357.

Chen, Y.P. (1985), 'Economic Status of the Aging' in Binstock, R.H. and E. Shanas (eds.), *Handbook of Aging and the Social Sciences*, Van Nostrand Reinhold, New York, pp. 641-665.

Chen, Y.P. (1995), 'Income Security a Key Concern for Elders', *Aging Today*, American Society on Aging, January/February, p. 7, 10.

Giarini, O. and W.R. Stahel (1993), *The Limits to Certainty*, Kluwer Academic Publishers, Dordrecht.

Goss, S.C. (1990), *Estimated Long-range OASDI Financial Effects of Advisory Council Staff Proposals*, Memorandum to Virginia Reno, Advisory Council Staff, October 17.

Grad, S. (1994), *Income of the Population 55 or Older, 1992* (Social Security Administration, Washington, D.C., SSA Publication no. 13-11871), May, p. 1.

Leavitt, T.D. and W.H. Crown (1994), *Labor Force Characteristics of Older Americans*, Manuscript, December.

Myers, R.J. (1995), *Statement on the Social Security Earnings Test*, Subcommittee on Social Security, Committee on Ways and Means, U.S. House of Representatives, January 9.

Public Trustees of the Social Security Board of Trustees (1995), *1995 Annual Report of the Federal Old Age and Survivors Insurance and Disability Insurance Trust Fund.*

Quinn, J.F. and R.V. Burkhauser (1993), 'Labor Market Obstacles to Aging Productivity' in Bass, S.A., F.G. Caro and Y.P. Chen (eds.), *Achieving A Productive Aging Society*, Auburn House, Westport, CT/London, pp. 43-59.

Radner, D.B. (1988), *The Wealth of the Aged and Nonaged*, 1984, Office of Research and Statistics Working Paper Series, no. 36 (Social Security Administration, Washington, D.C.).

Reday-Mulvey, G. (1990), 'Work and Retirement; Future Prospects for the Baby-boom Generation', *The Geneva Papers on Risk and Insurance*, no. 55, pp. 100-114.

Schieber, S.J. (1993), 'Retirement policy schizophrenia: Does America want its elderly to work or retire?', *Contingencies*, March/April, pp. 20-24.

ssa (1994), *Income of the Aged Chartbook*, 1992, Social Security Administration, Washington, D.C., ssa Publication no. 13-11727, December, 20,22.

Social Security and Medicare Boards of Trustees (1995), *Status of the Social Security and Medicare Programs: A summary of The 1995 Annual Reports*, Washington, D.C., April.

Trowbridge, C.L. (1986), 'Principal Indicators of Prospective Change in Social Security Costs' in Chen, Y.P. and G.F. Rohrlich (eds.), *Checks and Balances in Social Security*, University Press of America, Lanham and London, pp. 61-70.

U.S. Department of Labor, Bureau of Labor Statistics (1994), *Employment and Earnings*, U.S. Government Printing Office, Washington, D.C., January.

U.S. Department of Labor (1989), *Older Worker Task Force: Key Policy Issues for the Future*, Report to the Secretary of Labor, U.S. Government Printing Office, Washington, D.C.

U.S. House of Representatives, Committee on Ways and Means (1983), *Actuarial Cost Estimates of the Effects of Public Law 98-21 on the Old Age, Survivors and Disability Insurance and Hospital Insurance Programs*, U.S. Government Printing Office, Washington, D.C., September 8.

11 Older worker voluntary part-time employment in the United States: selected micro aspects

Harold L. Sheppard

11.1 Recent trends

What are the facts about trends, if any, in part-time employment in the United States over the past several years? The emphasis in this chapter is on voluntary part-time employment (VPT), especially as a proportion of all employed Americans. Our attention should be on voluntary part-time employment on the assumption that it is, to a great extent, a matter of free and unfettered choice. Admittedly, there are large numbers of persons working part-time on an involuntary basis, primarily because of a general lack of full-time jobs. But results of various surveys, confirmed more recently by Commonwealth Fund research reports, showed that most older workers prefer, seek, and many find part-time employment, and on a voluntary basis. But that is not the focus of this chapter.

An important 'micro'-nuance of VPT, in my opinion, lies in a concentration of fine-tuned age differences, with gender taken into consideration at the same time; and in changes over several years in these differences, for each of these age/gender categories. Tables 11.1, 11.2, and 11.3, form the basis of this section of the chapter.

First of all, it is absolutely necessary to consider separately the information on men and women. Combining these two gender categories obscures substantial empirical realities and policy implications. Table 11.1 suggests that overall, including even the total working population of men 16 and older, there has been a gradual rise in male VPT. While the percentages are low (slightly over

8 per cent as of 1993), we are talking about more than five million men working part-time on a voluntary basis.

Table 11.1

Voluntary part-time employment in the United States as a per cent of all male workers, by age, 1976-1993

Year	16 +	25-54	55-59	60-64	65 +
1976	7.7	1.85	3.00	8.00	41.4
1979	7.6	1.93	3.20	8.42	43.3
1982	7.7	2.11	3.18	9.00	43.9
1985	7.5	2.15	3.77	10.15	43.4
1988	7.9	2.35	4.67	12.62	42.5
1991	7.8	2.46	4.37	12.76	44.3
1993	8.1	2.67	5.09	13.30	44.2

Figures refer to voluntary part-time workers as a per cent of all employed.
Source: Bureau of Labor Statistics, U.S. Department of Labor.

Even in the primary, core age-group of any labour force, those 25-54, there has been an increase, albeit with very low percentages. We should least expect any large proportion in this core working-age-group, but the fact that it has been increasing steadily bears watching over the next several years.

In this core group, there is no doubt that voluntary part-time employment is eminently the domain of women. However, over the seventeen-year period covered in this analysis, that title has been steadily diminishing. From 1976 to 1993, the female proportion of all employed 25-54 year-old VPTs declined from 87.5 to 83.1 per cent. Starting in 1976, 12.5 per cent of the core VPT work force consisted of men, and their proportion increased steadily over the ensuing seventeen years to 16.9 per cent by 1993. And yet we know very little about the characteristics, the motives, and other dimensions of that increasing male proportion now working on a part-time basis voluntarily.

The phenomenon may be a reflection of a sort of phased retirement among men, beginning in the later years of this 25-54 year-old age-group. That is, they are now in the position of leaving full-time work, thanks perhaps to very-early-retirement pension opportunities in their regular place of employment, which allows them a chance to remain in the paid labour force, but only on a part-time basis – and by choice. But this is only speculation at this time. In the relatively 'young-old' group of men aged 55-59 years old, VPT stood at 5.1 per cent in 1993, reflecting a modest rate of increase since 1976. The greatest rate of increase, however, shows up in the case of the 60-64 year-old population, nearly 6 per cent, using a more technical measure of rates of increase in percentages. Currently, two out of every 15 working men are working voluntarily on a part-time basis. In 1976, the ratio was only about one out of every thirty-three.

Finally, as we should expect, the highest proportions of VPT are to be found in the 65-plus group. The fact that the increase over time has not been dramatic – from 41 to 44 per cent – might be due partly to the fact that this category, the 65-plus population, is itself aging; the proportion of the very-old is becoming a greater segment of that group, a segment which traditionally has a lower percentage in the active population. We need more fine-tuned data for future analyses, policy analysis, and programme development (e.g. 65-69; 70-74; 75-79; and 80 and older).

Table 11.2
Voluntary part-time employment in the United States as a per cent of all female workers, by age, 1976-1993

Year	16 +	25-54	55-59	60-64	65 +
1976	24.1	20.6	19.3	26.5	55.2
1979	23.4	19.6	20.3	27.1	55.7
1982	22.9	18.8	19.7	27.7	55.1
1985	21.7	17.6	20.4	27.0	56.2
1988	21.8	17.5	21.8	28.8	55.3
1991	21.5	16.6	20.6	30.5	55.9
1993	20.7	15.7	18.5	30.3	56.5

Source: Bureau of Labor Statistics, U.S. Department of Labor.

In the case of women, we find somewhat contrasting trends, when compared to those characterising men. First of all the percentage of VPT has been declining for the total employed population as a whole; also for the primary core working-age employed group (25-54); and it has remained relatively unchanged over the seventeen years represented in table 11.2. On the other hand, there has been an increase in VPT per cent in the 60-64 years-old group of women, from 27 to 30 per cent. But for the oldest category shown in that table, we see hardly any increase in VPT per cent. Again, the caveat stated above about the limitations of a '65-plus' category applies here to women as well.

Table 11.3 provides a comparison between men and women in the different age-groups over the seventeen-year period. It shows, for example, the contrasting trend directions in VPT per cent. In brief, these contrasts are as follows:
– overall, VPT is increasing among men, while decreasing among women;
– this is occurring even in the primary, core working age-groups;

- an increase in the percentage of VPT for men 55-59, with a plateauing for women of the same ages;
- increases for the 60-years old of both genders, with the rate of increase slightly greater among the men; and
- hardly any change for women 65-plus; but a relatively high rate of increase among men.

Table 11.3

Gender differences in voluntary part-time work trends in the United States, by age, 1976-1993

Age	1976	1979	1982	1985	1988	1991	1993
16+							
M	7.7	7.6	7.7	7.5	7.9	7.8	8.1
F	24.1	23.4	22.9	21.7	21.8	21.5	20.7
25-54							
M	1.85	1.93	2.11	2.15	2.35	2.46	2.67
F	20.6	19.6	18.8	17.6	17.5	16.6	15.7
55-59							
M	3.00	3.20	3.18	3.77	4.67	4.37	5.09
F	19.3	20.3	19.7	20.4	21.8	20.6	18.5
60-64							
M	8.00	8.42	9.00	10.2	12.6	12.8	13.3
F	26.5	27.1	27.7	27.0	28.6	30.5	30.3
65+							
M	41.4	43.3	43.9	43.4	42.5	44.3	44.2
F	55.2	55.7	55.1	56.2	55.3	55.9	56.5

Source: Bureau of Labor Statistics, U.S. Department of Labor.

Part-time employment as a percentage of all employed Americans, however, has not been increasing. Involuntary part-time employment rises and falls in accordance with general unemployment-rate conditions. As for voluntary part-time employment, a focus of this chapter, it actually has declined as a percentage of all Americans at work. The more relevant kinds of data, however, are with respect to specific age-gender classifications, as discussed above. For specific age-gender categories, voluntary part-time employment has been on the rise, as a proportion of all persons in those categories.

11.2 An example of best practice in part-time for older workers

The classical, ideal case of part-time work in America that is cited more frequently than any other is the Travelers Insurance Group story. Essentially, it consists of the re-employment of the company's own retirees on a regular, permanent, part-time basis, and with the right to continue a full Travelers pension. This right did not prevail until the Board of Directors of the company formally made changes in the pension rules and regulations to make such pension receipt possible. It was partly after a survey of Travelers' recent retirees showing their keen desire to continue working, but on a part-time basis, at their former place of employment, that the new policy was introduced. This particular case is another concrete example of survey findings revealing that if older workers do want to continue working after 'retirement,' but on a part-time basis, they would much prefer to do so with their previous employer. There is little systematic evidence, however, one way or the other, concerning the extent to which VPTS work in the place of their pre-retirement employment.

In greater detail, there are several ways in which the Travelers Insurance Group stands out as far as its policies and programmes for the utilisation of older workers are concerned. First, and unlike many other employers, this programme employs on a part-time basis its own retirees, as well as some retirees from other insurance companies when needed. 'Part-time' in this case may include some persons working on a full-time basis, but not for a full twelve months. The use of for-profit 'temps' agencies is much more frequent and typical among the vast majority of other employers.

The general tendency of employers not to re-employ their retirees on a part-time basis should be the basis for further policy scrutiny.

Second, the Travelers example is not simply a case of reaching out for retirees only on a seasonal basis, or only when the demand for labour may be unexpectedly high. The Travelers Group actually employs many of such persons on an almost yearround, permanent basis.

Third, such part-time re-employment retirees are allowed to continue receipt of their regular pensions, as long as they work no more than roughly 1,000 hours per year, i.e. on a maximum half-time basis. Retirees from other organisations become eligible after 500 hours per year for vacation pay and limited health insurance benefits, under Travelers.

Fourth, the numbers of such workers are substantial, at least when compared to the preponderance of other employers known for their positive older worker programmes. At the time of a mid-1991 report by ICF, Inc. (McNaught *et al.*, 1989) for the Commonwealth Fund, there were slightly more than 400 such persons, and more than three fifths were themselves retirees from Travelers. These figures were applicable for any given week. By definition, the total number would be higher when the full twelve-months period is considered.

From the standpoint of the individual workers themselves, the average age of whom was 67 at time of the study, their hourly wages are higher than what they typically could obtain through other employment avenues. For the ex-Travelers retirees alone, the programme provides some degree of psychological compensation. Re-employment in familiar circumstances associated with positive experiences of the past is welcomed by them.

The benefits to Travelers itself, on the financial side, are also positive, in that the recruitment costs are obviously much lower than if outside, commercial temporary agencies were used. In addition, lower 'learning curve' costs are incurred, through the re-employment of former Travelers employees. The McNaught *et al.* (1989) study found that when comparisons were made between the latter and retirees from outside agencies (a recruitment policy re-initiated), the company incurred a net savings of $870,000, as of 1989.

Just as important, in the roughly 20 types of jobs filled by this programme's employees, the study found that the 'TravTemps' workers exhibited no less productivity than the more permanent, full-time employees.

As stated above, the average age of these permanent part-time workers formerly employed full-time at Travelers was 67. Seventy per cent were women. The types of their jobs were heavily unskilled production tasks (more than two fifths); one sixth were receptionists/typists; another sixth were data entry operatives; one eighth, in administrative support positions; and the balance were distributed among secretarial, professional, word processing, and technical occupations.

11.3 Other examples of part-time employment

Examples of acceptable part-time and other non-traditional work-time allocations abound. Some of these can be found in an inventory kept up-to-date by the American Association for Retired Persons' National Older Workers Information System (NOWIS).

One such example involves more than just one enterprise as an employer. A nationwide Operation ABLE (Abilities Based on Long Experience), originating in Chicago, is special in that it 'prepares and links job seekers age 50 and older with jobs in business and industry,' and finds meaningful employment in private and public sector organisations, frequently for relatively permanent part-time jobs. Participants in this programme include professional, technical and administrative workers. Operation ABLE's own professional staff consists primarily of older workers, many of them on a part-time basis, with adequate benefits.

Operation ABLE is not the only organisation specialising in the temporary, as well as the permanent, placement of older workers – including persons as young as 40. Prime Timers of Dallas, Texas, for example, provides training, 'hands-on' skill updating, and benefits such as contributory life and health insurance coverage, bonuses, and even paid vacations and holidays – a rare personnel practice in the United States, even for full-time employees.

A somewhat unique example is the Elder Craftsmen organisation (New York City) that, since 1955, provides permanent exhibit retail-sale sites for artisans and craftsmen 55 years of age and older, with an extensive range of support services. These services include workshop training, and the encouragement of older persons to use their 'leisure time' creatively, and on a paid basis, through the design, creation, and selling of arts and craft products.

In brief, insurance companies, intermediary job-placement agencies, and banks are not the only industries represented in AARP's NOWIS. Other industries include:
- upscale specialty retail outlets;
- municipal governments;
- community and vocational colleges;
- grocery supermarket chains;
- income tax-service organisations;
- light packaging and assembly work companies;
- casino entertainment companies;
- services-to-the-elderly programmes.

Banks are a frequent employer of older workers on a part-time basis. In some cases, incidentally, Operation ABLE is involved in this job-match process (which includes training and counseling). Examples include Baybank of Berlington, Massachusetts, which actively recruits older workers and itself provides on-the-job training and bank-located formal classroom training.

The M & I Bank of Beloit, Wisconsin, has committed itself to hiring older workers for part-time and/or consulting assignments. Among the reasons for such a personnel policy is that the bank management believes that 'some customers may feel more comfortable with someone their own age.' Equally important, the bank recognises that their older employees prefer a phased retirement, moving to part-time work, and eventually to full-time retirement. The bank recognises clearly that many have skills and experience to offer and are still physically able to work at least a part-time schedule.

Another bank, PNC of Philadelphia, a commercial lending institution, has been employing and re-hiring retirees as temporary employees for more than a decade, with a programme that provides older workers opportunities to work a few hours a week at high hourly rates.

In many government and nonprofit service organisations with management-union collective bargaining units, it has been found that savings in benefits and wages were not important in hiring part-time employees. But this may be due to their placing greater priority on providing services than in making profits as their major objective. Kaiser-Permanente Health Care of California is one of the prominent examples of acceptable part-time employment.

11.4   Conclusion

There is no question that part-time employment can have its problems and limitations for both employee and employer. The lack of, or inadequacy of, social benefits is an obvious matter (health insurance coverage typically requires being employed in firms that provide such protection). Part-time employment need not to be synonymous with poor working conditions, inadequate benefits, low wages, etc. Instead of advocating any reversal of part-time employment, one might instead actively work towards a policy of changing and improving the status of part-time jobs, as is done in several European countries.

For some enterprises, part-time workers can actually be more costly and not as productive as full-time employees (Jondrow *et al.*, 1983). This explains why such workers tend to be offered lower wages.

Another neglected point is that, at least in the United States, employers, in times of declining product or service demand, may tend to dismiss large segments of their work force completely, rather than reduce hours of work, thereby creating a cadre of temporary (or perhaps permanent) part-time employees even if they are not labeled as such. The recent German steel industry adaptation by reducing hours of work instead of dismissing workers completely may be a portent of 'things to come.'

In this connection, a mid-1994 newsletter of the Work Force Programs Department of the American Association for Retired Persons – Working Age – dedicated that entire issue to 'Alternatives to Downsizing.' It reported a survey by a management consulting firm revealing that nearly three fourths of the survey's companies had tried job-sharing, shorter work weeks, or similar forms of reduction per worker in hours or days worked. Again, we do not know what per cent of the work force in these companies was affected, nor the degree to which such arrangements may be retained in the future. Alternatives to downsizing, apparently, are rarely put into effect, claims the author of the survey, 'because of poor planning.'

> 'Decision makers get involved too late in the game – when there is red ink all over the floor ... Then they have to make quick decisions. The problem is that most companies are not achieving the desired financial results. Poor planning and poor communications lead to poor morale, before, during and afterwards. The company's future depends on the troops that remain.' (Right Associates, 1992)

An historical note. These attempts at adaptation by some employers should, in my opinion, provoke some thought about the history of working hours, something I am sure someone such as Jean Fourastié has dealt with. In the United States now, for example, 'part-time' refers to less than 35 hours a week. In earlier decades, especially before World War II, part-time referred to something more than 35 hours – say, less than 40 hours. And before that, to something more than 40 hours. We know that in the 19th Century, 'full-time' referred to as many as 60 hours per week. Is it possible, due to the challenges stemming from chronic unemployment, and/or to the potential of technology-driven productivity increases, that we are on the verge of new re-definitions of what is full-time, perhaps to the point where working less than thirty hours per week will be categorised as 'full-time', to the point where something that is now considered part-time will be categorised as full-time?

Given the current pressures of OECD-type economies driven in part by globalisation, and bearing in mind this historical perspective, such a scenario might at first entail a minor downturn, or a freeze, in standards of living. But such a policy could be one salutary adaptation among others, to the challenges of system-wide joblessness.

References

Bartowiak, J. (1993), 'Trends Toward Part-Time Employment: Ethical Issues', *Journal of Business Ethics*, pp. 811-815.

Jondrow, M., F. Brechling and A. Marus (1983), *Older Workers in the Market for Part-Time Employment*. National Commission for Employment, Washington.

McNaught, W., M.C. Barth and P.H. Henderson (1989), 'The Human Resource Potential of Americans Over 50', *Human Resource Management*, vol. 28, no. 4, pp. 455-473.

Right Associates (1992), *Lessons Learned: Dispelling the Myths of Downsizing*, Washington.

PART IV

POTENTIAL
FOR GRADUAL RETIREMENT
AND RECOMMENDATIONS

12 Potential for gradual retirement and recommendations

Lei Delsen and Geneviève Reday-Mulvey

The situation in the countries selected for study shows that extension of working life is seen everywhere as a crucial policy for reducing the burden of social expenditure in years to come. Because of its flexible nature which is well suited to end of career, gradual retirement is finding increasing favour with the majority of workers, and growing acceptance with management and trade unions. There are, of course, features common to all the countries studied. And yet the situation as observed in 1995 varies greatly from one country to another. In this, Part IV of our study, we shall:

1 assess the extent of, and potential for, gradual retirement in the countries considered, by classifying them in four categories;
2 make recommendations for both public and company policies, and stress the need for their better integration; and finally
3 say a few words about the now evident need for rethinking the issues of work and retirement as part of a new approach to welfare in our societies.

12.1 The situation in the countries studied

In order better to understand the main trends and features of the current situation in the countries studied and therefore the potential of each for gradual retirement, we propose a tentative typology of four models: the Swedish, Japanese, Continental and Anglo-Saxon models.

The Swedish model has worked successfully for almost 20 years. In that country, labour force participation rates have decreased less than elsewhere and, in 1994, in spite of the severe recession, for men in the 60-64 age-group they were still at over 56 per cent and at 82 per cent for the 55-59 age-group. Almost one half of workers between 60 and 65 are in some form of gradual retirement, on generous financial and professional terms. There are three main reasons why this model has been successful: availability of part-time jobs and the habit of working flexibly, a good partnership between the State and enterprise, and the high replacement rate of partial pension arrangements. In Sweden, although no direct legislation on the issue exists, there is little age discrimination compared to countries such as the UK, France or Germany. And it can be said that a culture of late and phased retirement has already been established there, even if the events of the recent past might seem to suggest otherwise. Firms, especially big ones, make impressive use of continuing training until end of career and the recent thrust of employer policy has been to strengthen the relationship between productivity and wages.

The fairly widespread practice of gradual retirement in Sweden has been made possible above all by legislation which dates back to 1976 and which has provided for the combination of a partial pension and part-time work with good replacement rates. Whenever, as in the past, the Government has tried to cut expenditure and reduce those replacement rates, there has been an almost immediate decrease in the use of gradual retirement.

Important reforms to the pension system were introduced in June 1994. These will raise the age of partial retirement from 60 to 61, reduce the partial pension replacement rate (from 65 to 55 per cent), and reduce the number of hours compensated. Moreover pensions will be based on lifetime earnings, furnishing an incentive to work longer. However, the flexible partial pension/part-time work scheme, being deemed too costly, is due to disappear in 2000, leaving, as the only options available, a part-time old age pension and a part-time disability pension, which are less attractive.

The potential for gradual retirement in Sweden is now not as great as in the other countries studied, for the simple reason that so much has been achieved already. What now appears important is to be able to follow along the narrow path of public savings so necessary to the country's economic well-being while, at the same time, conserving its practice of gradual retirement and the other socio-economic policies that have made it in recent decades a model for so many other countries.

The Japanese model has in common with Sweden high participation rates for older workers. It is well-known that this is due in part to the 'shukko' system of employment normally operated by big firms. Under this system, large numbers of employees work on after the pension age of 60, frequently up to 65 if not later, and mostly part-time, often in a subsidiary of their previous employer. The financial and professional conditions offered to workers are not as generous as previously, but their income from this work is additional to the pension which for some of them is still too low. Self employment is also developed in Japan among older workers, and there exist 'silver centres' where workers, usually from smaller firms, can obtain information and support in finding part-time employment after the pension age. It is common knowledge that Japanese workers value the social 'inclusion' that this type of employment after pension age confers. Various surveys show that Japanese workers would like to continue even later than is nowadays possible.

The seniority rule which used to be very strong in Japan has been made more flexible, and now 50 is becoming the age as of which there is no further increase in the basic wage; sometimes there is even a decrease. I. Shimowada points in his chapter to the trend towards 'more flexible management policies' which 'will help to rectify the imbalance between performance and wages which is thought to constitute a major obstacle to more widespread employment of older workers'. More training, more flexible work and more job redesign are being offered, it appears, by an increasing proportion of firms.

The reforms of 1986 and 1994 have been highly instrumental in promoting employment of older workers. They have made early retirement less attractive, have modified the earnings tests, have made the future state pension obtainable in full only at the age of 65 instead of 60 (this change will come into force between 2001 and 2013), and have provided various subsidies to companies wishing to employ workers after the age of 60. There can be said to exist in Japan a government-led global policy and strong incentives from the State to encourage enterprise to extend work-life in a land whose life expectancy in good health is one of the highest in the world. Japan's labour force, it should be repeated, is aging earlier than those of Europe or America and, it seems, with no loss of productivity. However, although practice of gradual retirement outside main employment is already widespread, the potential for more gradual retirement is considerable since Japan's goal in this matter is to go from 'a society which retires at 60 to one that works until 65'. This will require extending and reinforcing many of the measures that have already been set in place.

The Continental approach is exemplified by France, Germany and the Netherlands. These three countries are characterised by a practice of very early retirement which has been encouraged over the last 15 years by public policies, and by a strong consensus between enterprise, the State and workers, resulting in very low activity rates for workers from the age of 55. It has been said, and rightly we believe, that labour force participation rates in these countries reflect more the availability of generous social-security provision than the situation of labour markets. In all three countries a strong early retirement culture exists. Over recent years, disability, unemployment and early retirement routes have been reduced significantly but they will have to be made even less accessible and more expensive in the future. In Germany (W. Schmähl *et al.*) and the Netherlands (L. Delsen), for example, invalidity and disability pension routes have been, and remain, loopholes for those who want to retire.

Public policies and collective agreements to encourage flexibility and phasing have been launched in these countries, for the time being more so perhaps in France than in Germany and the Netherlands. And there are the beginnings of a trend away from early retirement, especially in France and the Netherlands. In France over 30,000 workers were on gradual retirement at the end of 1994 and a fair number of examples of satisfactory practice already exist in this area; they show how important financial help from the State and a good partnership with enterprise really are. The task, however, of convincing workers who have got used to the idea of very early retirement of the virtues of extending work-life is not an easy one.

In Germany, recent legislation (Pension Reform Act of 1992) provides the basis for gradual retirement-oriented policies, but for the time being implementation has had only a very limited impact due to labour market difficulties (German reunification) and to the lack of sufficiently strong and flexible financial incentives (for example, the age at which phased retirement becomes possible is too late). Future measures to reduce exit routes in order to create more incentives to later and phased retirement are to be announced by the Government, and over recent months labour unions have also been proposing measures to promote gradual retirement.

In the Netherlands, collective agreements have recently been concluded and reflect the growing trend away from early retirement (VUT) towards more flexible occupational pension schemes allowing partial pensions. Flexible work patterns are widespread which is, of course, one of the important conditions for gradual retirement, and, since 1994, part-timers may no longer be excluded from pension provision. A major obstacle to any real progress, however, is the fact that the majority of pension funds remain final-salary based, but the Government now appears to favour a move towards average-pay systems. Other necessary company measures are, as in Germany and France, more training for older workers and more flexible pay systems.

In all three countries the potential for gradual retirement is considerable, and we shall be indicating below what we believe is required to make it a large-scale reality.

The Anglo-Saxon approach is exemplified by the UK and USA, where no strong public policies exist, but where flexibility is common. In both these countries part-time work and self employment among older workers have been increasing.

In the USA, due to the downsizing of firms and to the collapse of the so-called 'career employment system' for older workers, many employees in their fifties have been losing their jobs (Doeringer, 1993). Between the ages of 55 and, all too rarely in practice, 65, when they can begin drawing their state pension, they have had to take 'bridge jobs' which are often part-time, frequently pay less, and almost always provide lower levels of protection than their previous employment. And yet, well-known cases of post retirement-age employment exist such as, for example, the Travelers where working conditions for 'retirees' are usually excellent. Other examples can be found in banks, insurance companies, town administrations, colleges and supermarkets. but the conditions in such cases are not always representative of average conditions. In one sense, gradual retirement can be said to exist to a certain extent in practice, often outside main career employment, but legal measures will need to be taken in order to create the proper statutory social and financial framework required for its propagation. Recent surveys show that the potential for further gradual retirement is still considerable.

In the UK, public early retirement policies were tightened up at the end of the 1980s due to financial constraints and, since then, official policy has consisted of attempts to convince large employers of the advantages of retaining older workers much later than they, the employers, would wish to do. Employers' practice produces some interesting examples of better management of older workers. But in the absence of proper legislation and sound financial incentives, the results of this policy have not been very encouraging. Existing pension rules are once again an obstacle, based as they so often are on final salary, and funded from contributions which increase with the age of the employee.

12.2 Recommendations for public policies

Although some of the necessary changes or reforms have just been mentioned, it seems important at this stage to examine more comprehensively the public and company policies needed for large-scale realisation of the potential for gradual retirement in the countries studied.

It has been asserted in Part I of our study that raising the retirement age or changing pension conditions and rules will not, of themselves, suffice to reverse the significant trend towards early retirement which has taken place over the last twenty years. Reference has been made, more especially, to a much-needed change in attitude since all countries have been deeply affected by the so-called 'early retirement culture', particularly the three continental countries and, to a lesser extent, the UK and the USA.

As was made clear in the introduction and in some detail in the respective country chapters, all the countries examined have now initiated moves towards pension reform. Yet on reading the country chapters what stands out as essential is that public policies need to be sufficiently comprehensive and accompanied by incentives at various levels if a significant change of direction is to be hoped for in the years to come. Those countries which so far have been more successful in implementing gradual retirement are probably the ones which have designed global public policies (Sweden and Japan, and very recently, France). The description of the raft of new public policies in France may give some idea of the reach and coherence of policy options the editors believe to be required.

First, it has been stated in most country chapters that it is essential to make early retirement options as well as disability and unemployment routes more difficult, more costly and their terms more stringent. Although the countries studied, especially the Netherlands, Germany, Sweden and France have all, in varying degrees, moved in that direction, much ground still remains to be covered. It will be objected that current labour market conditions, and especially high rates of unemployment, make any progress in the desired direction at this time very difficult. It is precisely for this reason, the editors believe, that gradual retirement cannot be handled outside the broader context of employment redesign and redistribution (see below).

A second set of policies has to do with gradual retirement itself. The USA and the UK do not as yet have any specific legislation in this field, and the American authors, at least, have called for some kind of statutory structure for social security within which to promote gradual retirement. In the USA, for example, earnings test rules have been described as too severe. Political change in the UK would almost certainly bring with it welcome legislation in this area.

In other countries, recent legislation (or, in the Netherlands, collective agreements) is beginning to promote replacement of full early retirement by gradual early retirement. But such legislation clearly needs to be accompanied by financial incentives from the State, and we can see the positive results of policy strategies allied with incentive measures in countries like Sweden, Japan and more recently France. The German authors indicate that one of the reasons why thus far implementation of new legislation has not been effective is because of insufficient financial incentives and of regulations that are too complicated. The age at which gradual retirement can commence is also crucially important. Changing the deeply-rooted mindsets of the early retirement culture requires drastic redesign and gradual implementation. Japan seems, in this respect, to be a very good example of how to do it.

Financial incentives can also help employers hire older unemployed workers, and this measure exists in at least two countries, France and, since July 1995, Sweden. They can help target older workers for continuing training until end of career. Practice in Japan and France is relevant here, as also is the German authors' call for older workers to be made 'an important target group for public-financed vocational training'. But in the final analysis it appears that a good partnership between the State and enterprise is vital to the development of gradual retirement.

12.3 Recommendations for company policies

'One can hardly overstress the importance of properly integrated public and company policies for promoting the employment of older people' (I. Shimowada). In this domain, as for public policies, the country chapters describe a number of changes over recent years. However, all too frequently, new management policies for older workers have concerned too few firms and, therefore, too few workers. All country chapters have referred to model firms and instances of good practice. These experiences need in future to become the norm. Among the many company measures whose promotion country authors have recommended, we can examine here only the most important: personnel age-specific management, occupational pensions, training, pay policy, and part-time and flexible work options.

Personnel management

'The need for better integration of older people into the work force is increasingly admitted in publications on personnel management and by employers in their statements' (W. Schmähl *et al.* in the chapter on Germany). Our provisional conclusion is that, for the time being, it is probably more awareness of future challenges that is developing in representative firms in the countries surveyed than new age-specific management practice. Whatever the case, it is a fact that in all countries a small number of dynamic firms, often big ones, have started new policies either for employees in mid-career (such as abilities assessment and the drawing up of training plans for workers aged 40 to 45) or for their better integration at end of career. Mid-career abilities and aptitudes assessments, the training plan, internal or external mobility, ergonomic methods, flexible work schedules or reduced workload at end of career (and sometimes earlier), are some of the instruments being used and there is no doubt that they will be developing over the next few years.

The justification for new age-specific policies must always be commercial and economic before it is social. Older workers, it has often been recognised, perform tasks better or differently than younger ones, and the 'differently' can be an advantage where, for example, customer relations, sheer expertise or team-work are involved. The best way to convince other firms or other departments within a firm of the validity of a new approach to work force aging is to show them the results of new practice. As P. Taylor and A. Walker in their chapter on the UK point out: 'in order to persuade management of the benefits of employing older workers, some personnel departments publicised examples of where the organisation had successfully deployed older people'.

If policies for enhancing the employment opportunites of older workers are to make any headway at all, they will need to serve as much the interests of

employers as of employees. Ideas, therefore, for improving the various varia-
bles which can make employment at end of career less expensive, more
flexible, more adaptable and equally productive, have to be marshalled and
built into corporate practice. Examples of good practice will be imitated and
as a result new norms established, as has, to some extent, already happened in
Sweden and Japan.

Occupational pensions

In some countries occupational pensions currently constitute an obstacle to
gradual retirement and in various ways. First, many Dutch, British and American pension funds are final-salary based and authors have called for changes
to the rules to make them average-earnings based. In the UK, in addition,
contributions from employers increase with age; this is another rule that will
need to be modified. In the countries studied, there seems to be an emerging
consensus about the need to make such changes, and it has also been suggested
that there is a need to align the payment rules of occupational pensions on
those of the statutory pension schemes for a more favourable impact on
gradual retirement. And finally, for Germany, the UK and the USA, it is recommended that the rules for occupational pensions should cease to be such a
strong incitement to very early retirement.

Training

In order for older workers to remain motivated and productive, continuing
training should not terminate at 45 or 50 years but should continue until end
of career. Countries where such company policies exist are in a much stronger
position when the decision to extend working life is taken, although all countries need to develop such policies further. The statistics for Sweden showed,
it will be remembered, how impressive training is even for older workers. In
bigger French companies, the same policy is beginning to be encountered. In
Japan, there are incentives for training older workers, and bigger firms are
running successful schemes to meet this need. In the Netherlands and Germany, training until end of career has also developed over recent years but
much more needs to be done. The situation appears less encouraging in the USA
and the UK, and will require more incentives, more carefully targeted, from the
authorities, and more challenging strategies from firms if things are to be
improved.

Pay policy

Another important variable is pay policy. It is perfectly clear from most
chapters that seniority-based policies, by raising the wage costs of workers at

end of career, constitute a real obstacle to all forms of extension of working life. In all countries, there is a growing trend in wage calculation today towards reducing the weight of the seniority factor and increasing that of performance. This trend is perhaps more prevalent in the United States and the UK, but is now to be found in France as well where, in some sectors such as insurance, the old seniority pay system has been recently scrapped. In Japan, where seniority is a revered social value, seniority calculation now frequently levels off at 50, work after the age of 60 being outside main and regular employment, with very different wage profiles. In Germany, Sweden and the Netherlands, employer policy has been to strengthen the relation between wages and productivity.

Part-time and flexible work

The development of part-time and flexible forms of employment is obviously important for gradual retirement. Most countries have seen such development at either end of the life-cycle. Countries such as the Netherlands and the UK have a high rate of part-timers. Some have improved legislation in this respect so as to provide better levels of protection for part-time work (for example, France and the Netherlands). In other countries, there is availability of part-time jobs for older workers either inside (e.g. Sweden) or outside main career employment (e.g. Japan, USA, UK), but social protection for part-time employment has to be improved in the latter cases. It has been recognised by many that part-time work is likely to improve the productivity of older workers, reduce absenteeism and increase motivation. Examples of good initiatives for promoting part-time work in a targeted fashion are Japan's 'silver centres' or the part-time jobs banks such as ABLE or NOWIS in the USA.

12.4 Rethinking work and retirement, or the need to coordinate employment and social policies

At the end of his chapter, H. Sheppard asks: 'Is it possible due to the challenges stemming from chronic unemployment and to the potential of technology-driven productivity increases, that we are on the verge of a redefinition of what constitutes full-time ... to a point where something that is now considered part-time will be categorised as *full* time? ... Such a policy, among others, could be salutory to the challenges of system-wide joblessness.'

It is very much the editors' conviction that demographic and financial pressures require that the welfare states define new social and employment policies. Advances in information technology make it imperative for our societies carefully to re-examine the concept of 'full' employment. While, over the last 25 years, the services sector has unquestionably proved prolific as a creator of jobs, current and foreseeable restructuring in certain branches of the service sector – for example, banks and insurance – is going to result in job losses which will not necessarily be offset by job-creation in other branches, to say nothing of further substantial job-losses in the years to come in industry and agriculture. Moreover, in spite of a reduction in the number of young persons entering the labour market, increased productivity and labour substitution by capital will oblige us sooner or later to face the issue of how much work the average citizen will need, or can expect, to do.

Given the overall volume and new quality of work the service functions offer, new employment policies could be devised around the notions of basic employment. This might mean a shift from 'full-time' employment and exclusion from the labour market of over 30 per cent of potential workers (those receiving social benefits in one form or another, that is the unemployed, early retirees, older people wishing to remain active after the retirement age, young students, mothers with family responsibilities, etc.) to a society where governments and firms are concerned with assuring *basic employment for all,* that is, *part-time work for all citizens of an age and ability to work.* This new profile for 'full employment' would be positive for both enterprise (higher productivity, less absenteeism) and the community (less exclusion, more time for community activities). Much less financial support would be needed for the unemployed, the student, the mother, the early retiree and so forth. With such an approach it might be possible to build a society where the average citizen, whether young or old, man or woman, would work at least 1,000 hours per year, more if he or she is able to find extra hours of work, and be integrated socially with free time for other activities, whether economic, social, cultural or artistic. It has actually been calculated that in France the average number of hours worked per year divided by the potentially active population (people from the age of 20 to the age of 65) is around that number. This new 'full' or 'basic' concept of employment is founded on the complimentarity of equality and efficiency. Indeed, basic employment, together with its complimentary entitlement – the basic income – would, if ever they were built into an integrated social/employment policy, be found to be gradual-retirement positive and would render the official retirement age obsolete (Delsen, 1995). Basic employment, then, with gradual retirement as one of its facets, constitutes an essential aspect of what could be called 'a new welfare deal'.

Social and employment policies, in other words, need to be combined or, at the very least, coordinated if we wish in future to promote a society less divided between two extremes: those who work too much and those who are excluded from productive activity of any sort (Chen, 1995). Therefore, gradual retirement seems to stand at the crossroads of two important issues:
– the need to extend working life for very sound reasons which have to do with the financing of pensions and the proper management of human resources and skills; and

– the need to develop well-protected and regular part-time work not only as a transition from full employment to full retirement, but also as a bridge towards a morally proper distribution of 'full' employment whose redefinition is now long over-due.

References

Chen, Y-P. (1995), *Partial Pensions for Partial Retirements: Need for Coordinating Social Security Policy with Employment Policy,* Paper presented at the Mini-White House Conference on Aging, Baltimore, National Council of Senior Citizens, 23-25 February.

Delsen, L. (1995), *Atypical Employment: an International Perspective. Causes, Consequences and Policy,* Wolters-Noordhoff, Groningen.

Doeringer, P. (1993), 'The Myths of Early Retirement and Second Carreers', *Etudes et Dossiers,* no. 179 (October), International Association for the Study of Insurance Economics, Geneva.

Reday-Mulvey, G. (1993), 'Facing Social Uncertainty: Towards a New Social Policy' in Giarini, O. and W. Stahel *Limits to Certainty,* Kluwer Academic Publishers, Dordrecht.

About the contributors

Yung-Ping Chen is Frank J. Manning Eminent Scholar's Chair in Gerontology at the University of Massachusetts in Boston. He is an economist and a founding member of the National Academy of Social Insurance. His research interests include social security and long-term care financing, and the role of social security in promoting partial retirement. His most recent book is *Choice and Constraints: Economic Decisionmaking*.

Lei Delsen is Assistant Professor at the Department of Applied Economics of the University of Nijmegen. His current research deals with a number of topical European labour market problems and issues, including atypical employment, gradual retirement and employment opportunities for disabled people. A recent publication is *Atypical Employment: An International Perspective. Causes, Consequences and Policy*.

Rainer George is Research Assistant at the Special Research Centre 186, University of Bremen. His areas of research are partial pension and retirement decisions of older workers and the labour market position of the disabled. A recent publication is 'Die Arbeitsmarktsituation Behinderter in der Bundesrepublik Deutschland zwischen Anspruch und Wirklichkeit', *Berufliche Rehabilitation*, 1995, 30-50.

Christiane Oswald is Research Assistant at the Special Research Centre 186, University of Bremen. Her areas of research are partial pensions and the retirement decisions of older workers and the labour market in East Germany.

Geneviève Reday-Mulvey, a social-economist, is Chargée de Recherche at the International Association for the Study of Insurance Economics (the Geneva Association). In her capacity as co-ordinator of the research programme on Work and Retirement called The Four Pillars, she has worked extensively on the potential for extending working life in several OECD countries. Recent publications include 'Facing Social Uncertainty: Towards a New Social Policy' in O. Giarini and W. Stahel, *Limits to Certainty.*

Winfried Schmähl is Professor of Economics, specialising in Social Policy, and Head of the Economics Department of the Centre for Social Policy Research at the University of Bremen. He is chairman of the Permanent Advisory Board on pension policy to the German Federal Government. His main areas of research are the economics of social policy, pension policy and social security policy in the EU. His most recent publications include papers on pension reforms, globalisation and social policy and on long-term-care insurance.

Harold L. Sheppard is Professor at the Department of Gerontology, University of South Florida, Tampa. His primary research interests are in the economics of aging and aging social policy. His recent publications include *The Future of Older Workers* and 'Work and retirement' in T. Shuman *et al., Population Aging: International Perspectives.*

Isao Shimowada is Professor at the Faculty of Commerce, Hitotsubashi University in Tokyo. His main research interests are the influence of pensions on employment and international comparative and historical analysis of life insurance and social security. He is author of *Structure and Development of German Public Pension Systems* and co-author of *Economic Security Systems and Life Insurance Industry* (in Japanese).

Noriyuki Takayama is Professor of Economics at the Institute of Economic Research, Hitotsubashi University in Tokyo. He has published numerous books and articles in international journals including Econometrica. He is co-author of *Equity and Poverty under Rapid Economic Growth: The Japanese Experience,* and author of *The Greying of Japan: An Economic Perspective on Public Pensions.*

Philip Taylor is a Research Fellow at the Policy Studies Institute in London. Research interests include employers' attitudes and practices towards older workers and the impact of redundancies on older workers. He is co-author of *Too Old at 50* and *Age and Employment: Policies, Attitudes and Practices.*

Eskil Wadensjö is Professor of Labour Economics at the Swedish Institute for Social Research, Stockholm University. His present research concerns the economics of immigration, groups with a weak position in the labour market and the economics of social and occupational insurance systems. He has published numerous books and articles on labour economics. A recent publication is *Labour Market Policy at the Crossroads*.

Alan Walker is Professor of Social Policy in the Department of Sociological Studies at the University of Sheffield and Chair of the EU Observatory on Ageing and Older People. His present research covers employers' policies towards older workers and the social care of older people with learning difficulties. His most recent publications include *Age and Attitudes; Older People in Europe – Social Integration and the New Generational Contract*.

Name index